The grant of ...

the ffaith &c. To all to whome these present shall come Greetinge, Whereas in the
fifth yeare of our raigne Betweene Sir Richard Sutton of london knight Richard
... wotton of london Gentleman of the one partie, And Samuell Martyn of Charterhouse
... rose aforesaid gentleman and Bryan wotton sonne of the foresaid John wotton of the
... brede Esquire by his Indenture of bargaine and sale bearinge date the eighteenth day
... deare and royall ffather kinge James over England &c. and inrolled in his Maiesties
... rein expressed did graunte bargaine and sell vnto the foresaid Richard Aldworth and
... he Mannor of Blacktoft with the right members and appurtenances whatsoever in the
... building demeasne land Mesuages tenement and hereditament whatsoever to the said
... en as parte parcell or member thereof or with the same or with any parte or parcell
... ed or enioyed then in the tenure or occupation of the said Richard Hairebrede or his
... all Mesuages of Eastblacktoft and Stadlethorp with theire and every of their right
... er of howses edifices building land demeasne land, meadowes ffeedinge pastures Comons
... itter or any of them belonginge or apperteyninge or reputed esteemed or taken as parte
... assignes. And also all that Sitte of the late dissolved Chappell or Chauntrye of the
... orke, and all land tenement meadowes ffeedinge pastures Comons and hereditament
... bers and appurtenances whatsoever. And also divers Mesuages land tenement and
... o hundred acres or thereabout more or lesse with theire and every of theire appurtenances
... blacktofte Stadlethorp holding Estrington and Bellases and in yonkefleete or
... Owse to the foresaid mannor or Mannors or to any of them or to any other the premisses
... ites building barnes stables Dovehowses yard orchard Gardens land tenement
... er theis waters ffishing fishinge plates waves pathes work of Rēnt, rent aswell free
... trayes good and chattell of felons and fugitives deodand estovers and Comons of
... erties priviledges tithes oblatons obuentons fruit proffitt comodities emolument
... er the premisses or to any of them or to any parte or parcell of them or any of them
... member of them or any of them or with the same or any of them as parte parcell or
... and every of theire appurtenances whatsoever, And all other Mesuages land tenement
... blacketofte, Stadlethorpe and Bellases aforesaid and in every or any of them with their
... or wherein he the said Richard Hairebrede had or might or ought to haue had any
... t to haue descended vnto the said Richard Hairebrede by and after the decease of
... mainder and remainders of all and euerie the premisses and of every parte and
... apperteyninge. And also all yearely rent yssues and proffitt reserved vpon any
... thereof, And the remainder of all that capitall messuage tenement or ffarme and
... whatsoever thereunto belonginge or apperteyninge Situate lyeinge and beinge in
... boke or his Assignes, As in and by the said Indenture of bargaine and sale more
... ture reciting, That whereas Sir Thomas Metham knight by his Indenture of bargaine
... said ffathers raigne over England &c. and inrolled in his said Courte of Exchequer at
... o the foresaid Sir Richard Sutton knight by the name of Richard Sutton of Acton in
... parcell of arrable land meadow and pasture conteyninge and amountinge in the
... g of Blacktoft in the said County of Yorke with all and singuler their right members
... on or his Assignes, As in and by the said last mentioned Indenture of bargaine and
... nd by the said first mentioned Indenture reciting, That whereas Sir Oliver Williams
... the said Sir Oliver by their Indenture of bargaine and sale bearinge date the third day
... nd inrolled in his high Courte of Chancery at westminster did for the consideratons
... knight then Esquire and John wotton theire heires and Assignes forever, All that
... ne or higney Graunge And all that litle Island or parcell of Ground invironed with

CHARTERHOUSE

A 400th anniversary portrait

CHARTERHOUSE

A 400th anniversary portrait

EDITOR **ERNST ZILLEKENS**

THIRD MILLENNIUM
PUBLISHING, LONDON

© Third Millennium Publishing Limited

First published in 2010 by
Third Millennium Publishing Limited, a subsidiary of
Third Millennium Information Limited

2–5 Benjamin Street
London
United Kingdom
EC1M 5QL
www.tmiltd.com

ISBN 978 1 906507 14 5

British Library Cataloguing in Publication Data
A CIP catalogue record for this book is available from the
British Library.

Managing Editor: Susan Millership
Designer: Helen Swansbourne
Production: Bonnie Murray
Repro by Studio Fasoli, Italy
Printed by Gorenjski Tisk, Slovenia

JACKET ILLUSTRATIONS
Front and back: Roger Smeeton
Back flap: George Titus

ENDPAPERS
Royal Charter of 1630 regarding properties owned by
Sutton's Hospital. Photograph by George Titus

Contents

Editor's Note

Major anniversaries are a milestone in the history of any institution. They call for celebration, but also reflection about the journey to this point and, in the case of Charterhouse, to the quatercentenary in 2011. This book celebrates Carthusian achievement and traces key developments and changes. Some of them were significant turning points, such as the move to Godalming. But there have also been some constant traditions; Eric Harrison aptly captures one: 'the tradition which encourages on the one hand self-expression and a questioning mind, and on the other a consciousness of responsibility for the well-being of the whole community and a tolerant respect for different points of view and different interests and excellence.'

I would like to thank all Old Carthusians who responded so enthusiastically to the request for recollections for this book, and I apologise that it has not been possible to refer to each of them in the text. The full contributions will, however, be kept in the Archives, as a permanent record of Carthusian life. A special thank you goes to all those who wrote chapters or shorter sections, especially Stephen Porter and Clive Carter, and to the school Archive team, particularly Catherine Smith, the Archivist, who researched and wrote about many Old Carthusians, reassembled the text with infinite patience and gathered illustrations from the Archives. I am extremely grateful to Roger Smeeton for his wonderful photographs, which capture the spirit of the School and its pupils so superbly. I would also like to thank Brian Rees and Peter Attenborough for the considerable personal support they gave me by writing accounts of their time as Headmasters, Susan Millership, the Third Millennium editor, for her excellent editorial support and Helen Swansbourne for her skilful design work. I am much indebted to all those who proof-read the book especially the Headmaster, John Witheridge, Matthew Armstrong, Sue Cole, Geoffrey Ford, John Herbert, Margaret Jacobs, Mary Olive and Peter Parkin.

This book is not a new critical appraisal of the School's history, although earlier historical assessments by A.H. Tod, Anthony Quick, W.H. Holden and E.M. Jameson were drawn on. Quotations in the text from Old Carthusians are followed by their name, the initial of their House and the year they left. A full list of contributors can be found at the back of the book. The authors of those boxes that were not written by the Archivist are given at the end of the boxed text. For those not steeped in Charterhouse vernacular, the short glossary in the First Impressions section may be invaluable. (Finally, I apologise for any errors or omissions.)

ERNST ZILLEKENS
July 2010

DOMUS
CARTHUSIANÆ
FUNDATOR
THOMAS
SUTTON
1611

Headmaster's Foreword

Any institution that survives and flourishes for 400 years must possess special and distinctive qualities. I would summarise those qualities at Charterhouse as a remarkable ability to combine continuity with change.

Our founder, Thomas Sutton, lived through brutally uncertain times. Born in the reign of King Henry VIII, he was 15 when Edward VI succeeded to the throne, in his early 20s when Mary Tudor was queen, 26 when Elizabeth I was crowned and 71 when James I became king. With extraordinary political and entrepreneurial skill, Sutton managed not only to survive but also to amass an unrivalled fortune. Is it any surprise that he packed Charterhouse's governing body with the great, the good and the powerful?

A century later, by 1711, the Stuarts had fallen and Queen Anne was nearing the end of her reign. It was the year when Addison and Steele launched *The Spectator* 'to enliven morality with wit, and to temper wit with morality'. By 1811 the Hanoverians had ruled for 97 years, George III had gone mad, and the Prince of Wales was made Regent. Carthusians who were serving in the army had just four years to prepare for Waterloo. In 1911 the country was already overshadowed by rumours of a far greater war, and three years later Robert Graves and his ill-fated contemporaries left Charterhouse for the Western Front. No school in Great Britain sacrificed a higher proportion of its old boys than Charterhouse – and for 'old' read mostly in their teens and 20s.

Charterhouse has survived the changes and chances of history because it has managed to combine resilience with adaptability, a respect for tradition with a readiness to modernise. This is an especially British quality, and we can see it at work not only in our ancient schools and universities but in our monarchy, parliamentary democracy, judiciary and armed forces. When the original site in London became too cramped and its neighbourhood too squalid, the School had the courage and foresight to pack its bags and migrate to green and pleasant acres of Surrey countryside. In the 20th century, Charterhouse had the confidence to admit girls to the sixth form, and instead of trying to rebuild the Victorian boarding Houses the School sold them, using the proceeds to build modern Houses with a room for each pupil and modern kitchens to feed them. Now, at the start of the 21st century, we have created Fletcherites, a 12th House for sixth form day pupils. Furthermore, Charterhouse is giving all schools an academic lead by abandoning the A level and replacing it with the new Pre-University examination and, in 2011, the International Baccalaureate, both excellent courses which will stretch our pupils and allow universities to see just how knowledgeable and well prepared they are. The same Charterhouse, the same high standards and ambitions, the same confidence and vision – but expressing itself in fresh ideas and new solutions.

In 1820 the Duke of Wellington (a governor of the School) heard that his adoring friend Lady Shelley intended to send her son to his old school, Eton. He wrote to her to protest: 'I am astonished that you don't send your son to the Charterhouse, which I believe is the best school of them all.' As in 1820, so in 2011.

THE REVD JOHN WITHERIDGE MA
July 2010

Thomas Sutton's statue, Founder's Court.

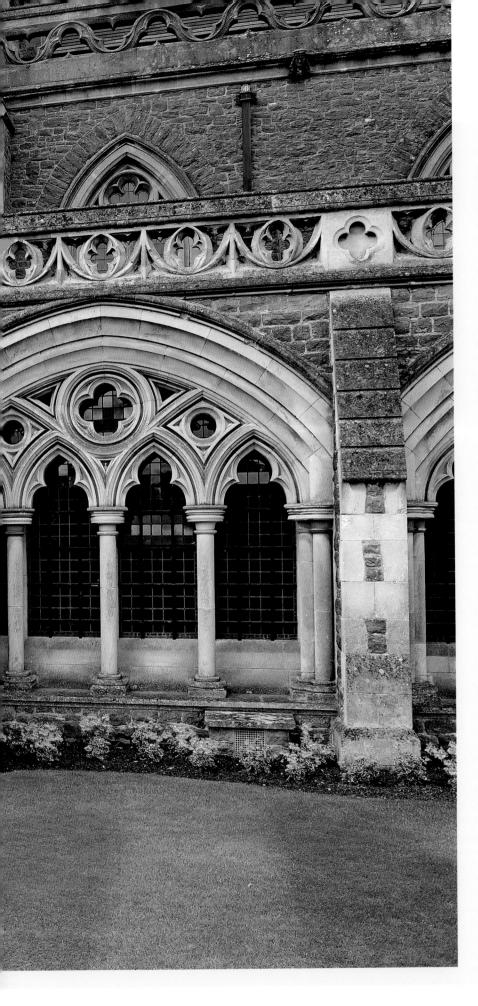

First impressions

I am probably one of the few to be accepted for Charterhouse who did not write and pass a Common Entrance exam. In 1944 – around early July – I was at school up in Darjeeling in India when I was told: 'Your mother will be here in a week to collect you. You are off to school in England.' It took five days by train down and across India to get from our home to Darjeeling. D-Day had occurred, and the authorities had just opened the sea lanes for persons with urgent business to travel from India to England. That trip is another story.

I had just turned 13, but, of course, first had to be vetted as suitable by the School. My mother and I duly reported to Duckites sometime in August. 'Lucy' Lovell, that most excellent Housemaster, was away as it was holiday time, and we were greeted by 'Bertie' Lee, the assistant Housemaster. My mother had to wait in Mr Lovell's drawing room while I was catechised in the entrance sun porch by a stern Bertie. At the end of the ordeal I was wheeled into the drawing room where Bertie pronounced in his usual dry manner: 'Christopher's arithmetic is reasonable; his English is passable; his Latin is execrable. We'll take him.' He was a man of few words but always to the point. Hey presto! The start to five very happy years at Charterhouse.

Christopher Hudson (G 1949)

*

Entrance to the South African Cloister and Old Music School (formerly the chapel).

I arrived at Hodgsonites at the end of August 1989. I was sharing a room with Ben Wakeham, son of the Conservative minister. We unpacked while our parents went to the Housemaster's private side for a drink. My mother had feared that it would be frightfully stand-offish but, with five of the 12 fathers being old boys, it was more of a reunion than anything else. After saying goodbye to our parents, we had supper in the House dining room and were taken for a swim by one of the House tutors – Pete Allison. We were then taken over to the Ralph Vaughan Williams Music School to ascertain whether we wanted to play a musical instrument. We had individual meetings with a new master – Russell Burton – who ran the choir. I stated that I had learned the piano at my prep school and simply wished to continue that. He asked, looking at my Scottish name, if I wished to learn the bagpipes. I declined. It was here that we encountered people from our year in other Houses. We went back to Hodgsonites for roll-call, or adsum. The monitor on duty read out the name of everyone in the House and they had to reply 'Sum' or 'I am'. This happened twice a day, at 7:30 in the morning and at 8:30 in the evening. We then went up to our bedrooms. Our first day had come to an end. The next day – our first full day at the School – began with chapel. We were then given a tour of the school. In the days that followed there were numerous meetings, mapping out the scope of our activities. We were also given a lecture on the School's history by Clive Carter.

Richard McMillan (H 1994)

*

It is the start of Oration 1943. Thirty Upper Shell boys, many of them new bugs, are assembled for their first Latin hash, under the jaundiced eye of Mr E.D.C. ('Bushy', on account of the walrus moustache) Lake. In the far corner, at the back of the room, sits a terrified new bug – terrified not only because he is a new bug, but also because he is acutely aware of his abject incompetence at Latin. To his great relief, it is soon apparent that this hash will be devoted, only, to the laborious noting of each boy's name and House. Eventually, it is the turn of the boy in the corner. His name and House are given. There is a pause. 'Bushy' lowers his spectacles and glares over the top of them: 'Oh yes. I remember your Common Entrance paper.' Twenty nine heads turn with interest – and no little glee – to inspect this curiosity in their midst. 'You have been admitted to the school against my recommendation.' After that, things could only get better.

Bill Flower (W 1947)

In 1944 my parents sent me to Charterhouse from Bermuda. The only way to get there was by Royal Naval warships. The individual skipper would be asked to take boys to England from this side of the Atlantic, Canada, the USA etc. They were usually English boys who had been sent over at the beginning of the war. My lot was to go on a frigate that was a convoy escort ship, and it took several weeks of dodging U-boats and horrendous weather to get to the UK.

When I arrived at Hodgsonites at the beginning of the summer term I was met by the Housemaster, V.S.H. Russell. He asked me what I was doing there, and I informed him that my parents had sent me. His reply was: 'You can't come in as you have not passed Common Entrance.' I did not have a clue what he was talking about. I asked him how I was to get home and explained how and where I had come from. Somewhat reluctantly he said, 'Oh all right, come in.' Needless to say I was rather shattered, particularly as I was ushered into his dining room and given a test on the spot. When it came to Latin I froze, and finally on being asked to read the preface I rather cheekily said that this would be simple as it was in English! In any event I was accepted into rather a low form and coasted for the next five years. On going into the House I ran into an older boy and asked him as follows in my rather American accent: 'Say bud, what do you do around this joint?' He was taken aback and speechless. I learned later that he was the Head of the School, captain of cricket and football. My Housemaster dined out on the story for years.

Michael Darling (H 1948)

Together with the other 'new hops' I was delivered by my parents, by road, complete with new uniforms and other items we had been told to bring, together with a tuck box and trunk. Earlier I had visited that wonderful establishment, Gorringes, the school outfitters, near to Victoria Station. We all arrived at tea time, which was presided over by our Housemaster, V.S.H. Russell, generally and affectionately known as 'Sniffy'. To us newcomers he appeared rather distant, aloof and somewhat forbidding. However, as can often be the case with first impressions, this turned out to be an inaccurate and unfair assessment.

Francis Monck-Mason (H 1952)

*

A little over 10 years ago I arrived at Charterhouse to begin my sixth form education. Having been born in Germany, I had spent my previous years at a grammar school in my home country. At the age of 16 I was frustrated by the experience of teachers' indifference towards their students, overcrowded classrooms and the clear-cut division between academic and personal education.

I had come to Charterhouse in the hope of finding change, and my very first impression was promising. At the induction session the Headmaster welcomed us with the words that we had come to the School to 'work hard and play hard', a motto I often recalled during the following two years. Because of the number of subjects I had chosen to study, a large proportion of my day was occupied with academic work. However, the enthusiasm that most teachers conveyed for their subjects and the attention individual students were given due to the small class sizes (including one-to-one tuition in a subject that would not fit into my daily timetable) meant that I suddenly experienced academic education as something challenging and enjoyable that awakened a curiosity to learn and understand. Of course, the second idea in the Headmaster's motto had to be addressed as well, and I remember vividly the fun I had playing the saxophone in the School's jazz band, taking part in piano competitions, making use of the – at the time newly opened – Charterhouse Sports Club and, at the end of my first year, successfully completing the Fifty-Mile Walk.

Daniel Schwarz (P 2001)

Glossary of Carthusian terms

Banco evening preparation for the next day's work

Beak Schoolmaster

Bloods leading sports players

Brick crush, queue

Brooke Hall the staff common room or a collective term for the teaching body

Bumming beating

Calling Over the termly assembly before the Headmaster when each pupil's work is reviewed

Carthusian a term for a pupil at Charterhouse

Carthusian, The title of official school magazine

Change changing room

Cocks downstairs basins

CQ cricket quarter (summer term)

Crown tuck shop

Cubes dormitory cubicles

Duckites nickname for Girdlestoneites

Exeat the break in the middle of the term

Fagging errands for monitor

Fags junior slaves

Fugshop carpentry shop

Greyfriar, The illustrated literary school magazine

Great (Gt) Comp sanatorium, medical centre

Hag House matron

Hash school work; lesson period

Hashroom classroom

Headman Headmaster

Homebill evening meal in Houses; when Houses were run by the Housemasters as a source of private income, the house butler provided extra food, which was charged to the boys' 'home bill'

Houseman Housemaster

LQ long quarter (spring term)

Master title of head of Sutton's Hospital

New bug new boy

New hop new boy

OC Old Carthusian (former pupil)

OQ oration quarter (autumn term)

Postees privileges

Private side private living quarters of a Housemaster and family

Quarter mid-morning break; a term

Schoolmaster Headmaster of school section of Sutton's Hospital

Specialist sixth form pupil

SQ summer quarter (summer term); now known as cricket quarter

Tool a run

Tosh bath

Usher assistant teacher at Sutton's Hospital

Under School pupils in the first three year groups

The Houses (in order of founding and with their school abbreviation): Gownboys G; Saunderites S; Verites V; Girdlestoneites g; Lockites L; Weekites W; Hodgsonites H; Daviesites D; Bodeites B; Pageites P; Robinites R; Fletcherites F.

The Founding of the School and the London Years, 1611–1872

DR STEPHEN PORTER

The Founding of the School and the London Years, 1611–1872

DR STEPHEN PORTER, ARCHIVIST OF CHARTERHOUSE, LONDON

Charterhouse was founded in 1611 by Thomas Sutton, one of the wealthiest men of his generation. 'Rich' Sutton, as he was known, had been planning to assign much of his fortune to endow a charity since the mid-1590s. His intention, summarised in a draft will of 1595, was the erection of 'a hospital, chapel and schoolhouse' at Little Hallingbury in Essex. Yet, after years of prevarication, in 1611 he acquired Howard House, the Earl of Suffolk's London mansion on the site of the former Carthusian priory. He died later that year, before it could be adapted as a home for the charity.

Sutton was born at Knaith, Lincolnshire, in 1532. His father, Richard Sutton, was clerk to the sheriff of Lincoln and his mother, Elizabeth Mering, came from a gentry family in Nottinghamshire. Thomas's patrons were Ambrose Dudley, Earl of Warwick, and his brother, Robert, Earl of Leicester, powerful members of the Elizabethan establishment. In his capacity as Master General of the Ordnance, Warwick secured for him the post of Master of the Ordnance in the North Parts, and he played a significant role in the defeat of the rebellion of the northern earls in 1569. Through Leicester's influence, in 1577 he obtained the leases of lucrative coalmines at Gateshead and Whickham in County Durham, formerly held by the Bishop of Durham. In 1582 he left the north of England, selling the lease of the mines for £12,000 in the following year, although retaining his post with the Ordnance until 1594.

He rode south with two horse-loads of money and added to his wealth later in 1582 by marrying Elizabeth Dudley, the widow of John Dudley of Stoke Newington, a cousin of the Earl of Leicester. Sutton now obtained control of Elizabeth's half-share of her late husband's estate and the profits of the other half while her only child, Anne, was a minor. He used his capital to expand his activities as a moneylender, becoming reputedly the

Left: Thomas Sutton.

Previous page: View of the London Charterhouse from Green, c. 1775, attributed to Thomas Malton.

Above: The London Charterhouse, 1756. In the foreground is Charterhouse Square, with the boarding house used by the early Masters (Crusius, Berdmore and Raine) facing and, to the left, the Porter's Lodge. The turquoise area beyond the buildings is the Green with the trees of Wilderness beyond it. To the left of Green is the School building and, on the far left, the brothers' quarters.

Right: A detail from an early document relating to the foundation of Charterhouse, depicting James I.

richest commoner in England. His wealth accumulated enormously, and he acquired property in Essex, Suffolk, Wiltshire, Lincolnshire and Cambridgeshire. At his death in 1611 he was worth £50,000, with an income of roughly £5,000 a year from property.

Elizabeth died in 1602, and Thomas's only child was an illegitimate son, Roger, to whom he gave no financial support after 1592. And so the outlet for the bulk of his fortune was to be his charity. Well aware of predatory interest in his wealth, in 1610 Sutton tried to secure the future of the foundation by obtaining an Act of Parliament and appointing as governors prominent figures in Church and State and in the law.

Despite his careful preparations, the purchase of the Charterhouse was a late decision, not finalised until early May 1611. As the Act referred specifically to Little Hallingbury, it could now be regarded as invalid, and so Sutton obtained Letters Patent specifying that the Charterhouse was to be the site of the foundation, with the name 'The Hospital of King James, founded in Charterhouse within the County of Middlesex'. These were granted on 22 June 1611, and the charity was then legally constituted. Although the title referred only to the almshouse, described by the contemporary term of hospital, a school had been intended throughout the

And gladly would he learne   *and gladly teach*

protracted planning of the charity. The Letters Patent described it as 'a free grammar school'.

After Sutton's death on 12 December 1611 Simon Baxter, Sutton's nephew and heir-at-law, claimed the whole of his fortune. In spite of Sir Francis Bacon's powerful support, the claim was dismissed in June 1613. The governors could then obtain possession of the buildings, where they met on 30 June to decide the practical arrangements. The 16 governors included the Master, the most senior figure in the charity and, although he had no direct participation in running the School, he was responsible for the overall condition of the hospital.

Sutton had not specified the numbers of almsmen and schoolboys, for they depended on the charity's income, and so it was the governors who decided that there should be 80 almsmen and 40 scholars. The boys were to be resident and supervised by just two members of staff, a Schoolmaster and his deputy, designated Usher. Sutton had appointed Francis Carter as surveyor, and the governors accepted his proposals for converting the buildings. A tennis court built during the 4th Duke of Norfolk's ownership of the house, between 1565 and his execution in 1572, was converted into a school. A schoolroom and hall were created on the

ground floor and dormitories on the newly inserted upper floors. They were later described as 'two long low pitched rooms one over the other, which are lined with rows of cabins on both sides with walls made of lath & plaster'. The Schoolmaster's and Usher's accommodation was within the same building. The alterations for the School cost £726; the total for the building work was approximately £8,000.

The School was opened in the autumn of 1614, with Nicholas Grey, a Classical scholar from Oxford, as the first Schoolmaster. He was 24 years old; statutes issued in 1627 ruled that the Schoolmaster should be at least 27. The scholars were to be nominated by the governors or the three royal governors, customarily the monarch, consort and heir. Someone who wished to place their son in the School would approach a governor, perhaps through an intermediary, who would then put his name forward. The qualifications were that the parents were poor and that the boy should be 'well entred in learninge' for his age. The scholars could be admitted between the ages of 10 and 14 and had to leave before they were 19. In 1613 the definition of poverty was that 'no children [were] to be placed there whose parents have any estate of lands to leave unto them, but onlie the children of poore men that want meanes to bringe them up'.

Left: Nicholas Grey, Schoolmaster 1614–24.

Below: The interior of the old Schoolroom, converted from the Duke of Norfolk's indoor tennis court into schoolrooms and dormitories in 1611.

Roger Williams

Roger Williams (c. 1606–83) was awarded a scholarship in 1621, having been nominated by Sir Edward Coke, for whom he had been taking shorthand notes of sermons and of speeches in the court of Star Chamber. Williams was admitted to Pembroke College, Oxford, in 1623 and graduated in 1626. He sailed to New England in 1630 and in 1637–8 founded the settlement of Providence, Rhode Island. There he established freedom of worship, the separation of Church and State and democratic government. He also took a close interest in the culture of the native Americans, publishing his findings in *A Key into the Language of America* (1643). Williams played an important role in the early history of the New England colonies and in the Puritan revolution, and his model for freedom of worship was to be adopted across the United States. A memorial tablet to him was placed in the chapel cloister at Sutton's Hospital in 1899 by Oscar S. Straus, the USA's minister for the Ottoman Empire.

The School quickly became very popular. Not only was there no difficulty in filling the scholars' places, but 'many towne boyes and outcommers from divers parts of the citty and suburbs' were also educated there. The statutes of 1627 restricted the number of such non-foundationers to 60 each for the Schoolmaster and Usher, implying a maximum of 160 pupils at this period. In 1669 it was estimated that roughly 900 boys had been educated at the School in its first 55 years; two-thirds of these were scholars, and so approximately 300 were non-foundationers who were mainly day boys, with just a few boarders. Boarding began only in the mid-17th century, although it had become an established practice by 1680, but there were few rooms available for boarders in the Schoolmaster's and Usher's accommodation.

A scholar's education was free, but competition was so intense that payments were made to secure a place. In 1630 this was commented on by Donald Lupton, who requested the governors 'not to suffer their men, or any other whom they affect, to get 30 or 40 pounds for the promise of the next vacant place for a youth to come in'. One reason for the pressure on scholars' places was that

the charity also provided an exhibition at university for eight years or paid the apprenticeship fees for those who were 'most unapt to learne' and so judged unsuitable for university. There were 24 exhibitions; after the Restoration the number was increased to 29. A place at university for eight years qualified the student for a career, most commonly in the Church, and an apprenticeship, successfully completed, gave the right to trade as a freeman of the City of London. As Edward Chamberlayne explained in 1682, once admitted to one of the principal schools, including Charterhouse, a boy was set on the path to a profession and 'will want little or no assistance from his parents all his lifetime after'. Seen in those terms, a payment to obtain a scholarship was a good long-term investment.

Because of the system of nomination by a governor, who typically could enter two boys every three years, a boy had to be placed on a list several years before he was old enough to enter. The process was explained in this way: 'It's requisite that they be sollicited especially for children 5 or 6 yeares before the children are capable of coming in … else ordinarily they will hardly have the benefit of their warrant.' Of course, the younger a boy was when admitted, within the permitted age range, the greater the benefit he would obtain from his time at the School, but that meant that a boy would need to be placed on a governor's list when he was six or seven years old, before his ability could have been properly assessed. However, the age limit did not apply to day boys, and parents who lived in London or who could secure lodgings nearby could send their son to the School in that capacity while waiting for his scholar's place. William Blackstone, who was only five when he was placed on Sir Robert Walpole's list in 1728, was a day boy at the School from 1730 but did not enter as a scholar until June 1735, when he was 12. Almost a century later John Leech was enrolled as a day boy when he was 7½ and as a boarder 18 months later. He did not obtain a scholarship and left when he was 14½.

The Act of 1610 specified that the Schoolmaster and Usher should teach the scholars 'reading, writing, and Latin and Greek grammar', and the statutes directed them to read to the pupils 'none but approved authors, Greek and Latin, such as are read in the best esteemed free schools' and to provide Greek testaments for those in the upper school. On Sundays members of the highest form were to present to the Schoolmaster, in the Great Hall, four Greek and four Latin verses on the second lesson for that day. Three lists of books from the first eight years of the School show that Latin authors predominated, especially Ovid, Terence and Cicero, with Mathurin Cordier's *Colloquia*, Aesop's *Fabuli* and Erasmus's *Colloquia*; comparatively few Greek books were bought.

A candidate for admission was examined by the Schoolmaster to make sure that he was adequately educated to benefit from the curriculum. Some were refused. But in 1653 the Schoolmaster's decision was challenged by the governors. Anxious to select children 'who may be the meetest objects of charity', they recognised that some had not reached the required standard because of the lack of means or opportunity, yet were capable of benefiting from a Charterhouse education. They considered that such boys could be admitted and taught 'reading, writing and ciphering' until apprenticed to a trade or profession. If placed in a separate form they would not hinder the more advanced pupils.

The admission of boys not able to reach the standard required for the sixth form created problems. In 1667 the Schoolmaster, Thomas Watson, explained that he had been compelled 'to receive some boyes who could not reade English; & many others, whose small progress in learning was nothing answerable to theire years; by reason whereof hee hath often wanted (& at this time doth want) scholars to supply the sixth forme'. That, in turn, limited the number of pupils qualified for university. The order of 1653 was therefore revoked, and the Schoolmaster was again permitted to decline applicants not well enough educated.

The priority was to prepare the scholars for a university education. An order of 1634 had ruled that there should be at least nine boys in the highest form, so that, 'upon any visitacon of the schoole & examinacon of the schollers in that forme for their abillityes to be sent to the universityes there may be a competent number in that forme, out of wch an Eleccon may be duly made of the best learned to be sent to the universityes'. The examinations were conducted by the Archbishop of Canterbury's and Bishop of London's chaplains, the Preacher and, on at least one occasion, a master of Westminster School. The position with regard to pupils unsuitable for university was stated in 1705 when 'a poor scholar' who wanted to go to sea was replaced by his brother, then at Eton and 'of a towardly disposition and good inclination towards his studyes'. The governors justified this with the statement that 'it is more answerable to the intent of this Foundation to Educate such scholars as may improve in Learning to their own advantage, and that

the maintaining such Boys at School as are not capable of Learning and must be put forth Apprentices is expensive & prejudicial to the Hospital'. Among the first 400 scholars admitted after 1680, when the earliest surviving register begins, more than twice as many went to university with an exhibition than were apprenticed.

Support for Charterhouse boys at the universities was increased by the bequest of Dame Elizabeth Holford. In her will of 1717 she bequeathed £4,700 for 11 exhibitions for scholars in Oxford at Christ Church, Pembroke and Worcester colleges and Hart Hall. These became available in 1728. The exhibitions at Hart Hall were transferred to University College in 1745. The Holford scholarships made Oxford more attractive than Cambridge for Charterhouse alumni, but until then both had been more or less equally popular.

Day boys also went to university but could not benefit from an exhibition. Among the day boys in the 17th century who achieved distinction were Richard Lovelace, Isaac Barrow and Joseph Addison. But Barrow's father withdrew him from the school because Robert Brooke, the Master, 'was negligent of him', despite being paid an extra fee. On the other hand, Richard Crashaw acknowledged Brooke's positive role. He entered as a scholar in 1629 and published his first collection of poems just five years later. In the preface he mentioned Brooke's influence in setting exercises imitating Latin and Greek authors. Crashaw embarked on an academic career at Cambridge with a fellowship at Peterhouse. Another of the scholars at the School in the early 17th century to achieve academic distinction was Thomas Greaves (or Graves), who was appointed Deputy Professor of Arabic at Oxford in 1637. In the following year the governors presented him to the rectory of Dunsby in Lincolnshire. This was one of the 11 benefices that Sutton had bequeathed to the charity, and it was the governors' policy to appoint Charterhouse alumni to them. The Schoolmasters, too, were drawn from the alumni, a practice that was maintained from the appointment of William Middleton in 1626 until 1863, when William Haig Brown was appointed.

Few parents withdrew their sons from the School – there were just two cases in the sample of 400 scholars who entered after 1680 – nor were many expelled, only six in the sample, the preferred form of punishment being a 'solemn and publick Recantation'. That is not to say that problems with discipline and behaviour did not occur. In 1635 the size of the glazier's bill for repairing broken

Opposite: View of the School from Upper Green by C.W. Radclyffe, 1844. The new School building (centre) was erected in 1803. On the left are the cloisters, Gownboys and the newly built Saunderites.

Above: (left) Richard Lovelace 1618–58, poet and Royalist cavalier; (right) Sir Richard Steele (1672–1729), MP and writer. Best known as editor of The Tatler *and* The Spectator, *on which he collaborated closely with Joseph Addison OC.*

windows prompted the governors to intervene, admonishing the Schoolmaster and Usher on the grounds that they were not imposing effective discipline.

The scholars could not leave the premises without permission, and some of those who were punished had defied this by climbing over the walls. Bullying of the junior pupils was common by the early 18th century. John Wesley entered as a scholar in 1714, when he was ten years old, and because the older boys snatched the younger ones' meat he later recalled that until he was 14: 'I had little but bread to eat and not great plenty of that.' The implication is that when he went into the upper school, which consisted of forms four, five and six, he could avoid such treatment.

Problems were also caused by boys who had a place at university but were still at the School. No longer willing to be subject to the Schoolmasters' discipline, they treated them disrespectfully. The domestic staff were subject not only to impertinence, but also violence. Having been informed 'that great disorders have been committed by several of the Scholars in assaulting & beating of the Servants of the House', in 1738 the governors ordered that any scholar who 'shall presume to assault any Officer Pensioner or Servant'

should be expelled. In February 1741 the matron's maid made a complaint against the captain of the school, John Roberts. When the Schoolmaster, James Hotchkis, told him he would be expelled, Roberts reacted by gathering most of the scholars, who found the maid in the wash-house, where they 'threw slops upon her, and after that water'. The matron remonstrated with them, so they again doused the maid and then broke the matron's windows. Roberts demanded that the maid be dismissed, and after he had confronted Hotchkis all the scholars burst out of the school 'and ran hollowing into the Green and other parts of the House'. It was a week before the School returned to normal. The governors punished the worst offenders – Roberts was expelled – also appointing a committee to investigate the state of the School, which concluded, rather surprisingly, that discipline was 'in an orderly State'.

The mid-18th century was a period of some turmoil at the School. Questions were asked about the boys' welfare and living conditions, and the teaching staff clashed with the Master and some of the officers. The late 17th and early 18th centuries had been a long period of stability, with Thomas Walker serving as Schoolmaster from 1679 until his death in 1728. His successor, Andrew Tooke, had

been his deputy as Usher since 1695 and was to remain as Schoolmaster until 1732, but Tooke and John Gough, his replacement as Usher, were not happy with the arrangements and petitioned the governors, complaining of the conduct of the Master, John King, and the manciple.

New appointments did not end the tensions. Hotchkis succeeded Tooke, and in 1737 Nicholas Mann was appointed Master. Hotchkis had a longstanding knowledge of the School, having entered as a scholar in 1714 and then held an exhibition. He returned as an assistant for almost seven years, before being appointed Usher. He was concerned about the boys' welfare and the staff's conditions, pointing out the difficulty of engaging a new Usher 'because of the nature of the appointment & the confinement'. Mann had no previous experience of the charity, yet was scathing about Hotchkis's abilities, referring to his 'deficiency and incapacity' and describing him as 'an ignorant weak creature whose knowledge is now daily questioned by his own scholars to his face and is out of all question at the Colleges where his ill-educated disciples appear'. There was nothing ill-educated about William Blackstone, whose talents were nurtured by Hotchkis while he was at the School in the 1730s.

John Wesley (1703–91)

John Wesley came to Charterhouse in 1714 as a foundation scholar. His father was chaplain to the Duke of Buckingham, a governor. He studied not only Latin and Greek, which were on the curriculum, but also Hebrew. After leaving the School he received a Charterhouse exhibition at Christ Church, Oxford. After a period in Georgia he returned to London and in 1738 underwent a profound spiritual experience during a service of the Moravians at a meeting house in Aldersgate Street. This convinced him that salvation comes only through an individual's faith in Christ. His connection with the charity was resumed, and in early 1739 he used a room in the buildings for study and quiet reflection. He split with the Moravians shortly afterwards and established Methodism, which developed into the most dynamic religious movement of the 18th century, not least through the strength of Wesley's convictions, his preaching abilities and boundless energy. A small plaster bust of him, dated 1770, is in the chapel cloister at Sutton's Hospital.

Blackstone was elected the world's first Professor of Common Law, at Oxford University, and between 1765 and 1769 he published the influential and enduring *Commentaries on the Laws of England*.

Hotchkis resigned in 1748 when the governors presented him to the living of Balsham. His successor, Lewis Crusius, attempted to improve standards. In his first year he insisted that the current sixth formers remain at school for an extra year because they were not well enough educated for university, but he also fell foul of the Master. Crusius's problems eased when Philip Bearcroft succeeded Mann in 1753. He had been a scholar and exhibitioner and had been Preacher since 1724, so had a close knowledge of the School.

Crusius took the opportunity to draw attention to its condition. In a memorandum presented in 1754 he complained that many scholars were 'not sufficiently qualified in learning for their age' when they were admitted, which he blamed on the lack of an entrance examination. He had found it necessary to reinstate 'many things' dropped by his predecessors and to add English exercises and geography 'as being necessary parts of Polite Learning'.

Part of the problem outlined by Crusius was that the School had too many pupils for the two staff to look after. The Usher taught the first, second and third forms, and the Schoolmaster the fourth, fifth and sixth. The upper school contained between 30 and 40 boys and was roughly half the size of the lower one, indicating a total of over 100 pupils, including the 44 scholars. In addition, the reading

Sir William Blackstone MP (Charterhouse 1731–38), author of the first codification of British law, Commentaries on the Laws of England, *is commemorated at Charterhouse by the annual Blackstone scholarship for sons of lawyers.*

master taught a junior class known as 'petties', designed to improve the literacy of new entrants. The governors were impressed by Crusius, 'by whose care and abilities the credit of the School hath already been much advanced', and allowed an extra £40 a year so that he could employ an Assistant Usher, and they decided that the School should be rebuilt because of the foul conditions in the existing one. But the new building was not erected, and the governors ordered only remedial work, including a new privy and 'such other repairs as are necessary to keep out wind and weather'.

Extra accommodation was, however, provided for the boarders. There were four boarding Houses by the 1750s, only one of which was run by a member of staff. That was the Master's house, on the south side of Chapel Court, which Crusius adapted for up to 23 boarders. When he resigned in 1769 the list of pupils for his successor, Samuel Berdmore, contained the names of 52 non-foundationers, both town-boys and boarders. The bill for a year for one boarder, in 1763, came to £19 8s, of which £12 10s was for boarding charges, £2 7s for tuition, £1 1s 6d for books and the remainder for a variety of fees.

Activities outside the formal curriculum included music and drama. One of the organist's duties was to 'bring up the Schollars to Musicke'. William Cosyn was the first organist, appointed in 1626, and from the appointment of Johann Christoph Pepusch in 1737 until the School was moved to Godalming in 1872 the post was held by a succession of distinguished musicians. The first record of a school play is a performance in 1729 of Terence's *The Eunuch*. Such productions seem to have become an annual event, attended by governors and other senior figures. Other entertainments were mounted, such as that staged for the Gunpowder Plot celebrations in 1732. An anti-papist, partisan work, entitled *A Dramatic Piece: By the Charter-House Scholars: In Memory of the Powder-Plot*, it was set in the Vatican, where the pope, assisted by the devil, schemes to revive Rome's pre-eminence.

Thomas Hull was a scholar from 1738 until 1745, when he was bound apprentice to his father, a London apothecary. Perhaps enthused by his experiences at School, he became an actor and dramatist, playing at the Smock Alley Theatre, Dublin, in 1753–4 and at Covent Garden from 1759 until shortly before his death in 1807. Hull's career choice was unusual, but those followed by Charterhouse scholars were changing during the 18th century. In the 1720s roughly equal numbers went on to

Programme for an early drama production by Charterhouse scholars.

careers in the Church or served apprenticeships, mostly in London. A few took posts in the universities, and some went into the law. By the 1770s the proportion of scholars who became clergymen was much the same as it had been 50 years earlier, but only a handful became apprentices, while roughly a fifth went directly into the armed forces. Of the scholars in the 18th century who entered the Church, John Wesley had a major impact as the founder of Methodism. Eight of them became bishops, while Charles Manners-Sutton, a boarder, was appointed Archbishop of Canterbury in 1805, the only Charterhouse boy to have achieved that distinction. Edward Law pursued a legal career, which culminated in his appointment as Attorney General in 1801 and Lord Chief Justice of England in the following year, when he was created Baron Ellenborough.

Among the few who followed political careers, Charles Jenkinson served as President of the Board of Trade from

Opposite: The north aisle of the Charterhouse chapel, built in 1614.

1786 until 1804 and, simultaneously, as Chancellor of the Duchy of Lancaster from 1786 until 1803. In 1796 he was created 1st Earl of Liverpool. His son, Robert Banks-Jenkinson, was a pupil in the 1780s and succeeded to the title in 1808. He was appointed Prime Minister in 1812 and held the post until 1827, during the final years of the Napoleonic War, the postwar recession and pressure for political reform and Catholic emancipation.

In the late 18th century the School grew in importance within the charity. The almshouse had commonly been regarded as the more prominent part, not least because of its significance as the largest almshouse ever founded in England. The changing attitude was helped by the appointment of William Ramsden as Master in 1778, promoted from the junior post of Usher, which he had held for 30 years. His long experience of the School no doubt improved its position, as well as easing the tensions between School and Master that had created difficulties earlier. He was Master until his death in 1804, having been Usher and then Master for 56 years.

Ramsden's successor was Philip Fisher, and in 1791 Berdmore's successor as Master was Matthew Raine. A fellow of Trinity College, Cambridge, Raine had been a scholar at Charterhouse in the 1770s.

In the 1790s the scholars still included the sons of the parish clergy and gentry, but with the emergence of the Charterhouse as one of the 'great schools' it also attracted the children of senior churchmen, members of the aristocracy, academics and diplomats. Nevertheless, when Fisher summarised the objectives of the charity in 1811 he stressed that the School should provide for those between the extremes of wealth and poverty, 'whose liberal habits and pursuits entitle them to expect for their sons those advantages of a learned education' that would otherwise be unavailable to them because of their modest incomes.

The number of pupils rose during Raine's time with the annual intake of non-foundationers being 30 or even 40, compared to the 20 that was typical when Berdmore was Schoolmaster. In 1802 the School contained 144 boys, and the balance between boarders and town-boys had changed, with 88 boarders but just 16 town-boys.

As the charity's rents of both its London and country estates increased during the late 18th and early 19th centuries, the problem of the deteriorating School building was at last addressed, and a new one was erected on the north side of Scholars' Green, which had been a

Left: Miniature of the 2nd Earl of Liverpool, Prime Minister 1812–27.

Below: Print by Radclyffe of the new Schoolroom, built in 1803.

formal garden but by that date was a sports field. The new School, built in 1802–3, was a single-storey building, containing a Schoolroom described as, 'very large – oblong, lofty, and well proportioned … lighted by a row of semicircular windows, placed very high up and running all round the building; and in the centre was a large skylight'. The room was laid out with two tiers of seating around the walls, with long tables and benches. Additional apartments for the Schoolmaster and Usher were added in 1805.

Right: Matthew Raine, Schoolmaster 1791–1811.

Alterations to the existing building were carried out at the same time. The scholars had become known as the

Gownboys, and that name was also applied to the building, which was described as 'of some antiquity … nearly as strong as Newgate'. Their hall on the ground floor was retained, and the former schoolroom was divided into a writing-school and a dormitory for the senior boys. On the first floor there was an open dormitory and rooms for the Usher and Preacher, and on the second floor a dormitory and two more rooms for the Usher. The three dormitories contained a total of 40 beds, reflecting the recently introduced reform to provide each boy with a separate bed.

In 1810 the governors presented Raine to the living of Little Hallingbury, and he asked if he could resign as Schoolmaster because of ill health. During Raine's final illness the Schoolmaster's duties were carried out by Dr John Russell, an assistant at the School since 1806. After Raine's death in 1811 the governors appointed Russell to the post, now designated Schoolmaster, even though at 25 he was two years below the minimum age specified in the statutes. He was to have a greater impact than any previous Schoolmaster.

Gownboys

Gownboys is the oldest Charterhouse boarding House, established to house the first scholars in 1614 (other pupils were initially day boys). They slept in dormitories above the first Schoolroom. Gownboys was named, not after the original Housemaster, but because the scholars wore gowns over their uniform (a short black jacket and knee breeches). Despite their status as 'scholars', the Gownboys were, at times, neglected by the Schoolmaster because he earned extra income directly from day pupils' fees, but not from the free scholars. Following the move to Godalming, the scholars were no longer placed in one House, but distributed throughout the various Houses, on a random but numerically equal basis.

Gownboys occupies the central position in the main school block on the east side of Founder's Court, built by P.C. Hardwick in 1872. The House has been modernised over the years, but the panelled dining-room and hall (with its 120-foot chimney) remains untouched and the two large tower studies occupied by the head monitor and deputy head monitor have also been preserved.

Dr John Russell.

The increase in the charity's income enabled the governors to consider adding four more scholars' places. Russell proposed that the new ones should be competed for by examination, not obtained through a governor's nomination. He had support from some of the governors but was opposed by others, including Fisher. Russell's proposal was defeated, and so the existing system of nomination was applied to the new places. Fisher was later remembered to have said that Charterhouse 'is not intended as a school of learning, it is a charitable foundation. We are not to seek out who is best. Poor boys and sons of poor men ought to be preferred to all the rest.' The Master's influence had outweighed that of the Schoolmaster, and the underlying uncertainty about the School's role had still not been resolved: it remained unclear whether it should be taking pupils who could be prepared for the universities or educating disadvantaged boys.

Russell was later described by one of his pupils, George Venables, as 'vigorous, unsympathetic and stern, though not severe'. But others remembered him as brutal. The author Martin Tupper wrote that he 'domineered over all to

William Makepeace Thackeray

The author William Makepeace Thackeray (1811–63) entered the School in 1822 as a lodger and left in 1828. He held the Schoolmaster, John Russell, personally responsible for his lack of progress, writing to his mother that 'he has thrown every possible object in my way to prevent my exerting myself'. He was critical of the staff's bullying and social pretensions, yet he subsequently became rather nostalgic for his schooldays. Thackeray was a distinguished essayist and editor, writing for *Punch* magazine – whose principal illustrator was John Leech, his contemporary and friend at Charterhouse – and he was the founding editor of the *Cornhill Magazine* in 1860. He found fame as one of the finest novelists of the 19th century and his books contain vivid depictions of English society, tinged with satire. They were popular, especially *Vanity Fair* (1847–8), *Pendennis* (1849–50), *The History of Henry Esmond* (1851–2) and *The Newcomes* (1853–5). In *The Newcomes* he presented an affectionate description of Charterhouse, and the connection with the author was fostered by the charity. A memorial to him was placed on the wall in the chapel cloister, and his centenary in 1911 was celebrated by an exhibition and a lecture by the Earl of Rosebery, Liberal Prime Minister in 1894–5.

The Newcomes paints a nostalgic picture of Charterhouse as the location for Clive Newcome's education and the sanctuary for Colonel Newcome in his old age. Thackeray describes Founder's Day, still celebrated on 12 December: 'To other than Cistercians, Grey Friars is a dreary place possibly. Nevertheless the pupils educated there love to revisit it; and the oldest of us grow young again for an hour or two as we come back into those scenes of childhood.

'The stewards of the day's dinner, according to an old-fashioned rite, have wands put into their hands, walk to church at the head of the procession, and sit there in places of honour. The boys are already in their seats, with smug fresh faces, and shining white collars; the old black-gowned pensioners are on their benches; the chapel is lighted, and Founder's Tomb, with its grotesque carvings, monsters, heraldries, darkles and shines with the most wonderful shadows and lights. There he lies, *Fundator Noster*, in his ruff and gown, awaiting the great Examination Day.

'Yonder sit 40 cherry-cheeked boys, thinking about home and holidays tomorrow. Yonder sit some threescore old gentlemen pensioners of the hospital, listening to the prayers and the psalms. You hear them coughing feebly in the twilight – the old reverend blackgowns.'

Above: Items from Thackeray's writing desk.

Left: A bust of Thackeray aged 11 by Boehm. It was modelled on a cast taken from the living face.

Below and right: Illustrations of Charterhouse from The Newcomes.

our universal terror', and he recalled Edward Churton, the Master of the upper school, 'affected to tears at the cruelty of his chief'. Yet Russell disliked corporal punishment and attempted to replace it with a system of fines, only to be defeated by the opposition of the boys themselves. His successor as Schoolmaster, Augustus Saunders, a pupil at the time, later explained their attitude with the comment: 'We thought flogging was very gentlemanly but fines most ungentlemanly.' Tupper attributed the nervous stammer that afflicted him until middle age to Russell's vindictive harassment. William Makepeace Thackeray was one of his contemporaries.

Pupils during Russell's time also recalled the uncomfortable conditions, the overcrowding, the poor food, the pranks in which they had indulged, the poring over smutty publications and the merciless bullying. Although Russell was 'a strong foe to all sorts of battles', fights broke out from time to time – Thackeray's nose was broken by Venables during one bout – and there was a more tragic

outcome to a traditional Good Friday rampage, known as 'pulling out', when a boy who was knocked over and trampled died of his injuries.

Some ill-treatment arose from the fagging system, with the junior boys carrying out chores for the older ones. Robert Smythe described it in his account of the charity published in 1808: 'Many a youth … has boiled the kettle, toasted the bread, and performed numberless menial offices, at the nod, and for the ease and pleasure, of an upper boy.' This he justified because it served 'in future life to check that spirit of domineering which the acquisition of power too often excites or generates in the possessors of it'. But not all boys did resist such behaviour while they were at School, and Alexander Tod later wrote that the senior boys 'could make the lives of fags a burden to them if they liked, and often they did'.

The conditions and disciplinary problems were partly due to the rapid increase in the numbers of pupils under Russell, after he introduced the Bell or Madras system in

Ackermann print of the new Charterhouse Schoolroom, viewed from the east end. Five boys are standing in front of the Schoolmaster's dais whilst the remaining pupils are taught by assistant masters and older pupils, as recommended by the Madras system.

Doodles drawn in a Charterhouse text book by John Leech who went on to become a famous cartoonist for Punch.

1818. This was devised by Andrew Bell, a clergyman, for use in the East India Company's Male Orphan Asylum at Madras. The older and more capable pupils taught the younger ones, in smaller groups than can be achieved in a form taught by a single teacher. The School was divided into 12 forms, subdivided into as many as 26 groups. Thomas Mozley remembered an occasion when Russell supervised the division of the School into groups, each containing 20 boys, and described the way in which the system worked. Each group was seated on three benches, which formed an open square, with a senior boy acting as the *praepositus* (monitor) on the fourth side as the teacher: 'When a boy made a fault he was forbidden to correct himself, and the chance was given to the next, and so on downwards, and the boy who corrected the fault … stepped past all the rest, and above the original fault-maker.' A boy could also lose his position for misbehaviour or inattention. The Schoolmaster's role was overseeing the classes and 'hearing each form in order, spending about half an hour or less with each'. John Leech wrote to his father: 'I went in to be examined by Dr Russell yesterday but did not get promoted but I did not lose more than one or two places.' But while the number of pupils rose from 238 in 1818, to 438 in 1822 and to 480 in 1825, the number of masters was increased only from five to eight.

Most of the increase in numbers consisted of boarders; three boarding Houses were added to the existing two in Charterhouse Square and two more were opened in Wilderness Row, north of the School. Additions were also made to the buildings, with an extension to the chapel and a building for the day boys, erected in 1825 close to the north end of Rutland Place. Also in that year work began to rebuild that part of the site where the Brothers' accommodation stood. The new quadrangles were designated Pensioners' Court and Preacher's Court. The governors would not erect accommodation for boarders because they were not part of the charity, but they

recognised that the boarders improved the standard of education for the Gownboys by providing greater competition. They also supplied extra remuneration for the staff because their fees, at least £80 a year, were divided among them, as they had been from the 17th century.

The boarding Houses were crowded, and the conditions partly explain the resentful memories of their schooldays nursed by Thackeray and his contemporaries. In his early fiction Thackeray described Charterhouse as the Slaughter House School, near Smithfield; only later did he designate it, more affectionately, as the Grey Friars. Former pupils were also critical of the curriculum, with its continued emphasis on Latin and Greek. Tupper described it as 'mainly waste of time and of very little service in the battle of life'.

Mozley was less severe, remembering with pleasure Russell's love of Greek and his teaching abilities, but he condemned the Bell system as 'a very bad one'. The problems it caused had been recognised at the time, and the numbers at Charterhouse fell steadily from the peak in

1825 to 289 in 1829 and 137 in 1832. Perhaps well suited to an elementary school, the system was not appropriate for a grammar school, and when Saunders succeeded Russell in 1832 he abandoned it completely.

Under Saunders the number of boys in the School gradually settled down to about 180. A governors' order of 1845 set the maximum number at 200, but in practice that figure was not reached. The boarding Houses were closed, and the House system evolved from the new arrangements put in place to lodge more than 100 boarders. Russell had not accommodated them in the Schoolmaster's house, rebuilt in 1829, but Saunders revived the practice, and the Usher from 1838, Oliver Walford, also took in boarders. His nickname was Old Ver, and Verites was hence adopted as the name of one of the school's Houses, along with Saunderites, Dickenites (Charles Dicken was assistant master in 1824–30 and reader in 1838–61; he took in 'a few private boarders'), and scholars.

Saunders revived Russell's scheme to increase the number of foundationers, who would be chosen by examination not nomination. In 1850 this was agreed to, but only two scholarships were to be competed for and candidates had to have been in the School for a year before the election. An investigation into the condition of the charity in 1860 showed that the annual surplus was £2,278 and that each Gownboy cost £100 per annum. The governors responded by implementing the largest increase

in the number of Gownboys since the establishment of the charity, raising the total to 60, and in 1862 a new building was erected to accommodate them. But the total number of boys did not increase, as Saunders had hoped, partly because parents were coming to prefer the new public schools that were being opened outside London, which provided a better environment and more facilities for sports. Football and cricket were both played at Charterhouse, for the site was large enough, and in his history of the charity published in 1849, M. Sewell wrote that: 'It is one of the few places, if not the only one, in the midst of the crowded habitations of London, where the schoolboy may still be seen enjoying, upon an ample green, the healthful and English game of cricket.' Nevertheless, the School was in the centre of the smoky and grimy metropolis, not in the spacious shires, and in 1862 Richard Elwyn, Schoolmaster from 1858 to 1863, commented: 'Of late years there has been a very strong feeling against London schools … even among many old Carthusians.'

Other criticisms were aired in an article in Charles Dickens's influential periodical *Household Words* in December 1855. It claimed that the School had come to dominate the charity at the expense of the almshouse and that the aristocracy and the Church's senior hierarchy were benefiting, not the parish clergy, whose sons should have been the recipients of its education. But almost half of the scholars admitted during the 1850s were sons of members

Saunderites

Saunderites was established in 1836 by Dr Augustus Page Saunders, himself a pupil in Chapman's from 1817 to 1819, and Schoolmaster from 1832 to 1853. Until the mid-20th century, the Headmaster was also the Housemaster of Saunderites; and the Headmaster still retains part of the House for his study and waiting rooms. When the School moved to Godalming, those Houses that already existed in London (Saunderites, Verites and Gownboys) were provided for in the architect's plans. The private side of Saunderites was planned by William Haig Brown to accommodate his wife, nine children and servants, and originally most of the boys slept in long dormitories. These are now gone, and boys are accommodated in either single or twin bedrooms.

Dr Augustus Saunders.

Verites

Verites House can claim a history dating back to 1794 when pupils first boarded in Rutland House on the south east side of Lower Green at the London Charterhouse. Rutland House was subsequently known as Chapman's and then Penny's House after its boarding house proprietors. In 1838 the House was taken over by Oliver Walford, known to the boys as 'Old Ver', an abbreviation of his first name. Walford died in 1858, but his nickname continues in the House name, Verites. Verites occupies one of the original three Victorian gothic 'block houses' at

Oliver Walford (Charterhouse 1827–31), Assistant Master 1836–38, Usher and Housemaster of Verites 1838–55.

Charterhouse, purpose-built for the School's move from London to its present site in Godalming in 1872.

of the lay professions and the armed forces, with slightly fewer being clergymen's sons, and most of their fathers were parish clergy, not senior churchmen. Boys from an aristocratic background formed less than one-seventh of the intake. The subsequent careers of Charterhouse boys contradicted the further claim in *Household Words* that the School had become a seminary for the Anglican Church, for they entered a wide range of professions and barely a fifth of them were ordained.

Among the Charterhouse alumni who went on to distinguished careers were Francis Turner Palgrave, who became Professor of Poetry at Oxford and is best known for his two volumes of *The Golden Treasury* of songs and lyrical poems, and Edwin Palmer, who became vice-president of Corpus Christi College, Oxford, and Professor of Latin Literature. George Ferguson Bowen was a Gownboy between 1833 and 1840; he was successively governor of Queensland, New Zealand, Victoria, Mauritius and Hong Kong, was knighted in 1856 and was made a Privy Councillor in 1886. Among his contemporaries was William Paget, who followed a career in the diplomatic service; he too received a knighthood, and was made a Privy Councillor in 1876. Their careers and those of other alumni could have been used to justify the existing system.

Saunders and Elwyn made their comments when they were witnesses at hearings of the Clarendon Commission, which investigated nine schools between 1861 and 1864. The commissioners enquired into all aspects of the School and questioned staff, officers, and present and past pupils. But two issues dominated. One was the possibility of separating the School from the almshouse and moving it out of London; the second was the way in which the scholars were selected. The suggestion that the School could be moved had been made as early as 1825, and it had since become a serious proposition. Those who favoured greater independence for the School as a separate branch of the charity clearly saw the Commission as an opportunity to air their views. Separation would allow it to develop and educate more boys. Saunders was unequivocal: 'I would take away the School, and take it into the country.'

Elwyn supported that view, describing Charterhouse as principally a boarding school already and adding that 'very few of our boys actually come from London'. Nor could he see any necessary connection between the School and the almshouse and thought that a separation could be made without damage to either and that it could be funded by

selling that part of the site occupied by the School. That would be relatively easy because the School and the almshouse were physically distinct. A move away from the capital without changing the character of the School was therefore a possibility. On the other hand, Elwyn wanted only limited change in respect of admissions. He believed that the nature of the School would be altered if all of the scholarships were competed for, and so he wished to retain some for boys nominated by the governors, 'because the fact of the governors having the power of nomination conduces to the gentlemanly character of the School'. Saunders thought that three places a year filled by competition would be appropriate. He stressed the difficulties of persuading the governors to make changes in the selection process.

The Master of the charity, William Hale Hale, was decidedly against change, describing himself as 'a very old-fashioned person'. He had been a pupil at the School from 1808 until 1811, was appointed Preacher in 1823 and succeeded Fisher as Master in 1842, holding the post until his death in 1870. The dominant figure in the charity for a generation or more, Hale was opposed to moving the School and changing the system of admissions, believing that 'competition would not be better than nomination'. He echoed Fisher: 'It was not, in my opinion, the object of the Founder to admit only such children as were good scholars.'

The commissioners had already heard evidence that Hale's long knowledge of the charity and his personality made him somewhat difficult for the Schoolmaster to deal with. While he did not have a direct involvement in the running of the School or discipline within it, he clearly had influence, as Master and a governor. Saunders said that Hale attended examinations and gave his opinion, and because of his status effectively presided over them. He also interfered with practical aspects of the School, without first consulting the Schoolmaster. Moving the School would end the Master's influence, for he would be left to supervise the almshouse.

Despite the apparent conservatism within the charity, changes had been made before the enquiry. By the early 1860s the subjects taught, in addition to Latin and Greek, included history (ancient and modern), geography, divinity, mathematics, drawing and French, to which chemistry and German had been added recently. The new subjects were not immediately popular with the boys. Nor did they want to see the most major change of all, the removal of the School to the country. One Gownboy told the commissioners

Above: Gownboys' Dining Room, London Charterhouse, watercolour by Frederick Smallfield. The room was created in 1613–14, partly on the site of the Friars' refectory. The room was the Gownboys' dining-hall from 1846 onwards.

Left: Brooke Hall, the London Charterhouse, 1868 by Frederick Smallfield.

that the pupils 'would like it to stay where it is … They think it could not be got up so well in the country'.

In 1864 the commissioners responded to the mass of evidence they had heard by recommending in their report that the School should be moved out of London and that all of the scholarships should be filled through open competition. The governors' response was that neither change would be implemented. They saw the removal of the School as unnecessary and also inexpedient, 'as it would entail the maintenance of two Establishments, an expenditure which the Funds of the Hospital could not meet'. *The Times* weighed in with a leader strongly in favour of a move, pointing out that parents would be reluctant to send their sons to a school 'in the very heart of the metropolis, and closely surrounded on all sides by its very worst districts'. It received letters agreeing with its stance, and a campaign supporting removal gathered momentum, with William Haig Brown, the new

Schoolmaster, to the fore. He and the Usher presented a memorial to the governors and canvassed the opinion of over 400 Old Carthusians; roughly 90 per cent of those who replied favoured moving the school.

The governors responded by setting up a committee to investigate the matter further. When it reported in favour of moving the School away from London, the governors changed their stance and accepted the recommendation. The Public Schools Act of 1868 provided for the division of the charity into two branches with separate boards of governors; that for the School was designated the Governing Body. The commissioners' proposal that all scholarships should be competed for was also accepted, and the last nominated Gownboy was admitted in 1873.

The sale of the School site to the Merchant Taylors' Company for £90,000, which was £30,000 under the price the governors had hoped to obtain, funded the purchase of 70 acres and the construction of the new buildings at Godalming in Surrey. The School met at Godalming for the first time on 18 June 1872, and the buildings were transferred to Merchant Taylors, which demolished them to erect their own. A few elements were taken to Godalming, including the stone door surround known as Gownboys' Arch, inscribed with the names of alumni, and a 17th-century chimneypiece from the writing-school.

The almshouse retains a few reminders of the long period during which it shared the site with the School. In the Great Hall the senior boys recited Latin and Greek verses to the Master every Sunday; the Old Library was the Gownboys' dining room from 1846 until 1872, reached from the School along the Norfolk Cloister, which was also the scene of hectic football matches; and the extension to the chapel erected for the boys still has its original pews, liberally inscribed with their graffiti. Schoolmasters and Ushers are more formally recorded, with memorials and ledger slabs to ten of them in the chapel and chapel cloister. These are tangible links between the two branches of Thomas Sutton's charity, which separated after 258 years together in the buildings that he had chosen for them.

1st XI Cricket team at London Charterhouse, 1867, outside the Norfolk Cloister.

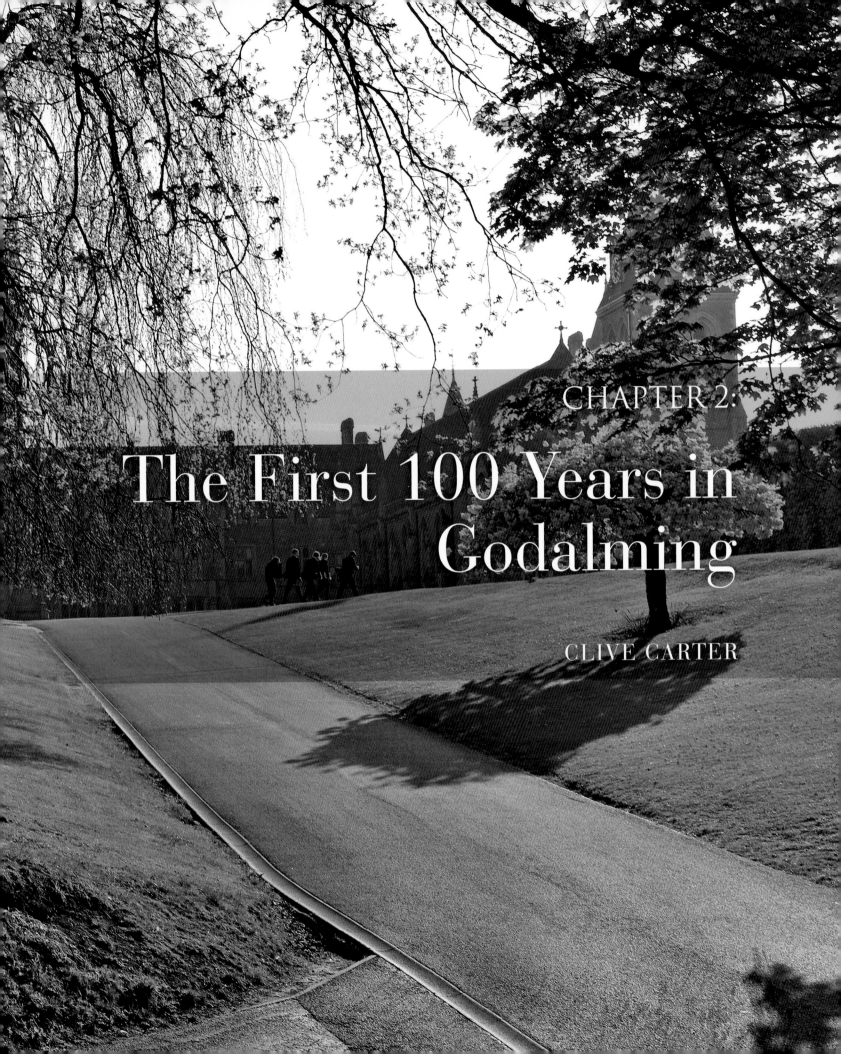

CHAPTER 2:

The First 100 Years in Godalming

CLIVE CARTER

The First 100 years in Godalming

CLIVE CARTER

Charterhouse has been so synonymous with Godalming for over a century that it is surprising to learn that this was not the first choice of site. The governors had begun by looking at their own lands, for they still held some of Sutton's original estates. Hallingbury, near Bishop's Stortford, where Sutton had originally founded the hospital, was initially considered, but rejected. Thereafter the brief they gave to the Foundation's architect, Philip Hardwick, instructed him to favour the Thames valley below Goring in Berkshire, the Liphook area or the region between Reigate and Guildford in Surrey. They wanted from 30 to 100 acres, with access to water and within three miles of a town. The first choice was a Taplow site, but the negotiations failed.

Haig Brown's wife, Annie Marion, was the daughter of the Revd Evan Edward Rowsell, rector of Hambledon. It was perhaps through this connection that Haig Brown came to hear of the Deanery Farm Estate in nearby Godalming. The British Land Company had bought the estate from the dean and chapter of Salisbury Cathedral and was selling it for development – its hill was said to be visible from Hambledon. The location fulfilled the conditions, except for water. It was said in the Masque (a historical pageant about Charterhouse) that when he was visiting the site with Hardwick, Haig Brown tripped and fell. Rising with a clod of earth in his hand, he said: 'I accept the omen; this must be Charterhouse soil.' Certainly Haig Brown's granddaughter, Hilda, has said that, having walked to the site from Hambledon, he brought back flowers and said: 'These are from where I am going to build my school.' The governors agreed.

The new site had no buildings on it, so Philip Hardwick was commissioned to provide a completely new design. The outcome was exceptionally fortunate. The site was rural but easily accessible from London by rail. It was near civilisation – Godalming – but sufficiently distinct to be remote from the fleshpots of Clerkenwell, which had worried the reformers. Mercifully, the site provided its own

building stone, the warm Bargate sandstone, so the hot red brick of less fortunate schools was avoided, and the design, probably by Hardwick's son, Philip Charles, in refined early Gothic, was distinctive without being overpowering. Some had hoped for a Roman style, like Euston Station (which Philip had designed in 1838) to echo the classicism of the London Gownboys and Big School, but they at least could relish the symmetry of the design and the Georgian proportions of the interiors. Though Charterhouse is no Stowe, it remains more practical and somehow more kindly.

Previous page: View from Racquet's Court Hill.

Below: Annie Marion Haig Brown and a page from one of her scrapbooks, in which she recorded every aspect of school life from 1863 to 1903.

THE NEW SCHOOL

The School that moved to Godalming was small. A total of 117 boys and seven masters came down to Godalming during the 'migration' on 18 June, Waterloo Day, 1872. They were to be joined by new pupils, who made the total up to 150, and three more beaks. Their premises, though much more open, rural and splendid, were, in general, the same as they had been in London, as the governors had specified. The three boarding Houses had a common room for seniors (Uppers) and one for juniors (Unders), called Upper-Long and Under-Long (room). Gownboys kept their old names of Hall and Writing School. Above this were two floors of large, open dormitories fitted out with wooden cubicles and a handful of individual studies.

William Haig Brown

The Revd Dr William Haig Brown (Headmaster, 1863–98) is rightly credited with being the second founder of Charterhouse. His skills as a businessman and as a manager of people were the keys to his success in moving the School from London to Godalming and turning its fortunes around. Haig Brown was educated at Christ's Hospital, was a fellow of Pembroke College, Cambridge, and, prior to his appointment at Charterhouse, had been headmaster of Kensington School. When he arrived at Charterhouse in 1863 the School was in a poor state with dwindling numbers. He played a crucial role in persuading the governors to abandon their opposition to the removal into the country that the Clarendon Commission had recommended in 1864.

Haig Brown proved to have the business acumen and personality to attract parents to the new School, doubling pupil numbers within two years. He overcame the lack of funds to build accommodation for extra pupils by allowing masters to build boarding Houses at their own expense as business ventures. As well as being Headmaster, Haig Brown was his own secretary, administrator and bursar, running the financial affairs of the school single-handedly. Once the School had moved he made sure that he informed and guided the governors' decisions. He was a good project manager, taking an interest in all the building developments. Haig Brown may not have been a particularly inspiring teacher, but he was good at appointing and managing his teaching staff. He was very happy to delegate much of the everyday running of the School to others, but he knew each boy by name and had a good overview.

Importantly for any leader, Haig Brown also had a tremendous personality and a good sense of humour, and he was regarded by the boys with a mixture of awe and affection. He was helped in his role by his wife, the indefatigable Annie Marion, who was devoted to the care of the boys, in addition to her own 12 children. She still found time to keep scrapbooks, gathering material on all aspects of School life and matters relating to Charterhouse. Haig Brown retired in 1897, after 34 years as Headmaster, to become Master of Sutton's Hospital, leaving a School that was successful and secure, both financially and academically.

Below left: A typical Charterhouse washroom, known as 'cocks'; (right) End of term packing in a Verites dormitory. Note the cubicles on either side of a central corridor.

Behind these main, three-storey blocks were lower, domestic premises. Service areas included kitchens, sculleries, a servants' hall, accommodation for the House butler and extensive cellars, while the boarders had changing rooms, a washing room – known as cocks, from the row of taps (cold) above the basins – and earth closets in open, internal courtyards.

The Houses kept their names: Saunderites (S) for the Headmaster, Verites (V) for the Usher and Gownboys for the Foundation scholars. S and V both had palatial premises for a Housemaster. William Veale, the son of Haig Brown's butler, names 20 staff in S. The plan for Gownboys had originally provided them with only a matron, which caused architectural anomalies that survive to this day. Perhaps surprisingly, there were no dining rooms. In London Gownboys, at least, had its own

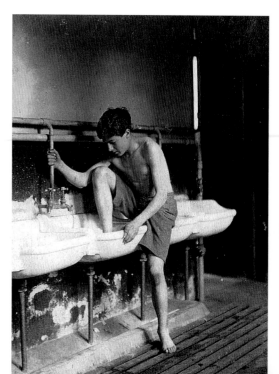

Left: The cloisters today.

Below: Brooke Hall Masters photographed in the cloisters of Scholars' Court, 1872, eight of whom have School Houses named after them.

separate room for eating, beside the Pensioners' Hall at the end of the cloister. Early plans for the new buildings incorporated a two-storey hall to the north of the main tower, perhaps to provide for meals, but this hall disappeared because the governors' perennial concern about lack of funds caused them to prune the design. All the pupils thus worked and ate on the same tables, clearing their books away into cupboards around the walls. This was to cause trouble later, being thought unhygienic. Nonetheless, the buildings were praised for being open, airy, well lit and with modern sanitation.

All the new buildings were connected by cloisters. This cloister system – two adjoining squares, some embedded, some external – made sure that everywhere was accessible under cover. For teaching there was the familiar Big School, laid out as in London, surrounded by six individual hashrooms and a general library, which combined the serious sections of the individual House collections. Both were accessible from the cloister around the transplanted Scholars' Court. Off the impressive, vaulted entrance hall under the tower was a staff common room, to replace Brooke Hall in the London chapel cloister. Another replacement was a room for the governors in Gownboys, with an entrance and lobby off the cloister.

Girdlestone Titmas Davies Hodgson Page Evans
Roulier Vyvyan Bode Buisson
Noon Haig Brown Lock Weekes

41

The School buildings were imposing, particularly Founder's Tower at 141 feet, but they were rather stark and isolated on their hilltop. It was a major change from the more domestic and incalculably more ancient London site. Nevertheless, the constituent parts and their layout would have been moderately familiar to the migrating pupils. The major difference, of course, was space. Although it has been justly claimed that 68½ acres (much of it steep 'hanger or copse, unsuitable for any known game, and indeed out of bounds', according to Jameson in *Charterhouse*) turned out to be seriously inadequate for a modern School, it did contrast markedly with the 5½ acres that the School had enjoyed in the old foundation. One of the reasons for the 'removal' had been the seriously unhealthy state of London for boarding pupils. Once the School had moved to what was later over-optimistically called 'Surrey Switzerland' on its dry, windswept hill, numbers increased rapidly.

It is hard now to think of these buildings as brand new (especially as they were designed to look medieval), but so they were. When the pupils arrived they were not even finished. 'Light was given by candles stuck in ginger-beer bottles … the buildings swarmed with earwigs and rats; to get rid of the rats boys were allowed to keep ferrets in the Houses,' noted A.H. Tod in *The History of Charterhouse*. Mrs Haig Brown's rooms were not painted until August, and she wrote in July: 'The French polishers are still in possession of the drawing room'.

View of the School from Big Ground, c. 1874. The Bargate stone quarry from which the School was built can be clearly seen.

The Haig Brown family's private drawing room in Saunderites.

Gas lighting was eventually supplied, and there was even heating.

The last part of the building programme, the chapel, was finally finished in 1874. Till then, daily worship was in Big School, and on Sundays the whole School walked the two miles to Shackleford church – rural, splendidly new and sufficiently large. The chapel was the most elaborate of all the new buildings, both inside and out, though it was smaller and less elaborate than Hardwick had planned. Outwardly there were crocketed pinnacles and canopied niches, and the interior looked like a splendid Victorian parish church, with an impressively roofed nave, carved corbels and a large east window presented by Queen Victoria in memory of Prince Albert. The seating was collegiate, which it had partly been in London. The single aisle to the south was, in effect, a gallery like the one in the London chapel built in the early 1800s as the number of pupils reached record levels under Dr Russell.

As usual, there was not enough money to furnish it, so windows, panelling, pews and plate were gradually added as gifts or memorials. There was one snag: the governors' pruning of the design for a larger chapel with its own cloister caused a problem. The School cloisters stopped at the chapel's east end, so those going to chapel, thus far sheltered, had to brave the weather to get to the entrance, which was under the tower at the far end of the building. Chapel proved to be too small as early as 1875. Reviving the original plan for a bigger chapel, with its connecting cloister to shelter the approaching congregation, was to become an architectural priority.

Above right: Original chapel under construction c. 1873. Note the Bargate stone stacked up outside Saunderites ready to be used.

Above: Interior of chapel.

Right: East window of chapel, presented by Queen Victoria.

Victorian method, logic and practicality informed the infrastructure. Founder's Tower resembles a bell tower, but it was really a water tower, supplied by a steam pump from the School's own 120 foot well. This well was dug beside the laundry, in a picturesque gaggle of service buildings, not often seen in the photographs, which sprawled along what was then the northern boundary of the new site and which included a maintenance workshop and the Headmaster's stables. The spoil from the earth closets became fertiliser for kitchen gardens.

THE HOUSES

Though provision had been made by the architect for three extra Houses, which would have produced an impressive and symmetrical campus, the new Governing Body felt that they had not enough money to build them. So, as had been the case in London, individual masters began accommodating boys in their own Houses. Those with private money, or those who could get a loan from the bank, bought the road frontage sites that the British Land Company had cannily excluded from the purchase – Dr Haig Brown had bravely secured four units at his own cost. These entrepreneurs built their own more or less palatial premises either side of the sandy track, appropriately called Sandy Lane, leading up the valley from Godalming. To the east of the School, this was once the haunt of nightingales. Buildings thus swiftly spread along the valley sides, altering the School's entire focus and ensuring that the grand entrance from Peperharow Road became the back door, destroying the architect's vision. The grand gates and two lodges were left in a backwater. In 1900 A.H. Tod observed: 'The architect followed nature, but the traffic followed convenience. Hence there is at present no lodge to mark the usual entrance to the School, only a gas meter.' These new, private Houses were joined to the School by a convenient bridge over the chasm, provided by the British Land Company. This eventually fell down and had to be replaced by the present, more glamorous, Gothic structure by Sir Arthur Blomfield, expressing the new found confidence of a rapidly expanding School.

Three of these new Houses were on the School side of Sandy Lane. Mr Girdlestone's House, north of the bridge, inevitably acquired his nickname, 'the Duck' and was universally called Duckites. Subsequent Housemasters fought a rearguard action against this, until Malcolm Bailey displayed model ducks everywhere in the 1990s. Below the bridge were Lockites and Weekites, whose pupils had no doubt a health-giving but precipitous climb up the steep valley slope to School.

On the opposite side of Sandy Lane were the gardens of Hodgsonites and Buissonites, but the Houses themselves were built on the valley crest, with access by another lane, Frith Hill Road, which led off the bridge.

View of Sandy Lane (now Charterhouse Road) up to school c. 1884. Market gardens still flank the road and immediately below the main school buildings are some small private houses, then occupied by Masters. On the left hand side, at the top of Sandy Lane, are (l–r) Weekites, Lockites and (on the skyline) Girdlestoneites. On the right are Hodgsonites and Bodeites (previously known as Buissonites).

44

Girdlestoneites

Frederic Girdlestone OC founded the House in 1874, having been associated with the School since 1853, and he continued as Housemaster until his retirement in 1912. He first became the Housemaster of Gownboys and on his move to Girdlestoneites persuaded a dozen Gownboys, including Robert Baden-Powell, to join him in his new House.

He was, all through his long mastership, the soul and essence of Charterhouse — always the moving spirit and generally the secretary, doing the spade work in various Carthusian events, trusted counsellor of the Headmaster, head of the choir and the School band, starter at the sports — all these and many other things. As a Housemaster he left the actual running of the House largely in the hands of the senior boys, but he was a shrewd judge of character and knew his boys well. Soon after one came as a new bug, he would talk to one very briefly in his study and at the end he would say, almost it would seem as an after thought, 'Do you ride?' If the answer was 'Yes, sir', one's name would go down in a little black book and once or twice each winter quarter one would be taken out hunting, followed by dinner with him and very cheery evenings they were. He kept three or four ponies at his own expense for the boys in his House to ride, a wonderfully generous hobby, and we usually hunted with the Chiddingfold or with the Milford Harriers …

All these things and the love and respect we bore him, made Duckites easily the happiest and most popular of Houses and left us for all time with deep and joyous memories. I suppose that there were few of his boys who would not have gone to the ends of the earth for Duck.

Hugh Fletcher (G 1894)

Above left: Girdlestone's coat of arms carved into the wall at Hall.

Centre: Frederic Girdlestone.

Below right: Cartoon of Girdlestone drawn by Max Beerbohm. He was known as 'the Duck' because of his distinctive waddle.

On the far side of this lane were to be found Daviesites, Pageites and Robinites. As in London, the House names fossilised round their founding masters. This led to some confusion when Mr Page abandoned Pageites for the larger and more remunerative Hodgsonites after the Revd James Hodgson moved on. The only name change was Buissonites. Founded by the French master, Monsieur B. Buisson, it was a more elaborate building, with a vague, understandable resemblance to a château. Some rumoured disgrace saw the departure of M. Buisson, and the House was taken over by John Bode, who was thus immortalised.

The School's Fire Brigade was formed in 1879 so that, in the event of fire, it was possible to respond immediately whilst waiting for the Godalming Fire Brigade to arrive. Membership of this elite body was limited to 20 leading sports players. They had their own uniform and hand-pulled fire engine and trained regularly, helping to fight a number of fires in the Charterhouse area, most notably the Verites fire of 1918.

Lockites

The House was founded in the summer of 1873 by Sidney W. Lock. For its first year of existence Lockites occupied Branksome House in Filmer Grove, Godalming, before moving into purpose-built accommodation on Sandy Lane (now Charterhouse Road) situated just southeast of the main school, with Weekites standing adjacent. The property was later overlooked by the Memorial Chapel, which was erected and dedicated in 1927. Originally owned by the Housemaster, the house was finally purchased by the School following a fire in 1919. During the Second World War Lockites was closed and its boys were redistributed among the other Houses. The building itself was taken over by Sir Walter St John's School, a boys' grammar school, which had been evacuated from Battersea. In 1974 the House moved to its current position overlooking Under Green.

Weekites

The Revd Charles Hampton Weekes started his House in Farncombe in LQ (spring term) 1873 with just nine boys, and they moved into a purpose-built house on Sandy Lane (now Charterhouse Road) in CQ (summer term) 1874 with 29 boys. Haig Brown's granddaughter, Miss Hilda Haig Brown, remembers Weekes as a very small man with a wicked smile. He was often late for early-morning school (perhaps because the climb from Weekites to the School was very steep), and the Headmaster once intervened to look after his class when he failed to arrive on time. When Weekes finally arrived, he put his head round the door, murmured, 'Sorry to disturb you, Sir', and went away, leaving Haig Brown to take the whole lesson. Mr Weekes was very wealthy, whether from private means or because of his business acumen in running the House is not known.

The Weekite House colour changed from brown and black to scarlet and black in 1897, a move that was not entirely appreciated by Weekites boys:

The Revd Carolus Weekes was a kindly soul and in the summer would come to the dormitories and ask us to speak low as his drawing room windows were open and words could be heard by the ladies. He did not leave until about 1896 when the Revd Romanis took over and promptly annoyed Weekites with a change of the cap piping from sepia brown to vermillion red, which would confuse with Gownboys' red piping.

S.A. Green (W 1897)

Above: The Revd Charles Weekes – cartoon by Beerbohm.

Left: Weekes' coat of arms.

Hodgsonites

The House was founded by J.T. Hodgson (G 1864) in 1872 with just four boys in a property on the south side of Godalming High Street. This meant a walk of 1½ miles up the hill to School for chapel at 7.45 am. They were allowed breakfast in Verites but were treated as outsiders. In 1873 the increased House population of ten boys were relieved to move to The Hermitage on Frith Hill Road, much closer to School.

In January 1874 a new home was ready for habitation, but, as all the boys were of Under School age, some seniors were imported from other Houses. The new building was designed by C.F. Hayward and included a mantelpiece dating from the 1850s and acquired by Mr Hodgson when part of the London Charterhouse was demolished. The Governing Body bought the property in 1888.

Hodgsonites was the final House to move into its new premises in 1974, and in 1977 the great stone mantelpiece was reconstructed within the boundary wall opposite the central dining rooms.

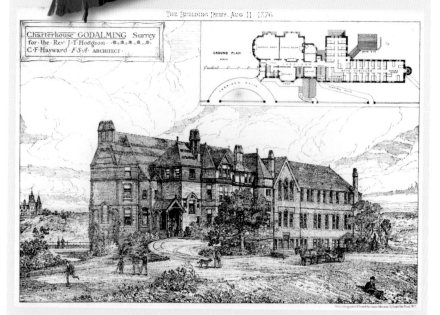

Bodeites

Bodeites c. 1882.

Founded by Monsieur Buisson in 1874, the House was originally known as Buissonites, but it was renamed after the new Housemaster, John E. Bode, in 1881. Bode taught the upper Fourth Form throughout his teaching career, making sure that his pupils had a sound grounding in Latin and Greek grammar. He was also an enthusiastic mountaineer until a knee injury prevented this.

Bodeites was one of the last Houses to remain in private ownership, but it was finally bought by the Governing Body in 1921. The original house was situated furthest from the main School. The architect is unknown, but was undoubtedly influenced by the style of French châteaux. The building was described as 'perched perilously on the edge of Charterhouse Hill in such a way that half the house commanded a splendid view from the other side and permanent sun in summer on a balcony, reserved for members of Authority only'.

These Houses were private enterprises, the last not becoming School property until 1921. As private property the pupils' fees went directly to the Housemaster, who paid a capitation fee to the School for tuition (this was the same system as in London). It was, therefore, actually possible to increase the profits by starving the boys. Some idea of the gains that were achievable may be had by comparing the first house bought by the Revd Charles Weekes in Farncombe with the gigantic mansion that he built at the top of the hill for his retirement and that still survives as a conference centre. Only one House failed to prosper. This was Uskites, built at the end of the new Peperharow Road by L.M. Stewart, the writing master. It was bought by the Governing Body and became a second sanatorium, either because it was held to be too far away for a boarding House or, if scandal is to be believed, because it degenerated into chaos. Conditions in these Houses were later declared to be unacceptably squalid, but for their time they were considered perfectly good, if not laudable, accommodation for Victorian pupils.

All the Houses were built on the same plan as those built by the governors, though they varied in size. They had the familiar rectangular boarding block of three storeys – the ground floor with common rooms, and two

Daviesites

The House was named after the founding Housemaster, the Revd G.S. Davies (known to the boys as 'Bogeye'). Davies was educated at the London Charterhouse and was orator in 1864, also winning a gold medal and the Elder and Talbot prizes before going to Christ's College, Cambridge. He had a wide knowledge of art and was instrumental in the establishment of the School Museum. He retired from the School in 1889 and returned to London as Master of Sutton's Hospital, a post he held until his death in 1927.

Daviesites was originally located in Farncombe, opening in May 1874 with just six boys, but it moved in 1875 to a building on the highest point of Frith Hill. The Daviesites building was bought by the Governing Body in 1905, when pupil numbers were increased from 25 to 40. It was the first 'new' House to move into its present building in November 1973.

In 1938 every Daviesite slept in a single cubicle with basin, jug and press. Until given a study, whether shared or not, in your 3rd or

Above: Daviesites approached over the bridge from Girdlestoneites, 1880.

Left: Davies's coat of arms.

4th year you relaxed, worked and did banco in 'longroom', called 'writing school' in some Houses, where there was a table tennis or billiards table. The room was administered by Top Table, a rank just below the monitors and 'Hall'. We also assembled here for morning adsum and evening jibs. The fag bell rang here, to be answered by the junior fag present. With the war no one slept on the third floor. Ground floor rooms were strengthened with huge oak beams and pillars and dormitories had to be introduced downstairs.

Christopher Ray (D 1942)

Pageites

One of the later Houses to be built, Pageites was founded in 1875 by T.E. Page, a renowned schoolmaster, Housemaster and classics scholar. It was originally situated on Frith Hill, a few hundred yards from the main School at the end of the bridge to Girdlestoneites. Pageites moved to its current building in 1974.

> [Page was] a tall, stooping figure, his greenish-black jacket, string tie, and shepherds-plaid trousers were a familiar sight to many generations of Carthusians. Rumour, indeed, averred that in his dashing youth he had once purchased a whole bolt of this curious material and that his tailor had been making trousers out of it for him ever since. Be that as it may, he was a classicist of the first rank (chosen by the American millionaire Loeb to be the first co-editor of the famous Loeb classical Library) and a fine teacher, to whom the School owed a regular annual harvest of university scholarships.
>
> John Staniforth (R 1912)

T.E. Page drawn by Beerbohm.

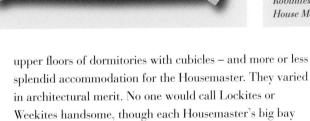

Robinites

The House was founded in 1872 by George H. Robinson, the music master, a talented pianist and organist, who could play all of Bach's fugues by heart. It was originally sited on Frith Hill and, for the first 30 years of its existence, was a 'waiting house', for pupils awaiting a transfer to another house. In 1904–5 it achieved full status within the School. In 1972 the House moved to its present site in purpose-built accommodation on Northbrook.

The Blackstone award was endowed by Bill Blackstone (R 1925) in memory of his distinguished ancestor, Sir William Blackstone, author of *Commentaries on the Laws of England*, the first codification of British law. It is an academic award for the sons of lawyers, and successful applicants are always placed in Robinites.

Robinites House photo, including Ralph Vaughan Williams, House Monitor, sitting to the left of Mr Robinson, 1889.

upper floors of dormitories with cubicles – and more or less splendid accommodation for the Housemaster. They varied in architectural merit. No one would call Lockites or Weekites handsome, though each Housemaster's big bay windows looking down the valley to Godalming must have been pleasant enough.

Some were converted private houses. Pageites acquired a handsome, almost Georgian front, and Daviesites remained slightly higgledy-piggledy, tile-hung and domestic. They were thus distinguished from the grander, cliff-edge, purpose-built dwellings of Hodgsonites and Bodeites. Eventually, most of the top of Frith Hill was

covered by new developments attached to the School: large School Houses; large private masters' houses and modest accommodation for School servants.

As well as their new home, the pupils found one major organisational difference: the scholars on the foundation were now selected by competitive examination. Instead of being grouped together in Gownboys in London and, one suspects, neglected as being not a source of personal income for the Housemaster, they were distributed evenly around the Houses to 'leaven the lump'. Many of those who migrated joined Mr Girdlestone's new House, which was conveniently near, more or less on the site envisioned by

Sunday afternoon

Ethelbert, William & Frederic out for a walk.

Left: Beerbohm cartoon of (l–r) Page, Haig Brown and Girdlestone stepping out for their regular Sunday afternoon walk.

Below: Mr Alexander Hay Tod, OC, Brooke Hall Master 1880–1920, Officer commanding the Cadet Corps 1881–1904, Housemaster of Verites 1906–20, author of The History of Charterhouse *in 1901 and photographer extraordinaire.*

the architect (though not as distinguished architecturally) and run by a man who had been a Gownboy himself and the Housemaster in London.

The Duck was to become one of the great figures of Charterhouse, along with Haig Brown and Thomas Page, with whom he enjoyed regular Sunday walks, caricatured by Max Beerbohm (the writer and cartoonist, who was a pupil between 1885 and 1890; see above). He remained Housemaster for 38 years and held open house on Thursday evenings, when he fed the more penurious bachelor masters.

Teaching was in Big School, very much on the same lines as in London, but within two years a major change saw its conversion to a library and the abandonment of communal teaching. This produced a need for more hashrooms, met first by building New School, later called C Block, for the army class and its new 'modern' subjects of maths and languages. Thereafter, every major new building had a fringe of teaching rooms, but there were never enough hashrooms. Not everyone appreciated the teaching, which remained resolutely classical: A.M. Powell

(W 1888) remarked that 'There were some, but not many, first rate teachers', and there was, 'in a word, no day-to-day incentive to do one's best, and every sort of temptation to slack and have a good time'.

EARLY DAYS

It was not just the buildings that were unfinished. There were no playing fields, for although what was now called Green, opposite Verites, had been cleared, flattened and turfed it had not yet settled, and what were to become the other pitches were still, according to Tod, 'a wild tangle of gorse, yellow broom and vipers bugloss'. Cocoa matting had to be laid as cricket wickets. There were not enough pupils for House matches, which were, in any case, considered prejudicial to School cohesion. The pupils spent most of their time wandering around Godalming, rambling in the countryside or bathing in the river Wey. 'As there was no possibility of every fellow being able to play a game every day, many of us tended to go for walks. This engendered an abiding love of the countryside, and how lucky we were in this particular countryside!' said A.M. Powell, who recalled walking to the Hog's Back in a snowstorm.

For those who are used to the idea of a rigid, sporting, public school system, these halcyon days may seem strange, but most of the organisation of life outside the hashroom was in the hands of the pupils, who were expected to be self-sufficient and who had indeed, in London, created and organised their own games. The 'safety elf' was nowhere to be seen – a monitor who got into difficulties in the river was rescued when he prudently thought to shout a fag call as he sank for the third time.

The School took enthusiastically to Surrey. Boys and masters collected insects, plants and birds' eggs, which became the basis for the School Natural History Museum. As late as the 1930s, when the A3 ran through Godalming,

southwest Surrey was still wild and rural, and nature study featured in the activities of many of the pupils. The library bought all the local histories, local cottagers' flower shows were held in Founder's Court, and Carthusians spent money in Godalming, which needed it. The School employed large numbers of the local population, either directly or as suppliers of anything from milk to kindling. Whole businesses were founded on its patronage: 'All Godalming town has called,' wrote Mrs Haig Brown a month after her arrival. And the beaks and staff became councillors and JPs.

The Charterhouse Museum

The Museum was founded in 1874 by the Revd G.S. Davies, first Housemaster of Daviesites. For over a century Old Carthusians and friends of the School donated artefacts from all over the world, reflecting their wide-ranging interests and experiences.

A purpose-built museum was erected in 1891–2 to house the growing collection. In 1972 the Museum was re-housed near Library, but this space was lost when Library was refurbished in 2004. Some of the most valuable Museum artefacts were sold in November 2002 to pay for this refurbishment, but the bulk of the Museum collection is in storage and is currently being re-catalogued and photographed.

Terracotta horse's head from Salamis, Cyprus, 1st millennium BC.

Attic black-figure ware ceramic cup, depicting a boy holding a fighting cock, c. 550–525 BC.

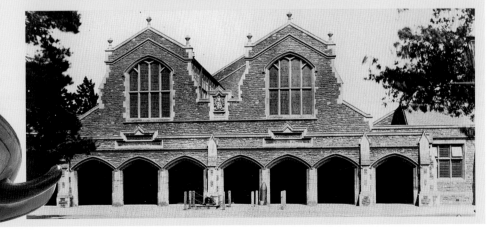

SETTLING IN

The early months were lived hand to mouth. Books were in eight-foot piles in what was to become the Library, and Tod remembered that it was as if all were new boys because nobody could find his way around. But this unstructured idyll was not to last, for the School's move to the country turned out to be a tremendous success, confounding the critics and surprising the promoters. Within 18 months of the move the number of pupils had doubled, and within four years it had reached 500, which was considered a prudent maximum. This enormous increase provoked a flurry of new buildings, many of them more splendid than the originals. The best example of this is Hall (local slang dropped the definite article for most names). There needed to be a building in which the whole School could be assembled, and to start with this was Big School, but, in 1875, when this became Library, a large barn had to be constructed to house School assemblies and the weekly entertainment on Saturday evenings. The new Hall abutted the east end of what was now the library and

was connected to it by vast arches, which incorporated a rising shutter mechanism so that the two buildings could act as one for popular events.

Hall is perhaps the most splendid of all the Victorian buildings. Very large, it had an elaborate hammerbeam roof and wonderfully carved exterior stonework, including gargoyles (which, alas, were only decorative) as well as six attached, generous hashrooms. Fitted with a stage and green room beneath, it became the venue of ever more ambitious dramatic productions, as well as a wonderful medley of events – lectures, concerts, entertainments, cinema shows, examinations, prize-givings, boxing competitions and gymnastics.

The frenzy of building caused by expansion went on well into the early 1900s and kept the School's architects employed. Hall was by Blomfield (a pupil of Hardwick),

Above: Interior of Library 1882; (top) The central fireplace has been preserved in today's library.

Left: Blomfield's architectural drawing of Hall, 1884.

Above and far right: Bathing spot used by the School on the River Wey.

Centre: Old Mr Dean teaching swimming, c. 1908.

Below: Eton fives court at Charterhouse, 1907.

who later designed the museum and lecture theatre block. This also had six hashrooms clustered around it, while an exotic T-shaped addition was made to the back of C Block to lighten that dull building and give four more. Though plans for an ambitious music school had to be shelved, a science block – with a staircase worthy of a French château (and an extraordinary smell) was created. This, unexpectedly, eventually sheltered the art department on its top floor. All these buildings cost a great deal of money and put the School heavily in debt by 1900.

It was not just the School buildings and playing fields that expanded between 1872 and 1911 but also the opportunities for pupils to pursue more individual activities. The bathing place on the river Wey was provided with concrete edging, changing shelters and springboards, while a heated swimming bath appeared in 1883, presided over by Mr Dean, a stonemason who had saved a boy from drowning in the Wey. This was believed to be the first public school pool, and it had an exotic air since it was partly paved with large marble discs. Legend had it that they had been acquired by Haig Brown from the makers of marble wash stands, which had to have a circle cut out for the basin. Here 'Old' Dean (so called to distinguish him from the son who succeeded him and was still called 'Young' Dean in his 80s) taught boys to swim by hanging them from a special harness that could still be seen in action 75 years later.

Eton fives courts (where gentlemanly behaviour was considered more important than skill) were fitted into the quarry from which the stone for the buildings had been hewn, the first four in 1874. Adjacent was an hourglass tennis court. A rather grand pair of rackets courts (1887, by OC subscription) graced the Peperharow Road entrance. They were surrounded by squash courts, built for practising of rackets in less lethal conditions. Designed to Harrovian dimensions, they were open air, like the fives courts, but they were too small once a national agreement was reached and were abandoned to casual use by junior pupils. There were plans for more: a real tennis court (which might have been considered appropriate since Gownboys had originally been built inside one) and a Greek theatre appeared on plans from time to time but never became reality.

And then there was shooting. This was a little dangerous for passers-by at first because the original range passed over their heads, but the sport was enthusiastically adopted. Some 100 volunteers founded the Charterhouse Rifle Corps as part of the Queen's West Surrey Volunteers in 1873. The Corps had its ups and downs – in 1880 only four men and six officers appeared at one parade – but it was rescued by Tod and Sergeant Grindle to become the pride of most pupils and to appear at national events, including Queen Victoria's Jubilee in 1887. The shooting team had sensational successes at Bisley, winning the Ashburton Shield four times in a row and the victorious team was cheered up the hill from the station by the population of Godalming. A commemorative fireplace with a replica of the shield was installed in Armoury, the latest occupant of the room off Scholars' Court, which had already served as library and museum.

Some 500 Carthusians served in the Boer War and the 35 who were killed needed commemoration. This was provided by a memorial cloister and a transept added to the chapel, built by subscription. The design was by W.D. Caroe, in a slightly more flamboyant Gothic style, which softened the southern aspect of the chapel and finally allowed the congregation dry-shod access. The cloister housed the war memorial itself, a plaque with the names of the fallen, as well as some private tablets to individual casualties. The South African Cloister eventually went on to house many more memorials to pupils and masters, and additions are still being made. The transept survives as the only remaining part of the original interior of the old chapel. It is still known as Hen Roost since its rather distant gallery was occupied mainly by

female visitors and Brooke Hall wives. The foundation stone, reputedly carved by Eric Gill, was laid with great ceremony by Baden-Powell, one of the boys who came down from London in 1872 and who pioneered scouting. His conduct of the siege of Mafeking had made him a national hero and his carriage was drawn up the hill by pupils. The relief of Mafeking in 1900 provoked wild scenes at the School and in Godalming, and briefly produced a new word in the English language to describe such outbursts – to maffick. After that, the scale of building declined, until the horrors of the First World War produced the School's most impressive building, Memorial Chapel.

Left: Hourglass tennis courts, 1883.

Below: Rifle Corps, Ashburton Shield winners, 1895.

Bottom: The Rifle Corps of 1874, including Baden-Powell (sixth from left).

Far left: Illustration on the front of The Graphic showing Charterhouse boys celebrating the relief of Mafeking, May 1900. Baden-Powell's handling of the siege led to him becoming a national hero.

Left: A large crowd watches Baden-Powell OC laying the foundation stone for the South African Cloister, 1901.

Below: The South African Cloister.

R.S.S. Baden-Powell

Robert Baden-Powell (1857–1941) attended Charterhouse from November 1870 to April 1876 and was thus one of the pupils who made the move to Godalming in 1872. He was originally in Gownboys under the housemastership of F.K.W. Girdlestone (Old Duck) and the Revd H.J. Evans. In 1874 Robert and his younger brother Baden were among those who moved into the new House set up by Girdlestone, where Baden-Powell's name can still be found on the honours board inside.

B-P himself tended to play down his academic ability, but he was certainly a keen sportsman. In his final year he was 1st XI goalkeeper, described as 'always keeping very cool', and he enjoyed shooting with the Rifle Corps.

He writes of canoeing on the river Wey, but there is no record that he played cricket. He was an able musician and singer, a talented actor and mimic, and an excellent artist, able to draw with either hand. As a member of an informal society known as the Druids (which seems to have done little more than meet occasionally), B-P acquired the nickname Lord Bathing Towel. More generally, and less elegantly, he was known as Bowel.

Already keen on outdoor activities with his brothers, he must have found the

Left: Portrait of Baden-Powell by G.F. Watts.

Above: The first issue of The Scout, *1908.*

Left: A picture drawn by Baden-Powell published in The Greyfriar.

Bronze scout by Sir William Goscombe John RA – the sculptor of the Thomas Sutton statue in Founder's Court. The statue was donated by an Old Carthusian who was a keen scout and wanted to mark the School's connection to the scout movement through Baden-Powell.

rural location a welcome change from London. According to his own accounts (notably in an article entitled 'The School of the Copse', written for *The Carthusian* magazine in 1922, 50 years after the move to Surrey), he enjoyed slipping away into the woods overlooking the Wey valley, watching birds, trapping and cooking rabbits and generally enjoying outdoor life.

When he was 19 B-P took entrance exams for the army, coming second in over 700 candidates and receiving a direct commission into the 13th Hussars. During a distinguished military career, spent largely in India and Africa, he remained a keen and active Old Carthusian. Just before sailing to South Africa in 1899 he took part in a charity matinée at the Haymarket Theatre in London in aid of the School's Mission in Southwark. In Mafeking in December 1899 he went looking for other OCs among his fellow officers to join him for a Founder's Day dinner. He couldn't find any (there had been one, but he had been killed a month or two earlier), but B-P had the dinner anyway. When he returned to Britain in 1901 one of his first visits was to his old School. Some months later he laid the foundation stone of the new South African Cloister in memory of OCs killed in the war, to be built alongside what was then the chapel.

By then B-P had become a national hero through his leadership and ingenuity when Mafeking was besieged, and B-P and 1,000 men had held out for 217 days against 6,000 Boers until relief arrived. He had used schoolboys to carry messages and supplies between the various command posts and had been impressed at their efficiency.

Back in England B-P originally planned to produce programme suggestions for existing youth organisations, and he tried out some of his ideas during an experimental camp on Brownsea Island in July 1907. He adapted one of his books on military scouting into *Scouting for Boys*, published in instalments during 1908. It was an immediate success, and its enthusiastic young readers formed themselves into patrols all over the country. An official framework followed, and subsequently the movement expanded to cater for Scouts' older and younger brothers and sisters. Today there are some 25 million Scouts and 9 million Guides all over the world, and *Scouting for Boys* is fourth in the list of all-time bestsellers, after the Bible, the Koran, and Mao Zedong's *Little Red Book*.

Lord Baden-Powell of Gilwell, Chief Scout of the World, died in 1941 at the age of 84. Alongside John Wesley, founder of the Methodist Church, he was undoubtedly one of the two most influential OCs ever.

Prince's Avenue today.

THE ESTATE

It was not just the buildings that had to expand to accommodate the 500 pupils. The 68½ largely uncultivated acres were not enough for games, even when the available land was eventually sorted into cricket and football pitches. Complaints about the quality of the pitches continued well into the 1880s. According to Tod, 'constant care is needed to keep this ground in good order, for the soil is light and sandy; grass does not get a good grip upon it, weeds do, and rabbits from the coppice play great havoc with the turf'.

In 1884 the ten acre field behind the Headmaster's garden was purchased from the Tottenham Charity and dedicated to junior School games, being called Under Green. Although the governors bought it, they did not have enough money to finish it properly. Masters, Old Carthusians and parents contributed, and the pavilion committee was formed. This was to make significant contributions to the site, using the profits of the tuck shop, for many years to come. The ten acres were covered in chalk and the entire School was lined up to tramp across it to even it up.

In 1897 Lessington Farm, which had been an uneasy neighbour to the School, sold 8 acres and the farmhouse to the pavilion committee (it still technically belonged to them

in 1904). This not only gave the football 2nd XI a home, but took the School's northern boundary up to the Hurtmore Road. The new access was dignified by a lodge and graced by planting an avenue of trees, to create Prince of Wales's Avenue. The last bit of Lessington Farm, the 17 acres known as Broom Field and Lees Field, fell to the committee in 1907. In 1914 a further 20 acres to the north of it, much of it woodland, were acquired and used for cultivation in order to encourage food supplies during the First World War. These 20 acres were later sold off in development plots, mostly to members of the School community. The larches planted for wood still have their descendants growing on the hanger.

By the tercentenary in 1911, the School buildings and grounds had assumed an appearance that would remain familiar to pupils for half a century, and the celebrations, including the specially composed Masque, were certainly justified.

Above left: Cricket watchers photographed by A.H. Tod.

Above: Cricket being played on Under Green.

SCHOOL LIFE

The tercentenary is a useful moment to stop and look at the School as it settled down to being one of the major public schools.

What was life like then? Perhaps the most unfamiliar aspect was that almost everything outside the hashroom was organised by pupils. This responsibility gave them an experience and independence that they might not otherwise have acquired and made them convincing and successful colonial administrators and officers in the services. The games captains picked their own teams, arranged their own fixtures and even organised the care and maintenance of the grounds. The House monitors ran the Houses, except for the catering and cleaning, so that a Housemaster would rarely venture beyond the green baize door except for the morning and evening roll-call, known as 'adsum' (from the reply, usually abbreviated to 'sum', to the boy's name being called). It was considered an insulting lack of trust for a Housemaster to check in person. On the whole this worked well, though it meant that a House could go downhill quickly before it was noticed.

The School was extremely hierarchical. The year, or even the term, of a boy's arrival would dictate his position in the School thereafter. Houses rarely mixed. In the novel *Basil Verely*, by 'a Carthusian', the hero asks his head monitor whether it is proper for him, a Verite, to have a friend in Robinites. The judgement is that, since the friend is noble and Basil a commoner, it is allowable. There was an elaborate system of privileges – for instance granted to the 'Bloods', the successful sportsmen. Anthony Quick quotes this description of a Blood in 'sportings' (home-going clothes): 'a tail coat, a top-hat, lavender kid gloves, cherry-wood walking stock and spats … the trousers had such a perfect crease that they hung like a plumb-line.'

Privilege dictated how one should dress, whether one could put one's hands in one's pocket or do up a number of buttons on one's coat; where one could walk; when one could have meals or enter chapel; and where one could be served in the tuck shop. And yet within this there are signs of liberality. Gerald Rendall, the Headmaster in 1911, disapproved of the dominance of the Bloods and granted the academic sixth form the same privileges, which they had claimed by a coup d'état. Max Beerbohm claimed later never to have changed for games, though it is recorded that two senior sportsmen held him down and played chess on his trousers, which they considered to be too vivid a check. It is true that those who remembered the School most

Cartoon of a typical Blood (centre) as seen by Beerbohm.

Classroom scenes photographed by A.H. Tod.

Right: Cartoon of A.H. Tod by a pupil drawn in the style of the cartoonist Leslie Ward, known as 'Spy'.

Below right: Headmasters (l–r) Rendall and Haig Brown with Baden-Powell, 1901.

fondly tended to be those who excelled at sport, and those who wrote later of their suffering were the intellectuals. Those who succeeded had enormous independence and an enviable quality of life, including the use of servants and great personal freedom.

The school day began with the ringing of a hand bell at 6.45 am, supplemented by the House butler banging an iron bar along the metal grids that capped the cubicles. There might be time for a hurried glass of milk and a biscuit, but then it was running for chapel, a quarter of a mile for some, possibly dressing on the way. 'Boys should not come to chapel in slippers, but yet they do,' noted Tod. The Headmaster waited in the ante chapel with his pocket watch in hand, and the doors were shut at 7.30 am. Fifteen minutes later, pupils rushed out again to hashrooms, and then breakfast at 8.30 am. This meal varied, depending on the generosity of the Housemaster, but in the Block Houses it was bread, butter and tea. Anything extra was provided by the House butler through a hatch and went on the boys' extras bill or 'home bill'.

After breakfast, shopkeepers from Godalming could be seen taking orders for clothing, stationery or books. In the summer sixth formers, who breakfasted at 9 am attended by their servants, might nip down to the river for a quick swim. The juniors went back into class at 9.30 am and the seniors at 10 am, both being released for a quarter of an hour ('the quarter') at 10.30 am. From 12.30 to 1.15 pm there was a slight lull, often filled by an informal football match in which anyone could participate, previously also a feature of games in London. Lunch in Houses included beer, another habit left over from London (where the drinking water might not have been safe), although Tod said it was left largely untouched. After lunch it would be back to the hashroom in summer until 4.30 pm, with games from 4.30 to 6.30 pm. In winter it was reversed, because of daylight, so that teaching began at 4 in the afternoon until 6 pm.

From 6 to 6.30 pm pupils would attempt to cram in whatever extracurricular activities they could before tea at 6.30 pm for the juniors and at 7 pm for the seniors, again

provided with toast from the toast fags. At 7.30 pm junior boys would settle down to their preparation ('banco', on the bench, from the schoolroom in London where preparation was on the benches at the back) supervised, of course, by seniors. At 9 pm came adsum and prayers. The juniors were in bed by 9.20 pm, where they were visited by the Housemaster and the monitor of the week. According to Tod, 'he looks into each cubicle, sees that its inmate is in bed – really in bed and not between the sheets with all his clothes – and says goodnight to each boy'. The little procession was completed by the House butler, who shut the cube doors and turned out the gas. The Uppers had lights out at 10.30 pm; the monitors went to bed when they pleased.

Games were more or less organised. Jameson records: 'Not that games are ever made compulsory by the School regulations, but it is generally understood that everyone is expected to play some game every day or nearly every day [for] all agree that a boy's leisure hours must be mapped out for him somehow.' Boys still rambled all over the countryside, and there was a roll-call at 4 pm for the entire School to make sure that no one had gone too far. The boundaries were the railway lines, slightly more extensive in 1911 than today – there was competition to see how far

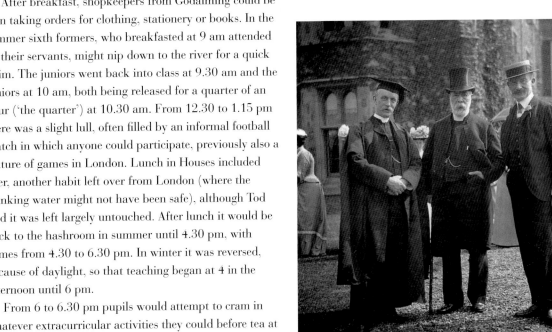

one could get without crossing one. 'Locking in' (at 6.30 pm in winter or 8.45 pm in summer) meant that all boys should be in their House unless there was something else that their Housemaster allowed. So there was, in fact, time for extracurricular activities on some evenings and, of course, there were the Saturday night entertainments, at which both masters and pupils sang and the audience stamped its feet and cried 'worp'. Sundays, though compulsory chapel happened twice, were a little more leisurely. There was private preparation before lunch and 30 minutes' teaching between 2 and 2.30 pm. Powell said that 'walks were a feature of our life on Sundays, when practically the whole School turned out in twos and threes'.

Hashroom work was largely focused on the classics. This could become a senseless grind of preparing a translation and then reading it aloud in class, which resulted, depending on the accuracy, in a physical change of place in the form, going 'to the top of the class', or in some sort of imposition, such as, 'write your con out and let me have it by tomorrow'.

The history of teaching at Charterhouse from 1872 was mainly comprised of unsuccessful attempts to broaden the curriculum, particularly into mathematics, science and foreign languages. 'Modern languages were somewhat neglected,' it was said.

What did I learn at Charterhouse? Sufficient Latin and Greek to be able to write hexameters and pentameters without the aid of a dictionary; and to help one to spell and distinguish between -ation and -ition. A supreme knowledge of French irregular verbs, but no knowledge of how to speak the language. Nothing of history that lasted. Of mathematics an ability to do mental arithmetic; but probably born not acquired; of English literature nothing; of modern languages, poetry, music – nothing. I could, I am sure, have taken away much more learning with me had I been better taught – and tried harder – and I cannot say

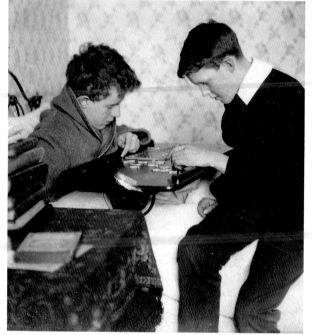

Left: Pupils in the Verites sick bay, photographed by Tod. In the days before antibiotics and mass inoculation deaths from common childhood ailments were not uncommon; each House had its own sick bay and the School Sanatorium (known as Great Comp) included quarantine wards.

Below: The statue of Thomas Sutton, by Sir William Goscombe John RA, was installed during the tercentenary of the School in 1911. It was purchased as a gift to the School by Old Carthusians.

that the lessons were made interesting. It seemed to me to be more of a tiresome routine, which some of the masters as well as the boys tried to get through with as little trouble as possible.

R.H. Eckersley (D 1903; *The Charterhouse we Knew*)

Yet 'saying your con' was still to be found in the upper forms, and moving places in two Fourth Forms (including Mr Wreford-Brown's celebrated 'Whizz-Bang', which irritated his underneath neighbour) as late as the 1950s.

Above: Cartoons of a typical school day in The Greyfriar, *1911.*

Sir Frank Fletcher

A born schoolmaster and a formidable Headmaster, Frank Fletcher (Headmaster, 1911–35) combined intellectual distinction, an understanding of boys, a capacity for perseverance, high moral principles and a gritty, no-nonsense realism. Fletcher came from a Lancashire colliery-owning family and won a scholarship to Rossall. There he proved a brilliant classicist and went on to win all the prizes – and a tutorship – at Jowett's Balliol (plus a hockey Blue) before starting his schoolmastering career at Rugby. Nine years later, at the age of 33, Fletcher was appointed Master of Marlborough, the first layman to head a leading public school. He modernised the school, which was still very Victorian, challenging its athleticism and brutality and dramatically improving its academic achievements.

Fletcher started as Headmaster of Charterhouse in the School's tercentenary year. He succeeded Gerald Rendall, whose donnish aloofness had allowed the School to degenerate into the philistine bear-garden ruled by the Bloods that Robert Graves describes in *Goodbye to All That.* As at Marlborough, Fletcher's first task was to restore order and discipline. He raised Charterhouse's academic standing, not least through his own demanding teaching of the classical sixth. All 18 of Fletcher's predecessors since 1626 had been ordained. Nevertheless, Fletcher gave the Christian ethos of the School his firm support, preaching and teaching divinity, and was always in his stall in chapel.

It was Fletcher's destiny to be Headmaster during the First World War. Some 3,500 Carthusians fought in the war, and every Sunday Fletcher read out in chapel the names of those who were wounded or missing, taken prisoner or killed. When the war was over he was determined that the School should have a new chapel in memory of the fallen. The architect Giles Gilbert Scott was commissioned and guided in his design by Fletcher, who wanted a modern chapel full of light and hope. The largest war memorial in Great Britain was consecrated in June 1927.

Three years earlier Fletcher had persuaded the Governing Body to purchase Northbrook House with its 50 acres, almost doubling the size of the School's grounds. Fletcher and his wife, Dorothy, moved out of Saunderites, and Northbrook became the Headmaster's house. After a spell as Great Comp, the School's sanatorium, it is now, appropriately, Fletcherites, the sixth form day House.

Fletcher retired in 1935, after 24 years at Charterhouse. He was knighted in 1937 for a lifetime's services to education.

John Witheridge

Robert Graves

The poet and novelist Robert Graves (1895–1985) attended Charterhouse (Gownboys) between 1909 and 1914. His experiences there are immortalised in his autobiography, *Goodbye to All That* (1929), in which he described the bullying he endured because of his high moral standards and his close friendship with a much younger boy, G.H. Johnstone, who inspired much of his early poetry. Graves found acceptance and inspiration in the school poetry society and a role model in George Mallory, with whom he went rock climbing. Graves' wartime service with the Royal Welsh Fusiliers, which is graphically depicted in his autobiography, had a profound impact on his poetry. He published his first volume, *Over the Brazier*, in 1916 and *Fairies and Fusiliers* in 1917. Graves became friends with Siegfried Sassoon, and when Sassoon threatened publicly to condemn the prolongation of the war, Graves intervened to persuade the authorities that his friend was suffering from nerves, thereby saving him from court martial.

Robert Graves photographed on his arrival at Charterhouse, 1909.

After demobilisation Graves initially failed to win popular approval as a poet, suffering from recurrent shell-shock and struggling to support his young family, but his fortunes looked up in 1926 when he was appointed Professor of English Literature at Cairo University, where he met the American poet, Laura Riding. She became his mistress, adviser and critic, encouraging him to write *Goodbye to All That*, novels, including the bestselling *I, Claudius* (1934), and his *Collected Poems* (1955). Graves moved to Majorca in 1929, leaving in 1936 on the outbreak of the Spanish Civil War. During the Second World War he lived in Devon with Beryl Hodge, with whom he worked on various literary projects. In 1946 he returned to Majorca with Beryl and their four children, and the couple married in 1953. Graves published *The White Goddess* in 1948 and, in 1955, *The Greek Myths*. He was Professor of Poetry at Oxford from 1961 to 1965, and in 1971 he was made an honorary fellow of St John's College. He died on Majorca having published more than 135 books.

Below: The Green Chartreuse, *a satirical magazine published by Graves and friends, July 1913.*

The Green Chartreuse.

JULY. 1913.

Lemmings' Exhilarating Tonic Wine.

ROUSES THE SLUGGISH BLOOD.
STRENGTHENS THE FAGGED.
CONDUCES TO FESTIVITY.
MAKES THE WORM PULL UP ITS SOCKS AND TURN.
PUTS OUT FIRE.
CURES THE STAGGERS.
And may be used as a Hair-restorer, thereby putting an end to Payne.

TESTIMONIALS.

Private Reasons, Corporal Punishment and Orderly Conduct of the 1st Blanks, write:—" We went on the spree last night with your stuff. Our Mess-room is now the messiest we've seen for years, strike us pink and blue if it ain't."

Pallas' Owl writes in the 'Schoolmaster':—" Can cordially recommend for sharpening the Beak, and brightening the Pupil."

The King of Siam's hereditary wine taster is convinced that Lemming's Tonic is not many streets behind Green Chartreuse.

This Space was reserved for
THE BLOODS,
but they need no advertisement.

HAVE YOU EVER VISITED

The Green Chartreuse

JULY, 1913.

EDITORIAL.

Green because it is not pink. A perfectly sufficient reason, though you mightn't think so; but then perhaps you were educated before the new method[1] was expounded. Of course there are ramifications in this kind of argument. Yellow might have been chosen: but this colour must approximate either to gilt or to mustard; the first won't do because we are too kind-hearted to wish to deprive the gingerbread, and the second won't do because we don't want to sting, and if we did we would keep it in our tail like a well-behaved wasp. Blue— either (i.) *sky* (standard too high or too low—saints have no sense of humour, and the laughter of the gods is always in bad taste); or (ii.) *marine* (suggests " sink or swim "—not a point of view we care to present to our readers); or (iii.) *ultra-marine* (transportation *ultra maria* is the proper remedy for imperialism and punning—but suppose we wanted to make a pun?) In any case the Blues won't suit us. Red is better; but red must approach either crimson or scarlet, and crimson[2] suggests Cabinet Ministers. Suffragettes. Brown—

THE LATE SEC.-LIEUT. T. K. DAVEY.
(Reprinted from the Bristol Times and Mirror, April 9th, 1918).

Sec.-Lieut. Thomas Kerrison Davey, Rifle Brigade (who, as previously announced, died of wounds on Easter Sunday), was born on October 8 1898, son of Mr. T. Ruding Davey, of Wrasall Court, Somerset, and was educated at Rowley's School, Clifton, and Charterhouse. He was in his House Eleven for cricket and football. Leaving school in April 1917, he joined the O.C.B., at Keble College, Oxford, and received his commission in October 1917. He was a nephew of the late Lieut. John Stanley Davey, of the North Somerset Yeomanry, who fell in the battle of Ypres on November 17 1914.

Gv RI

HE whom this scroll commemorates was numbered among those who, at the call of King and Country, left all that was dear to them, endured hardness, faced danger, and finally passed out of the sight of men by the path of duty and self-sacrifice, giving up their own lives that others might live in freedom. Let those who come after see to it that his name be not forgotten.

2/Lieut. Thomas Kerrison Davey
Rifle Brigade

THE FIRST WORLD WAR

The First World War had a profound and unparalleled effect on Charterhouse. Analysis of the Gownboy House photo of 1912 shows that all but one of the pupils served in the forces and, of those, a third were killed and a third wounded. Many pupils left the School early to join up. Three members of Brooke Hall left at once, and a steady trickle followed through the war, three were awarded MCs and three were killed.

Rationing and inflation meant that life was simpler and less colourful. Gone were the more exotic House colours and even the pink cover of *The Carthusian*, which, because of paper rationing, was the only Charterhouse magazine to survive. The 20 acres beyond Broom and Lees were planted with potatoes, oats and larch trees. Oswald Latter, Housemaster of Robinites, led the whole School in gangs, planting, nurturing and lifting tons of potatoes. Some pupils found themselves also working on the land in School Agricultural Camps. Other pupils took over the duties of the grounds staff who had left to join up, and they did their own mowing and rolling of the pitches.

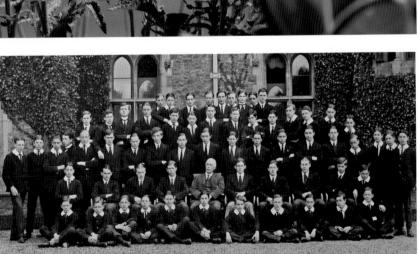

Charterhouse suffered heavy losses during the First World War. A third of the boys in this Gownboys House photograph of 1912 were killed and another third wounded.

Charterhouse pupils at OTC camp, 1909–10.

There were some unexpected consequences – the shortage of bread, for example, meant that the toast fags no longer had to do their duties. In 1919 Tod thought that some of this simplicity would last:

Time alone will show in what respects the Carthusian life is permanently changed. There are now no boys in the School who knew it before the war, i.e., War conditions are looked upon as more or less normal. It may be assumed that in the future, as now, slightly less time will be spent in School than before – whether shorter hours mean better results remains to be seen. Anyhow, intellectual pursuits, in spite of temporary cessation of university careers, have not flagged, indeed they have been encouraged by the new subjects dealt with in the newspapers, and interest in history has been awakened by public events. Ways of life have certainly been made more simple for the time by restrictions on luxuries of diet and clothing. The knowledge that all would soon have to take their share in the country's defence, and the preparation for it, the wider sympathies evoked by mingling with others in agricultural and the like occupations, the recognition of duties common to all, have certainly combined to modify the Carthusian modes of life and thought.

There was a great deal of military training. All pupils were obliged to join the Officers Training Corps (OTC) to be instructed for 12 hours a week in signalling, bayonet-fighting, drill, field instruction and battalion work. Physical training was eventually organised for the whole School during the 'quarter' – then from 11.15 to 11.30 am – which certainly raised the temperature (and aroma) of the following classes. A Zeppelin appeared over the School one evening in October 1915, but it dropped its bombs well away, perhaps aimed at the Chilworth gunpowder factories.

One great excitement was the burning of two Houses, Verites and Lockites. The Verite fire was a tremendous event. Pupils hurled the furniture out of the windows as the roof burned – one, not a Verite, was discovered flinging the Housemaster's trousers out of his bedroom window. 'It's very good of you fellows to help,' said Tod (H 1915–19; *The Charterhouse we Knew*).

Right: The Officers Cadet Corp marching past Founder's Court, 1912.

Below: The Verites fire, 1918.

Visible marks of the war were few, but the greatest effect was personal. Of the 3,200 Carthusians who fought, 687 lost their lives. 'The appalling slaughter of that war, the continuous anxiety in almost every home for some near relation, perhaps the nearest, over there in the trenches of northern France' (W.W.S. Adams, H 1923; *The Charterhouse we Knew*). To lose so many of one's friends was a personal disaster that was to affect the lives of the surviving Carthusians forever. Adams continued: 'My own brother fell. He had been head monitor of Hodgsonites, and I think I am right in saying that all those who sat at the monitors' table, when he had joined them, were now dead.'

H.C.D. Kimber (W 1912), killed near Aix Noulettes, 22 June 1916.

R.J.P. Rodakowski (R 1914), killed at Passchendaele, 9 October 1917.

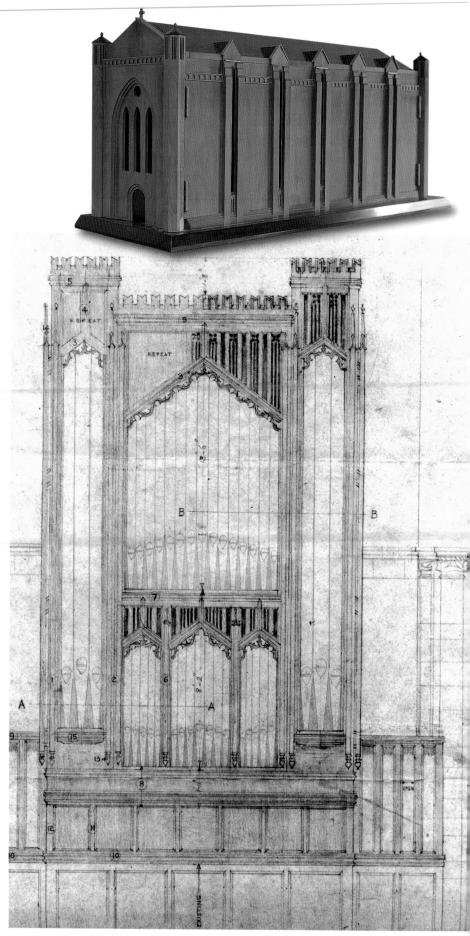

The feeling that there should be a tangible witness of the awful nature of the First World War, the sacrifice that it involved throughout the land and the determination that it should never happen again can be seen on every village green, and even the tiniest of churches has its memorial for the many families who lost all their children. The disproportionately large casualty rates among public-schoolboys, who, as junior officers, led from the front, made this feeling exceptionally strong at Charterhouse. Chapel was far too small. The last time the School had suffered war casualties the chapel's expansion had been the way of creating a memorial, and this no doubt suggested the creation of what was to become a new Memorial Chapel. The prime mover was the Headmaster, Frank Fletcher, and it was he, too, who guided the choice of architect to Giles Gilbert Scott, the infant prodigy who had won the competition for Liverpool Cathedral. Fletcher's opinion was that, of course, there should be a competition to design the new chapel but the Governing Body should be certain that Scott was to win it. It was Fletcher's idea to begin building Chapel – 'against considerable opposition and cold water,' according to Adams – before he had full financing for it, a gamble that was amply justified.

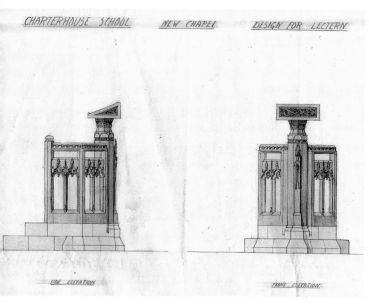

Designs by Gilbert Scott for Chapel lectern (above) and organ (right).

Top: Scale model of Chapel, designed to store cutlery.

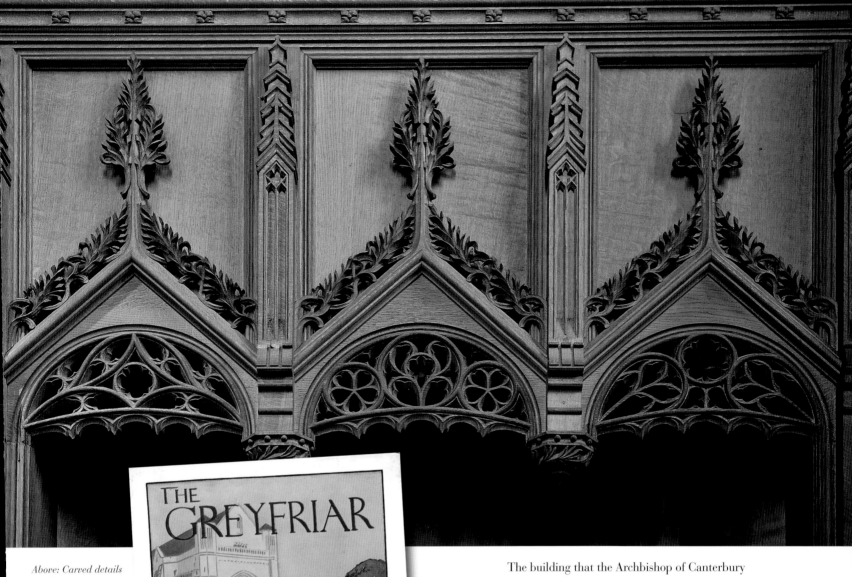

Above: Carved details in Chapel.

Right: The front of The Greyfriar celebrating the opening of Chapel, July 1927.

Below: A recent addition to Chapel's war memorial.

THE GREYFRIAR

VOL 8   JULY 1927   Nº 122

The building that the Archbishop of Canterbury consecrated on 17 June 1927, the anniversary of the migration (when the School moved to Godalming) and five years to the day after the laying of the foundation stone, was undeniably impressive. Scott designed everything down to the finest detail, and he produced a serious building for a serious purpose, although, at Fletcher's insistence, it is warm, light and airy. He even persuaded the donor of the altar cross to change its central stone from red to yellow, although he lost the fight to have no stained glass at all. The building is full of symbolism, from the flame motif on the altar and the wood carving, to the pelican, high in the apse, standing for sacrifice. It is a fitting memorial.

M. L. EVISON
R. 1998 - 2000   WELSH GUARDS   AFGHANISTAN
2009

BETWEEN THE WARS

Although it was possible for Oliver Van Oss to describe the 1930s as a time in which the clock of progress and change had been stopped, a different idea of what was going on at Charterhouse between the wars can be gained by consulting Jameson's history. This describes a pervading sense of informality and relaxation, coupled with an increase in efficiency and in the business-like administration and organisation of the School as a whole. Frank Fletcher, the Headmaster, was in a position by the mid-1920s to do a great deal to impose more universal standards on the independent feudalism of Houses and Housemasters at a time when House spirit was seen to predominate. A commission of enquiry by the Governing Body brought about the final buying-in of private Houses and the consequent establishment of all Housemasters as salaried employees of the School. The Houses became 'more home-like and cheerful', notes Jameson, as a result of improvements, such as the building of separate dining rooms.

Gownboys colonised the ground-floor rooms beyond the tower, freeing their panelled writing school for eating. Saunderites built an impressive separate hall, now the Saunders Room. Verites had to make do with an internal courtyard roofed over. Better heating and the provision of plentiful supplies of hot water were arranged, although cold baths were still compulsory in Hodgsonites in the early part of this period, and Gownboys still had chamber pots in cubes in 1937.

Homebill was abolished, so that all boys were fed roughly the same, and the appointment of tutors in each House and encouragement of matrons (the widow of the poet Edward Thomas was one) led to a much greater knowledge of the pupils themselves by those who were in charge of them. Jameson thought House tutors, who were originally resident, were a 'useful link between the boy and the Housemaster', and would get to know the character of the boys and be able to offer advice and encouragement. Housemasters were described as now 'much more business like, more methodical and more vigilant', though they took care to foster the idea that the senior boys were responsible for running the House.

It was during this period that Walter Sellar (joint author of *1066 and All That*) became Housemaster of Daviesites. He could be found wandering round his House on his own, chatting to his boys and taking an interest in their progress in a way that would have been

Above: Dunbar and Dames Longworth, Charterhouse athletics, relay 1931.

Right: Cartoon in The Greyfriar lampooning the introduction of daily physical drill in all Houses, 1927.

THE NEW P.T.

MARCHING WITH HEELS RAISING

WHAT ABOUT A MIXTURE?

TRUNK BENDING FORWARD WITH ARMS SWINGING BACKWARDS & FORWARDS

Returning from games, Northbrook playing fields.

MARCHING WITH OPPOSITE KNEE AND ARM RAISING

ARMS AND LEG SWINGING

considered insulting before the First World War. It was noticed, in general, that relations between masters and boys had become less formal. The 'Charterhouse Salute', the pupils' greeting to masters, gradually changed. In London, one removed one's cap or mortarboard; in Godalming, one touched the peak of the cap, worn at the back. After the disappearance of most caps during the war, a vague wave in the vicinity of the right ear sufficed. Visitors remarked on the general friendliness of the atmosphere.

Coupled with this was an expansion of opportunity both in the hashroom and outside it. A block of new hashrooms, appropriately called New Block, provided eight rooms in 1928, and the science block was greatly enlarged. A new sixth form room with an archway, modelled on Brooke Hall, provided an austere theatre for the Headmaster's teaching. The master's dais had disappeared, and pupils had individual desks designed by the William Morris Company.

By far the most impressive alteration to the School, however, was the purchase of the Northbrook estate in 1924. This house and its extensive grounds were offered to the School on the death of its owner, Mrs Ewart, who had cordial relations with the School and would often ask boys to tea. Pressure on the School to buy the estate and save it from development was applied by the heirs, who laid out access roads and drains and began selling off acre plots. The Governing Body could afford no more than £10,000 out of the £16,000 purchase price demanded. The remaining £6,000 was provided by the Pavilion Committee, a loan from Brooke Hall and a personal guarantee from Frank Fletcher. Fletcher gave up Saunderites and moved to Northbrook House, where he lived in some state, dining visiting teams in evening dress. The 20 acres that formed the nearest of the three fields acquired, which already had a cricket pitch, became a welcome addition to the playing fields. This rather scrambled acquisition was to have the most enormous consequences.

Although Fletcher had the reputation of being stern, he was also described as someone who disliked rules, and it was in his period, notes Jameson, that the famous admonition, 'a breach of common sense is a breach of the School rules', appeared. This was said to be an era in which personal liberty was extended in a way unthinkable before the war. Though there was still

morning School in summer, chapel was now after breakfast, lasted for 10 minutes and was designed, as the chaplain put it, to be more relevant to the pupils and at a time when they were awake.

The afternoon adsum disappeared because there were so many pupils who had good reason for doing other things in the middle of the afternoon. New tennis courts were laid out, and there was golf, boxing and fencing. In 1936 the first School sailing boat, presented by the Old Carthusian Yacht Club, appeared on Frensham Pond, while the league system for major sports meant that 'the whole of football and cricket and hockey of the School is arranged in House competitions planned out on a system as complicated and infallible as a railway timetable'. This system was part of the general organisation by which, wrote Jameson, 'a boy may come to look on turning up as a sort of School engagement instead of as a recreation for which he himself is responsible'.

There was more sports coaching, despite the fear that this would compromise the amateur nature of the top game. Those under 15 were not obliged to join the OTC, and the Scouts, music, drawing and the workshop were offered as alternatives. Punishment was said to be no longer excessive, and attempts were made to get away from laborious lines. Lines were often pre-written by pupils in their spare time because some masters could be relied on to set the same ones – 'Hummingbirds flit from tree to tree in the glorious tropical sunshine,' was E.A. Malaher's favourite.

The inter-war years were a time of transition at Charterhouse, as they were for the nation as a whole. On the one hand, there was less formality and more opportunity; and on the other, a more consistent, universal and business-like approach. Though some regretted the loss of a Corinthian atmosphere and a 'school of hard knocks' – 'sooner or later, the youth must be prepared for the knocks and shocks of the outside world,' wrote Revd L. Patterson (P/B 1903) – the influence of parents who were no longer prepared to fire their infants off into Spartan exile could not be ignored and nor could the influence of the motorcar and the wireless. Parties would still come from abroad to look at Charterhouse as the acme of education and Anthony Quick in his *Charterhouse – A History of the School* could say that during Birley's time: 'Charterhouse would return to the forefront of the public schools'.

Sir Robert Birley

A respected and influential educationalist and tireless campaigner for political and racial freedom, Sir Robert Birley (Headmaster, 1935–47) was also a charismatic and inspirational teacher. He was educated at Rugby and Balliol College, Oxford, where he gained a first in History. Having taught as an assistant master at Eton, Birley was appointed Headmaster of Charterhouse in 1935 when he was only 32 years old, succeeding Frank Fletcher and becoming the first non-classicist Headmaster.

The tall, youthful Headmaster with his young family and relaxed, informal approach created quite a stir at Charterhouse. He regarded teaching as an essential part of the Headmaster's role, enabling him to know each pupil personally, and, thanks to his enthusiastic encouragement, School societies multiplied and flourished. Birley provided firm, calm and inspiring leadership during the difficult years of the Second World War, insisting on moving his home from Northbrook back to Saunderites so that he was at the heart of the School and taking on the additional role of Housemaster of Saunderites. He successfully fought government plans to commandeer Charterhouse for military use.

While he was at Charterhouse, Birley was asked to represent the Headmasters' Conference on the Fleming Committee, and he contributed substantially to the 1944 Fleming Report on bridging the gap between public schools and the state system. In 1945 he was granted a sabbatical in order to assess the prospects for rebuilding the German education system, and he was subsequently invited to become educational adviser to the Allied Control Commission in Germany. Birley left Charterhouse in 1947 and was headmaster of Eton from 1949 to 1963, during which time he served twice as chairman of the Headmasters' Conference. In 1964 he became Visiting Professor of Education at Witwatersrand University, South Africa, where he was a beacon of inspiration and encouragement to those seeking reform. He returned to England in 1967 and became Professor and Head of Social Sciences and Humanities at the new City University, where he found a new outlet for his enthusiasm and academic rigour. He 'retired' in 1971 but continued an energetic programme of writing and public speaking until arthritis limited his mobility.

Anthony Quick summarised Sir Robert Birley's legacy at Charterhouse as follows: 'His vast intellectual energy and range, his passion for the great issues of the contemporary world grounded on strong Christian principles, his gifts as a teacher, his unpretentiousness, his belief in discussion and thought rather than edict, all left an indelible impression on Charterhouse.'

Right: Charterhouse ambulance, presented to the Red Cross at Charterhouse on 9 March 1940; shown here at Buckingham Palace with Queen Elizabeth on 15 March 1940. It was No 1 of the first convoy to be sent abroad and later had to be abandoned in France.

Below: The Corps Home Guard, c. 1942.

THE SECOND WORLD WAR

Many of the problems caused by the Second World War would have been familiar from 1914 – shortages, rationing, an emphasis on military training, pioneering and agriculture (a future minister of agriculture remembered climbing out of House at night to tend to his sick pigs) – but this time there were added horrors, which made the influence of the war on the School itself more noticeable. Bombing and the threat of invasion brought Charterhouse closer to the immediate dangers of war than it had been before. To training in the Junior Training Corps (later, CCF – Combined Cadet Force) were added Home Guard duties. B.D. Wilson (D 1942) remembers: 'Older boys were required from time to time to stand guard over the Godalming waterworks with a workable Lee-Enfield and five rounds of live ammunition (to be kept in the pocket and not in the rifle's magazine).' Shelter trenches were dug in the gardens and the Houses were reorganised; ground floors were reinforced with props, cubes were removed as a fire risk (some never returned), and there was considerable use of the cellars.

In Daviesites we were required to dig slit trenches in the garden, as air raid shelters. These were then roofed with

corrugated iron on which was piled earth and turves. An opening for entry was left at either end. In 1939 or 1940, suffering from flu in Great Comp, I heard my first air raid alert (warbling siren). I stayed where I was in bed. But in Daviesites in 1940–41 alerts during the night could occur once or twice a week. On hearing it, we put on dressing gowns and slippers and made our way with torches to our allotted trench, were counted, and sat there in the dark till the All Clear (single siren note) was sounded.

Brian Wilson (D 1942)

The apparent vulnerability of the School (in the south of England, not that far from the coast and on the Southern Defence Line, based on the river Wey, which it was hoped would hold up the Panzer divisions) meant that numbers dropped off more markedly than they had the last time. Some pupils still struggled through from overseas, one by convoy-escort frigate, another by flying-boat. Omar Pound, the son of Ezra Pound who was broadcasting for the Nazis in Italy, appeared in Daviesites.

The advent of WW2 brought changes that became more apparent as the war continued. The first and most important concerned food, as a result of food rationing. Meat was limited to about once a week. The rest of the time, we tended to exist on vegetarian meals (Woolton pie, after Lord Woolton, minister for food). We seldom saw eggs or confectionery. Sugar was in short supply. There was enough bread, in the form of the wholemeal 'standard' loaf. But butter was limited. We could buy jam in Crown. But we survived and suffered no ill-effects.

To deter airborne landings by glider, the most visible measures at Charterhouse were innumerable pine posts erected in all open spaces, except for the middle of the cricket and football pitches. Some of the pine poles had been cut and set the ground so rapidly that they later started to sprout small branches; a surprising and charming sight.

Brian Wilson (D 1942)

There was a threat that the buildings would be requisitioned by one of the services as were those of other public schools, like Marlborough. Charterhouse was due to be occupied by the Admiralty, but this was headed off by the Archbishop of Canterbury, chairman of the governors, who had access to the cabinet. Though the Panzer divisions never came, the School was struck. 'Our bomb,' said B.K. Hartshorne (G 1937), who qualified as a dispatch rider at

17, 'landed in Founder's Court at 7 minutes past 8 pm on 15 October, during banco: it was about 25 yards away, but as the ground was soft, most of the force of the explosion was upwards, shattering windows but doing no structural damage: I heard it coming and emerged unscathed from under my study desk'. The impact was outside the Headmaster's study, now back in Saunderites. J.C.S. Mackie (R 1940) remembered:

One evening in early 1941 during banco we heard the whistling sound of a stick of bombs falling. They seemed to come down quite slowly and to pass right over the House. Instinctively, the boys leaned forward and put their hands over their heads, waiting for the explosions. These sounded very close but not loud … One was in Founder's Court, close to Saunderites. The ground was so soft that the bomb made a huge crater, but mercifully it had no impact on the side of the building. The tiled roof was very badly damaged by stones which had been thrown up into the air and came crashing down on to the tiles. Canadian soldiers at a nearby camp donated a maple tree which was planted in the centre of the crater … A fraction of a second's difference, and the casualties would have been awful.

A Gownboy fortunately took a picture, though it was then illegal. The Victorian presentation fountain, which had hitherto graced the Court, though it was said to be undamaged, nonetheless disappeared: it was rumoured that the Headmaster disliked it.

Considering how prominent the School was and its position under the flight path of V1s – 'Wizard Doodle, Sir!' (there was much interest in identifying aircraft, often by sound alone) – it was remarkably fortunate to escape further damage.

The overall impression of life in the Houses was one of considerable inconvenience, like the nightly trudges to the shelter trenches during the constant air raid warnings. But since life was relatively basic anyway, the differences were not as marked as they might have been. 'It was very, very cold in the winters … Actually we didn't notice it much, being used to it in the first place, and we wore much heavier clothing in those days,' remembered B. Russell (G 1940). Some found it exciting. In *The Charterhouse we Knew* Gerald Priestland (D 1945) wrote: 'Life there had always seemed passionate and intense, it never ran at an even temperature: both pleasures and pains were extreme, and there was no intermediate … [I remember the School] in a stormy October twilight, with branches straining across the distant towers and the roads deserted, hostile with the terror of whom one might meet upon them.'

Food must have been a constant headache for the staff.

We certainly were not badly fed, if rather monotonously. There were always plenty of vegetables, and bread was not rationed until much later. However, one certainly learned to eat fast. Only last year my wife, observing that a fellow guest was quite speedy, asked him innocently if he was a Carthusian. 'How did you know?' was the astonished reply.

Brian Russell OBE (D 1945)

Opposite: Two panels of the War memorial in Chapel which records the names of the 340 Old Carthusians and masters who died in the Second World War.

Left: Crater created by bomb falling in Founder's Court, 25 October 1940.

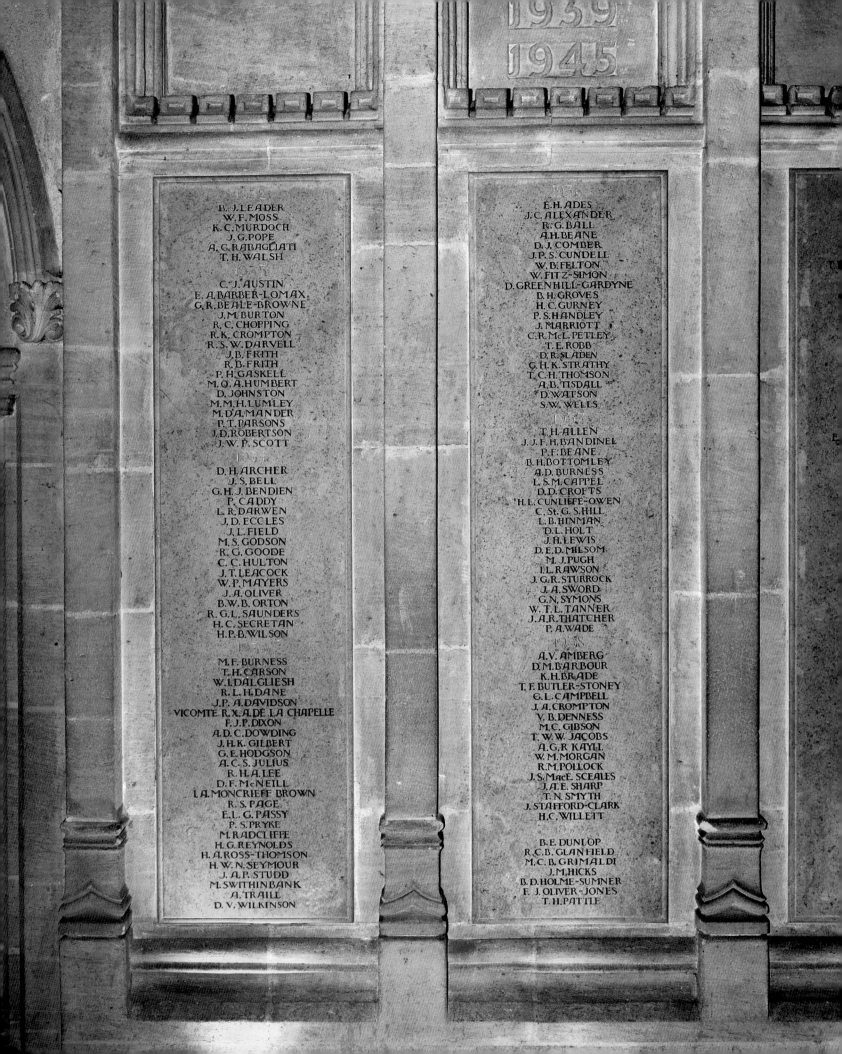

1939
1945

1932

B. J. LEADER
W. F. MOSS
K. C. MURDOCH
J. G. POPE
A. G. RABAGLIATI
T. H. WALSH

1933

C. J. AUSTIN
E. A. BARBER-LOMAX
G. R. BEALE-BROWNE
J. M. BURTON
R. C. CHOPPING
R. K. CROMPTON
R. S. W. DARVELL
J. B. FRITH
R. B. FRITH
P. H. GASKELL
M. O. A. HUMBERT
D. JOHNSTON
M. M. H. LUMLEY
M. D'A. MANDER
P. T. PARSONS
J. D. ROBERTSON
J. W. P. SCOTT

1934

D. H. ARCHER
J. S. BELL
G. H. J. BENDIEN
P. CADDY
L. R. DARWEN
J. D. ECCLES
J. L. FIELD
M. S. GODSON
R. G. GOODE
C. C. HULTON
J. T. LEACOCK
W. P. MAYERS
J. A. OLIVER
B. W. B. ORTON
R. G. L. SAUNDERS
H. C. SECRETAN
H. P. B. WILSON

1935

M. F. BURNESS
T. H. CARSON
W. I. DALGLIESH
R. L. H. DANE
J. P. A. DAVIDSON
VICOMTE R. X. A. DE LA CHAPELLE
F. J. P. DIXON
A. D. C. DOWDING
J. H. K. GILBERT
G. E. HODGSON
A. C. S. JULIUS
R. H. A. LEE
D. F. McNEILL
I. A. MONCRIEFF BROWN
R. S. PAGE
E. L. G. PASSY
P. S. PRYKE
M. RADCLIFFE
H. G. REYNOLDS
H. A. ROSS-THOMSON
H. W. N. SEYMOUR
J. A. P. STUDD
M. SWITHINBANK
A. TRAILL
D. V. WILKINSON

1935

E. H. ADES
J. C. ALEXANDER
R. G. BALL
A. H. BEANE
D. J. COMBER
J. P. S. CUNDELL
W. B. FELTON
W. FITZ-SIMON
D. GREENHILL-GARDYNE
B. H. GROVES
H. C. GURNEY
P. S. HANDLEY
J. MARRIOTT
C. R. McL. PETLEY
T. E. ROBB
D. R. SLADEN
G. H. K. STRATHY
T. C. H. THOMSON
A. B. TISDALL
D. WATSON
S. W. WELLS

1937

T. H. ALLEN
J. J. F. H. BANDINEL
P. F. BEANE
B. H. BOTTOMLEY
A. D. BURNESS
L. S. M. CAPPEL
D. D. CROFTS
H. L. CUNLIFFE-OWEN
C. St. G. S. HILL
L. B. HINMAN
D. L. HOLT
J. H. LEWIS
D. E. D. MILSOM
M. J. PUGH
I. L. RAWSON
J. G. R. STURROCK
J. A. SWORD
G. N. SYMONS
W. T. L. TANNER
J. A. R. THATCHER
P. A. WADE

1938

A. V. AMBERG
D. M. BARBOUR
K. H. BRADE
T. F. BUTLER-STONEY
G. L. CAMPBELL
J. A. CROMPTON
V. B. DENNESS
M. C. GIBSON
T. W. W. JACOBS
A. G. R KAYLL
W. M. MORGAN
R. M. POLLOCK
J. S. MacE. SCEALES
J. A. E. SHARP
T. N. SMYTH
J. STAFFORD-CLARK
H. C. WILLETT

1939

B. E. DUNLOP
R. C. B. GLANFIELD
M. C. B. GRIMALDI
J. M. HICKS
B. D. HOLME-SUMNER
F. J. OLIVER-JONES
T. H. PATTLE

Wartime memories

The 'new bug's test' (knowledge of School's geography and traditions) determined your seniority. Surnames were 'de rigueur'. Apart from hash, games, art, fugshop, music or drama, there was little mixing with those senior or junior to us; the School was intensely tribal, each House had its own postees and fagging. There were general School rules, whose breaking involved a bumming by the head man or the House man; no other beaks could use the cane, but in House head monitors were allowed to, mostly only with Housemaster's permission.

Compulsory turning-up and voluntary minor sports, including a tool round Jaggers, were needed for exercises requirements to be fulfilled. Exercise was compulsory daily. Yearlings, scouting and OTC activities (later called JTC) were on Tuesday with an hour-long hash after it. Home Guard (1940) became compulsory at 17; we had two weekly parades, one on Sundays. There were two half-holidays, Wednesday and Saturday (Tuesday, Thursday and Saturday half-holidays began in about 1966).

Hash was the same in 1965 except that no scripture was taught in hashrooms on Sundays and hash before breakfast in SQ (7.30–8.10) had been discontinued. Daily chapel was compulsory with two compulsory services on the first and last Sundays of the quarter.

PT took place regularly in the morning quarter, taken by senior boys, and there was a weekly PT hash in change. Books for hash were carried; no one had bags. Fagging varied between Houses. Scholars were required only to fag for one year, everyone else for two. Running errands for monitors and getting provisions from Crown were a fag's main duty and you also had to make toast for Hall and monitors' homebill – which followed everyone else's – at

Charterhouse scouts supporting the war effort by helping with the harvest at Forde Abbey Farm, Chard, Somerset.

7 pm. Some were also required to clean a monitor's study regularly.

The food, even with the wartime rationing, was well managed in D. All the Houses had individual catering arrangements. We had our own food lockers so could keep control of our very small rations of butter, sugar, jam and milk each week. We could still get eggs from Godalming and our butler would cook them for us at homebill. Bread, sweets and clothes were rationed in 1942.

Tradesmen and the barber visited each House regularly to take orders but some even went to other shops to get us things we asked them for, even our dry cleaning. There was no school shop until the late forties when Gorringe's first ran it after the war. Three firms in Godalming were authorised in my time to sell the school uniform. Cycling down the hill to Godalming was allowed (but a boy's death in a collision with a car just before my return prohibited this).

Until we were senior enough to have a study space – only monitors had individual studies – we lived in longroom. Each had a desk and we sat in the order in which we passed our new bugs exam after the first fortnight. The test was to make sure we knew the slang and where everything was in the school, taught to us by a boy in his first year referred to as our father.

Travelling to and from home was mostly by train. Few parents picked boys up in cars. Luggage was sent by P(assengers) L(uggage) in A(dvance) or goods train.

We *did* have free time, but our organised days did not seem irksome. There were no expeditions and no nights could be spent away except during the one annual 'exeat' in SQ up to the outbreak of war. Thereafter we had to stay at school till the holidays. I always felt happy and secure in my House throughout my time in Daviesites and made a lot of life-long friends.

Chris Ray (D 1942; Brooke Hall 1965–85)

(See *Glossary*, page 13, for an explanation of the terms used)

Music flourished. It was, as George Giri (B 1941) noted, 'an intensely musical School'. The London Symphony Orchestra came down, and, on another occasion, Vaughan Williams famously failed to operate the cuckoo-call in the *Toy Symphony* put on for him. George Draper, blown out of bed by a bomb in London and not knowing for a week that his wife had survived, arrived with no possessions to electrify the brass and woodwind players. A.F.T. Monck-Mason (H 1948) recalled: 'Nobody seemed sure how many instruments he played – mostly woodwind – but they were many.'

Perhaps it was the staff who felt the effect most. Extra worries were piled on the Headmaster and the other Housemasters, who were constantly battling with ever more complex regulations from government bodies, while attempting to feed their Houses. There was also the business of black-out, for which large Gothic windows were unsuitable. The overall impression is one of joyless worrying, sleeplessness and irritation, and yet, according to B. Russell:

It was exciting. From 1940, when we stood with the Commonwealth alone against an apparently triumphant Germany – and almost the whole of Europe – to 1945. We were fighting for the preservation of what we believed in. Very many died for it. We who survived could feel the thrill of ultimate success, of preservation against almost impossible odds.

The School losses were not as terrible as they had been in the First World War, but they were no less significant for that, as the six panels of 340 names that had to be added in the ante-chapel attest.

Brigadier Dudley Clarke OBE, CBE, CB, American Legion of Merit

One of the great unsung heroes of the Second World War, Dudley Clarke was said by Field Marshal Alexander to have done as much to win the war as any other single officer. He was educated at Charterhouse, in Pageites, from 1912 to 1915, joining the Royal Horse Artillery in 1916 before transferring to the Royal Flying Corps in November 1917.

On the outbreak of the Second World War his remarkable skills came into play. He had charm and dramatic flair, plus an ingenious imagination and a photographic memory, and it was these attributes that made him a master of espionage and strategic deception. Following the withdrawal from Dunkirk, he came up with the idea of mounting guerrilla raids on the coast of occupied France, using specially trained small raiding groups that he named 'Commandos'. Churchill approved his scheme in June 1940 and put Clarke in charge of recruiting, training and deploying the Commandos. Once the Commandos were established, Clarke was head-hunted by General Sir Archibald Wavell to establish A Force, a deception organisation in the Middle East. Clarke and his team set up misleading clues and false information across the Mediterranean theatre, leading the enemy to over-estimate Allied strength there by nearly a quarter of a million men and to tie down troops that might otherwise have been redeployed to France to resist the Allied invasion.

Dudley Clarke is credited with naming the SAS. When Lieutenant David Stirling was seeking permission to form a new raiding regiment in North Africa, Clarke promised his support if Stirling would name it after a fictitious parachute brigade, the Special Air Service, which Clarke had invented to convince the Germans that there were British paratroopers in North Africa. It was Clarke who had the inspired idea of using a 'double', the actor, M.E. Clifton James, to impersonate Field Marshal Montgomery in Gibraltar and to distract the Germans, while the real Monty was preparing for the D-Day invasion of Normandy.

Because of the secret nature of his work, Dudley Clarke was not permitted to publish his memoirs and his important contribution to the war effort was largely unrecognised during his lifetime.

Major General Orde Wingate

Orde Wingate (S 1920), who organised and led the Chindits in Burma during the Second World War, is commemorated in the Memorial Chapel. Described by Churchill as 'a man of genius who might well have become also a man of destiny', Wingate was killed in a plane crash in 1944.

Left: Lord Mountbatten inspects the Corps at the unveiling of Wingate's memorial, March 1951.

The effects of the war on the School lasted a long time. Michael Darling (H 1948) remembers bread and potato rationing in 1947, and even in the 1950s boys were still being given the equivalent of wartime rations. The School buildings remained unkempt, unpainted and run down for many years. What the war and the resulting political upheaval did do, however, was to emphasise those changes that Tod – who never beat boys in his House – had hoped would result from the First World War. Charterhouse was seen to be distinctly insular in a way that may have suited life in 1900 but that was out of place in postwar Labour austerity. But it is easy to typecast, and it was a Carthusian, Lord Beveridge, who was largely responsible for the welfare reforms that followed the war (see page 168).

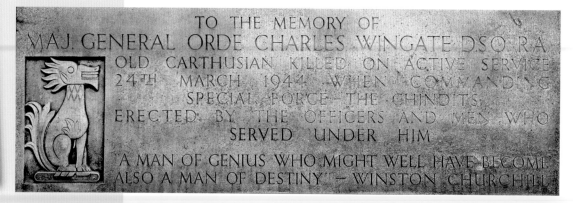

Lord Ismay

In the Second World War, Hastings Ismay rose to particular prominence as a general and as Deputy Secretary (Military) to the War Cabinet, effectively acting as Churchill's number two. He was later appointed to be Chief of Staff to the last viceroy of India, Lord Mountbatten, and subsequently served as Secretary of State for Commonwealth Relations. The fine senior common room in Verites, known as Ismays, was named in his honour.

Chiefs of Staff at Downing Street, 7 May 1945.
Back row (l–r): Major General Hollis and General Sir Hastings Ismay (OC); front row: Sir Charles Portal, Marshal of the RAF, Field Marshal Sir Alan Brooke, Prime Minister Winston Churchill, Admiral of the Fleet and Sir Andrew Cunningham.

THE 1950s ONWARDS

In the late 1950s it was possible to recognise many of the features of the School still surviving from before the First World War. In the upper fourth E.A. Malaher's pupils moved position physically, depending on their answers to questions delivered from his desk on the raised dais, form order being taken at midday on Friday. R.L. Arrowsmith's Latin classes memorised a page of Latin grammar every day and 'said their con' as their predecessors had. Privileges continued over a wide field – School monitors kept their jackets open everywhere, House monitors in House, while the rest had to have theirs buttoned.

Sir Brian Young

Brian Young (Headmaster, 1952–65) surely belongs to that select band of great Headmasters of Charterhouse, alongside Haig Brown, Frank Fletcher and Robert Birley. He arrived, aged 31, at the beginning of my second year. Tall, dark and strikingly good looking, he made his mark in no time. It was his singular eloquence, whether in the pulpit or at 'Final Calling-Over' or, as I later discovered, when speaking after Founder's Day dinners, that first stamped him as exceptional.

In the years that followed, I was fortunate to get to know him about as well as any boy could, since I was a Classics Specialist and therefore a beneficiary of his outstanding teaching. To read Aeschylus, Aristophanes, Demosthenes and Lucretius, *inter alios*, with him was a privilege, but it was when he appointed me as Head of School in my final two quarters that I grew to realise the breadth of his interests, his astonishing memory and his mastery of every aspect of Carthusian life.

A brilliant scholar (Porson prizewinner at Cambridge), a fine athlete (hurdler and fives player) and, for good measure, endowed with a bass voice good enough for Boris Ord to have engaged him in the King's College Choir, he could do almost everything better than anyone else. Just as well, I thought, since any member of Brooke Hall aged 50 or more was old enough to have been his father when he was appointed Headmaster.

Three illustrations 'get him' for me. The first came when he asked the senior year in the Classical Sixth what their university ambitions were. 'Oxford, or Cambridge?' he asked, and when anyone replied 'Cambridge', he said, 'Which college?' As an afterthought he added, 'Would Oxford be a possible alternative?' Receiving an emphatic 'No' from one boy, he smilingly said: 'Ah, I had rather be a doorkeeper in the house of the Lord than to dwell in the tents of ungodliness.'

Second, when reviewing the events of cricket quarter 1956, he came to the performance of the Cricket XI. It happened that 1956 was an Ashes year and, in the hope that the Revd David Shepherd, later Bishop of Liverpool, might regain enough form to return to the England side, MCC chose him to play against the School. He made an elegant 56 and in due course was selected to play for England in Laker's 19-for-90 test match at Old Trafford. He promptly made 133, which led Brian Young to opine that our 1st XI had proved itself to be 'almost exactly twice as good as the Australians'.

Third, on the morning after the death of Vincent ('Sniffy') Russell while playing the part of Judge Jeffries in the Masque that same quarter, he delivered a tribute to him of such sensitivity, insight and felicity of phrase as to leave us all – and senior Hodgsonites in particular – as moved as we were stunned. It was an outstanding achievement by the most brilliant man I have ever known.

Michael Seligman (H 1956)

Above: Headmaster, Brian Young, with monitors of 1956, including Michael Seligman (seated fourth from left).

Daviesites still walked on the right-hand pavement approaching Brooke Hall, all others on the left hand, except monitors, who occupied the centre of the road. Bloods were still the only people allowed down Bloods' Steps and had their separate serving hatch at Crown. Monitors still beat, as did Housemasters themselves, though not all of them. Leave to Godalming or to go home was severely restricted. There were 300 members of the Railway Society, because it showed films on Saturdays. Trunks still arrived by Passenger Luggage in Advance, and tradesmen were still in attendance in the mornings.

Personal fagging existed in many Houses, though in Daviesites there was general fagging. (Daviesites considered themselves humane; Robinites considered themselves to be humane and intellectual.) It was not done in some Houses for a boy to address anyone in the year above him unless spoken to first, and a fag on message duty was expected to wait in the entrance hall of another

Friends on Weekites roof and rowing on the Wey, photographed by Jon Wilkie, 1958.

House, which was foreign territory to him, until somebody deigned to notice him. Surnames were the rule. One master, F.W. Ives, wrote to a successful university scholarship winner: 'Dear ——, I am afraid I do not know your Christian name, but in my day to be addressed by one's surname was a sign of affection.'

Although there was nominal heating in the Houses, it was still powered by a coke boiler, stoked by the pupils, and face-flannels froze on bedside lockers overnight. There were no study-bedrooms. The junior boys usually had a

The First Drugs Bust

By 1970 we were aware that drugs were becoming a problem, but we were naive and ignorant — at least I was as a new Housemaster. Strange, unaccountable things were happening in the House, like the burning of sash cords, but their meaning eluded me.

It was the end of CQ with late evening chapel. At adsum back in House two boys were missing. I had decided to sit at the bottom of the stairs, waiting for them, when the phone rang. 'Guildford Police here, we've got two of your lads, picked up on the top of the multi-storey car park smoking cannabis. Will you come and pick them up?' I drove to the police station and was about to bring them back when the head of the Guildford drug squad intervened. 'Hang on to those boys. I want to talk to them.' Their story was that it was a typical end-of-term prank, and the first time they'd tried drugs. Their story was ripped to pieces. 'How do you manage to roll a joint like this if it was your first time? Do you really think that someone would pass over an illegal drug to a complete stranger?'

The upshot was that he said that he had to go through the House. I rang the Headmaster to put him in the picture and back we came. The result was that the drug squad spent the entire night combing the House, interviewing boys, including some brought in from three other Houses. The extent of drug taking, including LSD, was laid bare. The pushers were expelled, while the others were dealt with leniently on the grounds that they were innocent experimenters. From my point of view I was happy to remain fairly neutral to pick up the pieces, while the drug squad were regarded as the protagonists. I was certainly a wiser man after that terrible night, and the House was a happier place.

I recall one amusing incident. At 3 am, as we toured the House, the matron burst out of her room, clothed in a Lady Macbeth-style nightgown and cap. 'What are you silly boys doing up at this hour?' I didn't quite let on that the 'silly boys' were actually members of the drug squad, but I calmed her down and she went back to bed.

Norman Evans
(Housemaster L 1970–85)

...dmaster, ...ng, ...s a pupil at ... Over, 1960.

Yet the 20 years that separate this period from the centenary of the School's move in 1872 were to produce changes just as dramatic as the move itself had done. It was a challenging period: the Labour Government's determination to abolish public schools, the 'swinging sixties', drugs, hippies, the idolisation of the individual – all these cut straight across the old-fashioned apparatus of the School.

If Charterhouse muddled through in a moderately amiable way, it was largely because of Headmaster Oliver van Oss. A man of sympathy and experience, he was held from the first in great affection by his pupils. He took a wide interest in everything that happened in the School and had the irreplaceable quality of making everyone feel that he appreciated what they did and felt that it was worthwhile. Outrageous teenage protest was defused. Though some of the masters and governors thought him far too lax, following the hard line that they advocated might have provoked disaster.

If we compare the School of 1955 with that of 1972 the changes are startling, but they were often gradual. Girls, for example, appeared in a Carthusian way. They started as science pupils cycling over from Priorsfield School, merged into the daughters of Brooke Hall joining as day girls, developed into sisters of pupils living with local families and finally moved into a girls' hostel. The grass-roots nature of this development led to sixth form-only entry and the absolute insistence that girls were full members of the boys' Houses. After being bombarded with minute prohibitions for their initial six weeks, the girls in Gownboys told their Housemaster that either he trusted them or he didn't and that they proposed to create their own rules: a combination of liberality and common sense that was typically Carthusian at the time.

The CCF became voluntary and was matched on Mondays by other activities, including pioneering and social services ('granny bashing'). Privilege and hierarchy diminished markedly, and there was a renewed insistence on the tradition that monitors had cure of souls rather than privilege. It was the monitors, led by Robinites, who abolished fagging and beating. Housemasters, too, gradually stopped beating. The adoption of first names, hitherto restricted to first XIs, Upper Sixths and Green Room, could be seen as an indicator of the general relaxation of hierarchy.

There was a broadening of the curriculum, with flexible arrangements that meant that most combinations of A-level

small dormitory, and the rest had cubicles, except for the very senior monitors who might share a couple of rooms. Housemasters could still be found who would visit the boys' side of the House only when escorted by the duty monitor for adsum, prayers and evening rounds. The Headmaster would not normally feel it appropriate to talk to parents, and Housemasters had virtually sole authority on which boys they took into their Houses. Despite nearly a century of attempts to get intellectualism prized above athletic prowess, scholars were still called 'hash pros', and it was possible to find a pupil reading a text book hidden behind a comic.

There had certainly been change, but it was gradual – after all, if you had a system that everyone, even foreigners, admired, why change it? As Jameson put it, change was gradual: 'Which could be reasonably taken as a sign of health by men of discernment.'

subjects could be studied. There was an increase in respect for scholarship and the encouragement of original thought, all of which provided a positive response to the challenges of ever-rising standards of university entry and public examinations, although, as C. Jonas (G 1959) remarked, it could still be said that: 'Charterhouse had a remarkable way of encouraging one's innate enthusiasm and went far beyond measuring its boys just by academic results.'

The first architectural signs of a general relaxation came thanks to the art master, Ian Fleming-Williams. He guided the building of the outrageously modern Studio – a Gold Flake packet resting on a matchbox, as it was described in *The Greyfriar* (see page 120). The Studio, with its light, warmth and spaciousness, welcomed even the most philistine Carthusian to give him much needed culture in an informal setting. The first steps were taken in modernising the Houses to give privacy, warmth and decent sanitation. It was only now that many Housemasters' private sides gained central heating and lost the drudgery of feeding dozens of open fires. In the 1960s the effects of post-war austerity began to wear off, both in terms of comfort and rations.

The greatest change was the gigantic upheaval caused by the building of the new Houses. This was an extraordinary leap of faith, since it involved painful financial and geographic sacrifices. In the end, after many vicissitudes, it proved to be a success. It meant that in

Oliver van Oss, Headmaster 1965–73.

seven Houses every pupil had an individual study-bedroom with a decent view, and this in itself led to important changes in habits of work and social integration. Many of the good points were thrashed out by a committee of those who were going to have to live with the results (a refreshing change), which threw up a number of important modifications – social areas, including the 'conversation pit' (instead of the lift), were encouraged in order to avoid pupils becoming isolated in their rooms.

Not everybody was happy with the move. Leap-frogging from gradual upgrading to complete modernisation meant abandoning two Houses that had already been part-modernised. The Housemaster of Pageites, who had spent two years planning the modernisation of his House only to see it destroyed, found it hard to take. It was not just the Houses that were sold. Gone too was 'Doddites', the slightly scruffy kickabout area behind D, P and R, with its eccentric, corrugated-iron-clad gym, where the ordeal of House boxing took

The Rolls-Royce Enthusiasts' Club

The Rolls-Royce Enthusiasts' Club came to the school in July 1960 for a Concours d'elegance. I was enthralled by the magnificent Edwardian (pre-1918) Silver Ghosts, especially the closed one which, I believe, belonged to Stanley Sears.

Later, in February 1962, the Vintage Sports Car Club ran a hill climb up Racquets Court Hill, and I was bitten with the bug from then on. This event was run by Tim Carson, himself an OC.

David Ryder Richardson (S 1962)

Architect's plans for south elevation and study for the new Houses.

View from a Verites study, illustration from The Greyfriar, *1959.*

place. The sanatorium, known as Great Comp, moved to Northbrook House in an act of architectural vandalism. Bernina, the bachelor colony, was replaced by the less collegiate tower. Laleham, which had belonged to the Huxleys, and Twycross, where the School doctor lived, vanished, and the Farm was swallowed up.

Falling land values necessitated further sales. The sale of land on the School side of Charterhouse Hill was a mistake, and the developer broke the covenants that the School had imposed, bringing understandable opprobrium for over-development and putting this development right beneath the chapel. These problems were familiar from the 1872 move when lack of money from the sale of the original site forced compromises.

As further Houses in Mark Way were sold, the School retreated to the southwest, only failing to sell Broom and Lees because of the opposition of local councils. It became, finally, a suburban school, and the new A3 cut the campus off from the countryside over which Edwardian pupils had roamed.

The architecture of the new Houses, much criticised at the time, has come to be seen in its proper context of delivering a spiky outline without incurring the impossible cost of Bargate stone and Gothic detail. The focus of the School shifted: Founder's Court was now the centre, and Duckites was on the edge.

All in all, the second move was essential for the School's survival. Mothers were reluctant to send their children to the gloomy Spartan atmosphere of the Victorian Houses – Bodeites was called 'the submarine', since, seen from the fag entrance, it uncannily resembled one. Recentering the School gave more space and room for the various developments, like the Queen's Sports Centre, which modern schools are expected to provide. Pressure was also put on the remaining old Houses to modernise, allowing all pupils to acquire their own space and privacy.

The 1960s saw a general broadening of scope. There was less in the way of compulsory team games, and more emphasis on individual sports and recreations. There was more breadth in the curriculum, with science, engineering and further modern languages. This was the kind of process by which the School reinvented itself almost every decade. The master in charge of football is reputed to have said to a 1st XI player who had been criticised for his academic effort, 'There are more things in life than football, boyo,' adding, *sotto voce*, 'I can't believe I said that.'

There were losses. 'I can't help being captain of cricket,' said one Verite, harassed by his intellectual friends, and a member of the English department wondered, after years of struggle to civilise the Bloods, whether he would prefer that they were playing bad football or writing bad poetry. Gone was the spaciousness of early times in which the Masque – a huge dramatic undertaking that occupied two-thirds of the masters and pupils – could be performed during the summer term of major national exams. Gone, too, were the Brooke Hall play and the long summer afternoons idled away playing languid Etcetera's cricket, one of the qualifications for which was the wearing of a boater that did not fall off. Public schools had once set the agenda for education, but times were changing, and training to govern the empire would no longer do.

In the summer of 1972, the centenary of the move to Godalming, the School was thrown open to visitors for a whole week of celebrations, with exhibitions, displays, presentations and tours. On the Saturday it was the turn of the Old Carthusians. They gathered on a perfect summer evening on Mrs Haig Brown's terrace overlooking Green to watch a firework display based on the 1911 programme. (The Headmaster was overheard to remark to the technician in charge of the fireworks: 'I have given you a junior master as an assistant. He has a degree in physics.' The technician replied: 'Damn that, can he run?') As they watched the fireworks, they had every reason to reflect that the School had weathered an enormously difficult period but had successfully carried out the biggest revolution since the 1872 migration.

CHAPTER 3:

The Recent Past, 1973–96

ERNST ZILLEKENS

CHAPTER 3:

The Recent Past, 1973–96

ERNST ZILLEKENS

THE NEW HOUSES

Following the celebrations of the first 100 years in Godalming and the laying of the foundation stone for the new Houses by HM The Queen in 1972, Brian Rees's term of office as Headmaster began in 1973 with the gradual migration of seven boarding Houses to their new sites. The reaction to this major development was mixed.

Previous page: Early morning at the modern Houses, Lockites (far right) and Weekites.

First, a Housemaster's point of view:
From the Old to the New Lockites

I took over Lockites as Housemaster in January 1970. The private side accommodation was dark, cold, but spacious. The boys' side was barbaric. The dormitories were long rows of horseboxes: each boy had his own box, and we were expected to shut them in last thing at night (needless to say, climbing over the top proved no problem). Banco was done by the juniors in the common room (Under-Long), sitting on benches at tables. The baths were communal, with the water being emptied into an open drain. Because of the shortage of baths, bath times had to be arranged. The lavatories were outside, now roofed with corrugated iron, but dripping with damp in the winter. I am told that the boys returning after the holidays gave a large gulp – and got on with life as best they could.

On our side of the house the accommodation was acceptable, but the duties of the Housemaster's wife were onerous. My poor wife, Margaret, with two small children to bring up, found herself in charge of the domestic side of the House. There was the kitchen department and the cleaning. Feeding was done in the House – so if the cook went ill she had to take over. There was Charles, released we believe from a mental home by clerical error, who was involved with laying the tables and washing-up (health and safety was not yet a mantra). In the holidays he took

to his bed and expected Margaret to look after him. There were the kitchen staff – at one time we had a pair of Yugoslavs who threatened to murder one another! Yes, the Housemaster's wife's life was hell – a tension of loyalties between family and House.

HM The Queen (seen here with retired Headmaster, Sir Robert Birley) visits Charterhouse to lay a foundation stone for the new Houses, 1972.

84

First, Housemasters used to give us great leeway in the decoration of our studies, with complete paint jobs and complex lighting systems refreshed almost term by term. My own study had a makeshift second floor at one stage, and others featured door controls that cut out illegal sound systems as required. We really did become quite 'creative' and it was a shock to find that we were not even allowed to apply Blu-tack to the walls of the new Houses.

Above all, though, being situated slightly outside the main School undoubtedly reinforced our sense of identity and independence. Robinites, being the most far-flung of all, had its own recreation area, a shop at the end of the lane and no end of nooks and crannies in which to hide out and hatch plans.

Of course, we liked and, I hope, appreciated the new Houses when they arrived, but I for one did rather hanker for Frith Hill and certainly shed a tear when the old Robinites burned down soon after our departure.

Life at Charterhouse was never going to be quite the same, and in the longer term there have certainly been indications that everything became a little more regimented. Sadly, and perhaps inevitably, I fear the move probably brought about the end of a 'hands-off' approach from Housemasters. Most of us appreciated this, and I am sure it helped in setting us up for life in the outside world.

So we moved to Northbrook and we moved with the times; but Frith Hill is home to many of the memories that still move me nearly 40 years on.

Nick Fitzherbert (R 1975)

Above: Lockites House photo with Norman Evans (centre), 1981.

Above right: The demolition of Lockites.

Below right: Traditional cubes in Verites.

Both boys and we were relieved to hear of plans to build new Houses. Then it happened. In 1974 we moved into the new Lockites – comparative luxury! Carpeting and warmth! Each boy had his own bedroom, with desk and wardrobe. Showers and kitchenettes on each corridor. A common room for adsums and TV watching, a small music room and a room for the two girls who had now joined the House. Nearby were the central dining rooms, with central cooking and with each House having its own space.

On the private side, luxury, too. No longer the anguish of worrying about catering. A view over Under Green and sunshine. Some pleasant rooms, suitable for the family. Space to create our own vegetable garden (useful for setting miscreants to work). The matron had pleasant quarters, too; as well as being concerned with health and the laundry, she now looked after the cleaning.

We were glad we were one of the later Houses to move across, as the teething problems which had beset some of the earlier ones had been dealt with. We were certainly ready for the move.

Norman Evans (Housemaster L 1970–85)

Next, a pupil's perspective:

Many Carthusians of the early 1970s generation experienced school life from two very different perspectives in that our time was divided between the 'old' Houses on Frith Hill and the brand 'new' Houses on Northbrook. Clearly there was a stark difference between the 'hotel-like' splendours of the new Houses and the quite primitive conditions of the old, but I believe the effects ran deeper.

Finally, the Headmaster's recollection:

When I arrived in 1973, the new Houses were already nearing completion but had not been occupied. The first few quarters were marked by long processions of Carthusians carrying lampshades and cushions and household bric-a-brac over the grounds behind the Headmaster's house, like a trail of refugees one saw in wartime newsreels. The full scope of the grand design and financing of this huge change in the School's outward appearance had been planned by the Governing Body, my predecessor OVO [Oliver van Oss] and the then bursar, John Daukes, who played a major role and had the necessary tough skin to deal with the businessmen at Bovis and other major contractors. But, as luck would have it, the first Houses to move were those whose current site was the most valuable building land, among them Daviesites, the prime site for new buildings. Like all three Houses farthest away, it had a grand private side and its Housemaster, Donald Stagg, was highly unwilling to exchange such fine apartments for the less impressive private sides of the new Houses, good by modern standards but subsumed into the general structure with the boys and girls. He endeavoured to procrastinate with every known ploy and drew up a list of structural faults, including a claim that the lintel of his frontdoor was not properly fixed and would fall and kill him on the first morning of occupation. In the end, all I could say was, 'Donald this is your finest hour,' and usher him out with a warm handshake. In the end, he did have the last laugh, as one of the subcontractors responsible for the damp courses had weirdly turned the endings inwards rather than outwards in the brickwork. Early in the days of occupation we had a torrential rainstorm and several Houses had floods. David Summerscale, Housemaster of Robinites, leapt out of bed that morning and found himself standing in a foot of icy water.

Brian Rees

Donald Stagg had also been one of the prime movers in the campaign to admit his and other masters' daughters into the sixth form at the end of Oliver van Oss's time as Headmaster. But it was in Brian Rees's time that the girls were admitted more widely, although the number remained at between 20 and 22 in each sixth form year for quite a long time. Initially, most girls came from local girls' schools and did not live far from the School, so they were day pupils, but as the geographical catchment area began to widen the School adopted a number of landladies, who were all friends or acquaintances of members of the school staff, with whom the girls lodged. They shared a study in boys' boarding Houses and went back to their 'digs' in the evening. There were opportunities to be found on many different levels: Belinda Knox (B 1978) recalls that she 'joined the corps, which not only allowed us to improve our khaki wardrobe but also allowed us to drive the school silver mini round the School grounds'.

Girls at Charterhouse, 1975–2005

Going to Charterhouse was a very positive experience for me – 'the making of her,' in my parents' words – and so I hoped it would do the same for my girls. Like them, I had come from an all-girls school, and what both generations needed was to escape undiluted girls.

Nowadays, I would never have got into Charterhouse. Not being especially academic, I would have failed the entrance exam miserably. Luckily, in those days there was no such thing. The old school tie was still extremely effective, and as a large proportion of the male members of my family had been to Charterhouse, the door was open for me. I also happened to be quite musical, which was in my favour. All I had to do was to chat to Philip Balkwill (who loved music) for about ten minutes. I guess he thought I was the right sort of chap(ess), and I was in.

Fortunately, my daughters are more academically inclined and sailed through the entrance exam, the eldest being awarded an exhibition. Contrarily, one of the things I wanted for the girls was a more relaxed attitude to study, and the boys certainly provided that.

Below left: One of the first female pupils, Susan Hamilton, joins her brother, Michael, at Charterhouse, 1974.

Do you approve of girls?
Yes 97%   No 3%

Do you approve of girls in Cha[rter] house?
Yes 79%   Don't know 8%   No 13%

Given the enthusiastic response to [the] abstract idea of women there wa[s] surprisingly large resistance to [their?] appearance inside Charterhouse, public opinion was still very much [on] their side. The general view is that [they] are not only decorative but help [to?] humanise their intensely masculine [sur]roundings.

Cartoons in The Carthusian *illustrating a jokey survey of boys' attitudes to the newly arrived girls, 1974. Drawn by Charles Peattie, now famous for his work for the* Daily Telegraph, *the survey's conclusion was that girls are welcome 'As long as they look decorative, speak when spoken to and keep their places'!*

w many girls should there be at
arterhouse?

swers varied between none and
70 (two girls to every boy) but there
med very little enthusiasm for com-
te co-education, Carthusians ap-
rently preferring to keep girls in a
trollable minority. The great con-
sus of opinion was for between 50
d 100 girls, with the lower figure
htly more favoured.

Top: Specialists history pupils on a field trip, 1977, including Katherine Armitage, Kate Forshall with Dr Fernandez-Armesto (at the back).

Right: Pupils leaving Chapel: whilst boys wore uniform, girls chose their own clothes until the introduction of a girls' black suit in 1997.

I am guessing that sports for girls are much better provided for now. Certainly our girls were able to play both netball and lacrosse – I seem to remember that squash and tennis were the only sports on offer in my day – and, of course, they have that very snazzy sports hall.

Today's girls also have a smart uniform, which is, of course, stretched to its boundaries at times. We were allowed to wear whatever we liked, and we mostly looked a pretty scruffy lot.

So, although many things have changed since the 1970s, the overall experience of being a girl at Charterhouse is pretty similar. Both our girls left with a great deal more self-confidence and manage, most importantly, to view boys as friends. Both generations left Charterhouse much better equipped to move on to the next stage in their life, which is surely what it is all about.

Shelley Phillips, née Howard (g 1977)

Coming from an all-girls school, where our lives had been cosy and protected from reality, I found Charterhouse an almighty shock. Having had one brother leave and another still there gave me a false sense of already knowing the School. How wrong could I have been? Being one of only 45

My first memory of Charterhouse was being dropped off by my landlady, Sue Cole (after my time renowned as 'Queen of Crack', the tuckshop, for many years), at the private side of Duckites, shaking so badly with nerves that it took some encouragement from Sue to just get out of the car. In I walked and was faced straight away with a queue of boys waiting to see Philip Balkwill. So terrified was I – and blinded by so many boys – that I failed to see the fire extinguisher and walked straight into it. Not a great start.

What I learned pretty quickly was that a sense of humour was vital and that I had to do away with girly sensitivity. There was a lot of teasing – or 'beating up', as it was known. This has not changed, except that it is now called 'rinsing'. Teenage boys seem to find this the only way to communicate with the opposite sex. Fortunately for me and my girls, we managed to see the funny side, but not all girls could cope with it.

So how have things changed? Rules and regulations are much more rigorous than I remember. Today, pupils have to sign in and out of House, and their whereabouts are always known. No sneaking off to the pub then … or getting up at dawn after A levels to meet for a celebration breakfast in a local farmer's field.

girls in nearly 700 boys, we were what I call the 'early girls' – still living in digs and having a room in the boys' Houses, teaching ourselves lacrosse and having no place of our own to hang out. We were a minority – something that today's School has addressed – but it was an incredible experience.

Charterhouse was the making of me. I think the greatest gift I was given was the ability to learn to think independently – I was inspired by teachers to develop my own mind, and as a result achieved great grades and a place at Bristol University. The array of opportunities presented to us to try new things opened my mind to a world of opportunity to be grasped if you had the will and the tenacity to fit it all in.

Juliet Slot, née Mellstrom (B 1986)

ACADEMIC LIFE

In the early 1980s the school took risks on some occasions to offer someone who had not made a success of their academic career in another school a chance to succeed at Charterhouse:

It was very decent of Charterhouse to accept me into the sixth form in 1980. Having been expelled from Cheltenham Ladies College with an appalling report suggesting I was mad, unteachable and dangerous, there weren't many institutions clamouring for the honour of furthering my education. I never saw this report, but during my two years at Charterhouse a number of teachers quoted extracts from it with amusement.

Compared to the prison-like regime at Cheltenham, Charterhouse offered considerable freedom. I lived with a

relaxed family called the Wrights and had an understanding and good-humoured Housemaster, Norman Evans, who allowed me total freedom at weekends. I was a lazy student and instinctively rebellious, but, treated with respect at Charterhouse, I lost the fury against authority that dominated my time at Cheltenham. I can't pretend that I ever engaged fully academically during my time at Charterhouse, and I undoubtedly annoyed some of my teachers, but I left with a love of Plath, Faulkner and Larkin, and I've been sitting reading on my sofa in Somerset ever since!

Charlotte Rees-Mogg (L 1982)

The academic ethos of the School was strong and was still shaped by the seventh-term Oxbridge entrance exam. Independent learning and detailed study were, therefore, important aspects of the approach to teaching in the sixth form. Apart from tackling a considerable volume of work, Specialists found time to develop and follow particular enthusiasms. But Specialists tended to divide into two distinct groups: those who acquired academic rigour and interest and those who focused more on the rich extracurricular programme, being quite happy with more modest academic achievements.

The day-to-day running of the School benefited from being supported by quite mature third year Specialists as School and House monitors until just before the end of OQ (autumn term), when the second years would take over. The mature outlook of the senior pupils was one of the reasons why a more relaxed and liberal attitude to the way in which teaching was delivered was possible. Finding ways of inspiring pupils was crucial and beaks could find idiosyncratic routes to achieving this goal.

Robin Totton (French) and Philip Balkwill (English) go together. Both real mavericks, who I suspect would not last five minutes in today's politically correct world (we almost never got any work marked by Mr Balkwill), but they made their subjects live, and their enthusiasm was infectious. They both taught me how to enjoy appreciating literature. My A-level subjects were Latin, Greek and History. Peter Baldwin was the Head of Classics then, and he was superb. He worked us hard and took no nonsense from us. He had a rather camp wit, which could be quite barbed, and all howlers were pounced upon mercilessly. However,

Feature on girls at Charterhouse, published in Woman and Home *magazine, 1980.*

I know that I learned a great deal from him about the appreciation of Latin and Greek literature. Lessons with him were never dull, as the intellectual fireworks would fly.

Among the historians, Felipe Fernandez-Armesto stands out. He was already something of a character: he liked to wear his DPhil gown to chapel, and his upper-class accent and esoteric vocabulary caused some amusement. The wicked might say he was something of a poser. But in my first year in the sixth form FFA came into his own. He made the point of teaching us one topic and making us write essays on another. Having to write essays on something we hadn't been taught? This was terrifying stuff, and my first essays for him were unimpressive. But eventually I learned how to swim rather than sink and started to enjoy going off to research and write up essays on subjects of my own choosing – and even sometimes got some complimentary comments for them. Once I got to university, I began to realise the depths of FFA's cunning: he was forcing us to think and work like university students two years early. He really taught us how to research and how to write essays.

Robin Darwall-Smith (G 1981)

Dr Darwall-Smith is now archivist of Magdalen College and University College, Oxford

Until the early 1980s admission to the Fourth Form took place each term. Four forms began the Fourth Form in September, another two in January and one at the beginning of CQ (summer term). This enabled academically weaker pupils to spend extra time at their prep schools, and if any of those who had arrived in the summer found their academic work hard they could be given the option of starting in the Fourth Form again the following autumn. The Fourth Form was not an introductory year; instead pupils had to choose their optional subjects before they came. Only two sciences, physics and chemistry, were compulsory. Biology was an optional subject together with a second foreign language, classics, history, geography, art and design and technology. Pupils' academic progress was monitored by form masters and through an internal review system, where each Under School form would appear before the Headmaster after they had been awarded grades for attainment and effort in all their subjects, something Brian Rees valued greatly:

Going over the progress of each form with the form master once or twice each quarter, either in Hall or in the summer under that enormous tree, was the system named 'calling over'. This was something new to me and immensely

Some of the students on their way to a class. BELOW: Tea in a cushioned-lined study.

Catherine Clancy and Emma Scoby at their study window. BELOW: Irene, at the head of the table, lunching in one of the houses.

What is it like, then, to be at a great public school for boys? More especially, IRENE HEATH wondered, what is it like to be a girl in one of these cloistered institutions?

valuable as a means of pushing along some of the laggards without fuss and a heavy hand.

A positive by-product of this process was that the Headmaster quite quickly knew all pupils in the School. In the 1970s there were still a number of form masters who taught more than one subject to their form, so they would know their pupils particularly well, seeing them for as many as 12 or 13 hashes a week. But they were gradually replaced by more subject-specialist teachers, which eventually led to the introduction of a tutor system to provide the support they had been giving.

The extracurricular programme was rich, with the possibilities for participating in sports seemingly limitless. Music was strong under Bill Llewellyn, and the results were certainly impressive. The standard of chapel singing was outstanding, as was that of many concerts. Studio offered all those interested in art the opportunity to develop their skills and enjoy working there throughout the weekend. Plays were few in number. There was a school play each year in OQ (autumn term), followed at the end of that term by the Oxbridge farce, French play in LQ (spring term) and in the summer the Lockite Art Festival. But a quite unique artistic event took place in OQ 1979, the premier of a large-scale opera, *King of Macedon*, written by our first composer-in-residence, Roger Steptoe, and conducted by Bill Llewellyn. Eric Harrison recounts what a special occasion this was in *A Charterhouse Miscellany*:

The first performance, given in Hall on 18 October and attended by Alice, Duchess of Gloucester, and the Greek ambassador, captured the magic and excitement of a world premiere that it indeed was. It was well received and reviewed in the national press, comments being made on the excellent preparation and ingenious staging of Geoffrey Ford's production. The point was made that it was not really a school opera, because, although it involved a large number of members of the School and Brooke Hall on and behind the scenes, the principal singers and the main body of the 36-piece orchestra were professional. One may ask whether such enterprises as this, costly as they are in both time and money, are justified. Whatever prudence may dictate, unique occasions like this one, with all its many facets – the experience of taking part in the development and perfection of a new work of art, the excitement of the actual performance, the distinguished visitors, the splendid refreshment marquee, beautifully decorated – are enormously worthwhile. Great and memorable experiences are an important part of a liberal education.

Below left: King of Macedon, *with Glyn Davenport in the title role, 1979.*

Below: Roger Steptoe (Composer in Residence), Ursula Vaughan Williams (Librettist) and Bill Llewellyn (Conductor) discuss the score for King of Macedon.

Pupil and Beak: A Lifetime at Charterhouse

When my father, Dr John Blatchly (JMB), took up his appointment as head of science in OQ (autumn term) 1966, we moved into Lower Kelstone; I was six years old. Founder's Tower, viewed through the trees in the front garden, was a totemic emblem of Charterhouse: with its back turned (like the portrait of OVO in Hall) it seemed mysterious, distant and powerful. That December I was impressed by the noise and crush of the carol service: a throng of large boys in half-darkness beneath Gilbert Scott's dingy lanterns, which shed pools of gloom. Soon I was attending subscription concerts in Hall – the Amadeus Quartet, the King's Singers – improvising origami in the balcony with my programme while the incomprehensible, interminable but nourishing music happened below. In the summers Brooke Hall families used the pool, run by the amazing Mr Dean, at the foot of Rackets Court Hill. Walking down the graceful curve of that lane by the fragrant box hedge was like being by the sea. The baths were as noisy as chapel, the marble surfaces like vast fishmongers' slabs, and the forested hill outside seemed to lean into it, dropping dead wood on to the glass roof.

My father's promotion to Headmaster of Ipswich left me here to enter Gownboys in 1973. His quondam colleagues were very kind to me always – and tactfully failed to marvel at my complete lack of scientific acumen.

New hops' tea in the garden of G private side was a stilted affair: sensible boys who understood the rules of the game said little or nothing; I foolishly tried to break the ice. All in G acknowledged that John Phillips (JCP) was a remarkable Housemaster, and as long as we tried to meet his high expectations, we had nothing else to fear. Music scholars were as much members of music school as of their own Houses. Bill Llewellyn (WBJL) presided over a humming department; we encompassed vast

Mark Blatchly as a 'woodcutter's boy' in Vaughan Williams' Pilgrim's Progress, 1972.

swathes of repertoire in choirs and orchestra, learning classics from the inside. Robin Wells (RJAW) was my unofficial tutor; he listened patiently and at length, then advised me wisely. Each evening in the last week of CQ (summer term) there was late chapel followed by a short concert – Monday band, Tuesday orchestra, Wednesday choir and so on – a series of jolly dins. Of course, these evenings were always warm, and the sun came in through the west windows just so.

I joined Brooke Hall in OQ (autumn term) 1996 and ran the choirs for seven years. Then I was happy to retire behind the organ console and apply all my choir-training energies to housemastering in Gownboys. Running the House has overwritten many of my schoolboy memories – and now G study bedrooms have been fashioned from former butteries and lavatories, and vice versa. Most confusingly, Saunderites eats in the old G tosh-room – and G (like all Houses) has a whole room dedicated to the watching of television, a pursuit permitted for half-an-hour on 1970s Saturday evenings if it was raining and you had broken your leg.

The School has not changed much in 40 years – although it seemed in the 1970s that Carthusians were allowed to fail, and it was certainly quite possible to get all the way through the School without donning a pair of footer shorts – a feat undreamed of in the modern era. The School now prohibits failure, striving always to produce the best outcome even for the determinedly unwilling. Society has changed, however – with the internet, the mobile phone, the cult of mediocrity fostered by 'reality' television and junk journalism, not to mention the passivity inculcated by hours of gawping at TV and PC screens and the commercialisation of sport. However, despite the apparent decline in academic rigour, young people hone their practical skills to levels that Carthusians in the 1970s would have gasped at. Their music-making, cabinet-making, art and footballing are unimaginably better now.

Mark Blatchly
(G 1979, Brooke Hall 1996–)

Following the move to the new Houses it became apparent that a number of other areas in the School were in need of modernisation. The wood and metal workshops were housed in a large wooden hut that had been put up as a temporary building in the First World War. After a successful appeal they were established in a new design and technology centre, named after John Derry OC, one of the first pilots to break the sound barrier. The huge growth in music and the beginning of a valuable association with the National Youth Orchestra rendered the teaching and practice facilities in music school inadequate. A new music school was built and named after Ralph Vaughan Williams OC, the distinguished composer. Hall and lecture theatre, where, even in the days of more liberal health and safety regulations, the mounting of stage equipment had to be classed as seriously risky, proved progressively less adequate as venues to stage plays. The need for a school theatre was eventually met by building the theatre named in honour of Ben Travers (1886–1980), who came to lay the foundation stone in his 90s (see page 129).

Left: The Ralph Vaughan Williams (RVW) Centre today.

Below: The opening of the RVW Centre, 12 July 1980, with Brian Rees in the foreground.

Left: John Derry OC, the first Briton to exceed the speed of sound, piloting a de Havilland DH 108. He was killed at the 1952 Farnborough Airshow when his aircraft broke up due to a design fault. The Technology Centre is named in his honour (see page 99).

Brooke Hall included a wide range of talent and interest, and most beaks had distinctive personalities. As an institution it was not dissimilar to a cross between an Oxbridge senior common room and a London gentlemen's club. Housemasters entertained regularly, and new colleagues were made welcome, the fabled members of Brooke Hall who would not speak to a beak until he had done at least five years' service in the School having retired by then. In Brian Rees's time the first female members of the full-time teaching staff joined Brooke Hall – Michèle Mather to teach French in 1977 and Jay Upton to teach Spanish in 1980. Recruiting new members of staff could sometimes be a source of amusement for Brian Rees:

Brooke Hall, 1981.

Front row (l–r): G.S. Howlett, P.G.T. Lewis, N.C. Evans, D.H. Darbishire, R.H. Crawford, W.J.B. Llewellyn, E.E. Harrison, B.F. Rees (Headmaster), J.B. Marriott, G. Ullyott, G.D. Stagg, A.S. Day, G.T. Ford, M.J. Woods, R.K. Totton, C.T.A. Ray.

Row 1: J.C. Daukes, J. Peters, R.G. Woodcock, W.M. Aitken, A.T. Cooke, D.R. Thorpe, C.B. Carter, R.J.A. Wells, C.E. Davies, P.G. Balkwill, P.N. Baldwin, C.T.B. Gilbart-Smith, B. Freake, J.H. Sparks, R.A. Wright, R.M. Butcher.

Row 2: B.R. Souter, P.A. Duncan, D.Q. Watson, D.G. Newman, R.A. Ingram, P.J. Clack, C.K. Wheeler, A.S. Morrison, R.A. Crowsley, M.J. Bailey, A.R. Wilson, R.A. Bogdan, G.H. Hallsmith, P.A. Johnson, D.C.R. Lincoln, H.W. Foot.

Row 3: J.U.V. Edwardes, T.C. Tang, M.F.D. Lloyd, I. Macdonald, A.P. Tyrer, R.P. Noble, W.J.K. Jenkins, A.R.K. Clayton, P.G. Allison, H.D. Gammell, C.J. Ellis, B.P. O'Donahoe, M.H. Davidge, E.H. Zillekens, A. Williams, E. Freake.

Back row: J.H. Morris, J.D. Baylis, S.J. Shuttleworth, P.S. Dinkenor, B.L. Frylinck, S.P. Fielder, D.G. Jeffreys, R.P. Allen, D.A. Swayne, C.J.B. O'Neill, S.J. Harker, K.D. Bingham, J.H. Upton, E.L.H. Vogel, R.W. Smeeton, M.G.P. Chignell.

As in all schools there were lighter moments. The interviews for the composer-in-residence elicited some eccentric applicants, including one gentleman who had composed a piece that required steel scaffolding for players at various heights. And I remember one temporary master who appeared to have gone into teaching solely for the purpose of producing the musical Cabaret *and had apparently no other interest. Another temporary master asked for leave the next morning 'to get married'. 'It'll be alright; I'll be back in the afternoon,' he added. He was last heard of having slipped off an escalator and never returned.*

At the end of CQ (summer term) 1981 Brian Rees left to become Headmaster of Rugby, and Peter Attenborough arrived from Sedbergh to take over as Headmaster at the beginning of LQ (spring term) 1982. The School he encountered was rather assured of its standing and value and may have appeared somewhat complacent to a critical outside observer at the time. The body of Housemasters was a strong force, united in their commitment to promote their pupils' academic progress as well as nurture any extracurricular achievements.

Houses had quite distinctive characters due to the nature and approach of the particular Housemaster. There was one who would not accept any social engagement in term time as he never left his House in the evening. At the other end of the scale there was a colleague who seemed committed to unbridled liberty, frequently leaving the senior boys in charge, who mostly rose to the challenge quite remarkably. Members of Brooke Hall often held strong views, which they would voice forcibly. One colleague, who always seemed shrouded in a certain gloom, had a sharp intellect and a caustic wit, and his remarks were all too often reminiscent of the dark rumblings of a smouldering volcano. Another was a self-styled guru who would expound his views at relentless length, confident of his listener's eventual acquiescence.

A number of colleagues were not natural team players, but during his time as Headmaster, Peter Attenborough achieved a remarkable degree of cooperation – had there have been a serious crisis, the teaching staff would have united behind him as one. He faced the difficult task of tackling the varied application of disciplinary rules, which in some instances failed to confront unsatisfactory pupil behaviour. He decided to address the School on a weekly basis in congregational practice to inculcate common standards. He also encouraged strongly all

Right: Peter Attenborough unveils his retirement portrait, painted by Johnny Jonas (G 1966), 1993.

members of Brooke Hall to promote high standards of discipline in the School.

Several significant changes were imposed from outside, which the entire private sector of education had to grapple with. The most significant was the abolition of the entrance examination to the universities of Oxford and Cambridge for post-A-level candidates:

Before that decision a group of academically gifted Specialists had stayed on at School for one further Quarter after their A levels to prepare intensively for intellectually demanding examinations. Freed of the constraints of examination syllabuses, they were able to explore special areas of interest in their subjects, a joy to them and to those who tutored them. They gave an intellectual, academic lead, especially to the Second Year Specialists, but also to the whole community. This pattern had been very exciting for both Carthusians and those who taught them.

It was a major concern to find alternative ways to encourage creative teaching to foster the spirit of intellectual enquiry, and to promote intellectual curiosity and enthusiasm for its own sake, which seemed to be threatened by the loss of the seventh-term course. The resulting gap was considerable and had not been successfully filled by the time I left Charterhouse.

Peter Attenborough

The other development was the advent of GCSEs, which proved to be noticeably less demanding than O levels. As all pupils entered the Fourth Form in September following the abolition of the seventh-term Oxbridge entrance examination and as GCSE courses were two-year syllabuses, the curriculum in the first year in the School was turned into an introductory year, where pupils had the chance to sample all subjects and then make up their minds which options to choose besides the compulsory core subjects for GCSE. The scholars, who had gone straight into the Remove, also joined the School in the Fourth Form now, which made it rather easier for them to integrate socially. But it is doubtful whether the Under School programme as a whole challenged them sufficiently.

The focus of learning changed gradually from studying a subject to gain a comprehensive knowledge to concentrating on the knowledge required to achieve a top grade in the examination. The advent of modular A levels and subsequently the AS/A2 system was to compound this change. In spite of this progressive shift in emphasis, much inspirational teaching continued:

The teaching was unforgettable – inspiring, original and just a touch eccentric. I remember with great fondness Harvey Hallsmith, whose English lessons taught me a lifelong love of Jane Austen and Shakespeare, even if he did cast me as a witch in Macbeth. *I like to think that learning my lines stood me in good stead for committing to memory the breaking news stories I now cover on a daily basis – even if Channnel 4 encourages me not to speak my prophecies in riddles like witches.*

And then there was Clive Carter, who'd advise us to improve our minds by reading the English dictionary. OK, so he didn't exactly stick to the history curriculum, but he gave us an enduring love of the English language. Who needs to know the finer points of Anglo-Saxon history when you can – if you so choose – sprinkle words like 'etiolated' and 'steatopygous' into everyday conversation?

Cathy Newman (B 1990)

The pastoral system was strong as was the sense of community and belonging. There were still vestiges from the past, such as remnants of the old fagging system, but they were gradually on their way out as pupils began to view their position in the School less hierarchically. The recollections of a head of House in the 1980s reveal the strong sense of responsibility that senior pupils felt:

Harvey Hallsmith and Christopher Wilkins (L 1982) in Thark, *1984.*

Life was a full-time juggling act: getting up early enough to perform at adsum without getting the names wrong, charming staff in the dining room into submission when the boys had upset them, ensuring that members of side table were carrying out their responsibilities suitably and that the fagging system was not abused by some of its more enthusiastic protagonists, catching miscreants before the Housemaster caught them to mend their ways without bribery, pleading for clemency for those destined for beatings and keeping the peace on all floors between boys, Housemaster and hag.

This had to be fitted in between the demands of watching House teams, ensuring that the House box had been emptied in cloisters, trying to find it important to win the House music competition, picking up litter, and making sure no one walked on the grass, listened to an illegal radio, chipped a snooker ball dangerously in the common room, undid their top button, watched television on a weekday or wore an earring in secret.

The only perk of the job was a double-study, affording the occupier two wardrobes for all meaningful ties and an extra bed on which to pile his laundry. It was a fearsomely responsible position, which left little time to cram for A levels, S levels and the seventh-term Oxbridge exams. The Weekite head of House in the 1980s should have been given a free pass into the Diplomatic Corps.

Christopher Harvie (W 1982)

The transfer from the Under School to the Specialists was always a difficult period. The boys remained Under School pupils in behaviour and outlook, and it was only in the course of their first year as Specialists that they matured into their new role. They felt territorial and slightly threatened by the new arrivals. In some Houses old-fashioned gender stereotyping was still allowed to determine mores, which did not aid the integration of girls:

Before I even set foot in a classroom, Charterhouse taught me an important lesson: that men really come from Mars and women from Venus. When I started as a First Year Specialist in Bodeites in 1990 the boys treated the girls as interlopers from outer space. We all arrived, keen to make new friends and settle in – and to our utter bemusement found ourselves totally ignored by the opposite sex. Our attempts to strike up conversation were met with a silence that suggested not just disapproval but downright hostility.

This lasted about ten days. And then I guess the boys gradually came to terms with the fact that we were sharing the same planet for the next two years so we might as well get along. And we did.

That lesson over, our education in the classroom could begin.

Cathy Newman (B 1990)

The start of OQ (autumn term) saw 40 unknown females trotting into chapel, scrutinised by 600 pairs of eyes. It is impressive that the whole School did not degenerate for

weeks thereafter, but the House system provided ownership and belonging. We were dealienised rapidly. It also helped that there were enough of us to have proper sports teams and to find close friends. We did not have to become ladettes. Trying to present the girls' point of view was therefore not always easy as we were not a homogenous unit. But it was obvious that some things were not to our liking. When I arrived in Verites there was a tradition of the new girls serving the boys at meals. Girls were integrated but the world was not yet politically correct, and mostly that gave the place a certain charm.

I think it also prepared us well for the working world, and particularly in my case for the male-dominated world of finance.

Annabel Rudebeck (V 1995)

In 1989 the question of full coeducation was examined by two committees, one composed of a group of Housemasters, and the other of a number of heads of department. The Housemasters' committee came out in favour of full coeducation, arguing it was more natural and the School would be attracting excellent girls, making Charterhouse the best school for girls in the area. The heads of department committee advocated the status quo because 13 was not a good age for girls to change schools; this was because boys' and girls' development diverged significantly

Yearlings on a School trip.

between the ages of 13 and 16 and because girls could be held back for reasons of social integration and distract the boys, slowing academic progress in both cases. This committee regarded it as unlikely that many girls would leave their excellent local girls' schools at the age of 13, and it also feared that the high calibre sixth form entry would wither. The Governing Body looked at a number of mixed boarding schools, which they found lacking in academic rigour, and decided that the status quo of a coeducational sixth form only should be maintained, but that the number of girls in the sixth form should be increased to make it more coeducational.

Many girls and a fair number of boys were applying to come into the sixth form in the 1980s, and by 1992 the need for sixth form scholarships on entry to the school was met by converting the Robert Birley Memorial Award, which had originally been set up with the help of the Carthusian Trust for the son of a preparatory school teacher at the age of 12, into a sixth form scholarship, to which further awards were added in due course.

The School also widened the access to the school by creating a number of special Sixth Form scholarships with the help of an Old Carthusian:

Peter Newton (P 1944) was grateful for his education at Charterhouse as a foundation scholar, not least for being taught to write so well that he landed a post with the Financial Times *to write the Lex column. He subsequently moved to the USA and had a highly successful career as an entrepreneur and visionary oenologist. Following a visit to Charterhouse in 1987 he decided to offer sixth form scholarships to boys and girls who would make an outstanding contribution to the School community provided that the School matched his offer. Accordingly, for the rest of my time as Headmaster we were able to award at least four scholarships to people joining the School in the sixth form, one or two were free places and two were worth two-thirds of the fee; these were often supplemented by other grants and awards, including from the Rank Foundation programme for potential leaders. The Peter Newton Awards resulted in dozens of applications annually and the award of four or five scholarships each year and usually other entries too. This generosity was an excellent means of attracting high calibre students – for example, in 1988 there were 82 applicants with seven entrants from this source.*

Peter Attenborough

These are the recollections of one of the early Newton scholars:

Most people have their school chosen for them and find themselves pigeonholed for a decision that their parents took. In 1988 I had the rare opportunity to choose my school when I was offered a Newton scholarship to attend

Newton scholars, 1988–91.

Pupils at work in the John Derry Centre.

the sixth form at Charterhouse. Now, 21 years on it seems like the most life-changing, important decision I ever made. My previous school was a determinedly mediocre comprehensive school in Prudhoe, a small town near Newcastle. As a gangly boy with a regional accent joining at the same time as a cohort of beautiful, cultured young women, you can imagine that I wasn't the first member of the new intake that the other boys wanted to meet. But generally people were very welcoming and didn't seem to notice or care that my background had less money than theirs. Eventually, I made a wide circle of friends, a few of whom were for life, for example Neil Davidson (V), with whom I set up a software company in 1999.

The big difference was not so much the people but the culture – somehow it seemed so much easier to make things happen and to be a more complete person. Would I have got the lab space at any other school to conduct experiments on why rivers meander? Would I have been able to sign out a load of camping equipment at an hour's notice and head off to the Lake District? Would any Headmaster (Mr Attenborough) answer in his study at 11 pm and calmly coach me into a better understanding of myself and the

world? Would any other Housemaster (Mr Balkwill) have asserted that he had given me permission to take a small bottle of whisky that singed a few eyebrows when ignited in a demonstration of the 'chemistry of cooking'?

Although it is hard to explain via tangible examples, there was an underlying humanity and belief in the power of us as individuals to do good that pervaded my experiences of Charterhouse. I am eternally grateful for the opportunity.

Simon Galbraith (G 1988)

Two facilities initiated in Brian Rees's time and opened under Peter Attenborough enhanced the range of extracurricular activities. These were the John Derry Technology Centre, which in no time was being used by 50 to 60 Carthusians in their free time, and the Ben Travers Theatre (BTT), which Peter Attenborough regarded as 'the most beneficial of all the new facilities', as the greater flexibility of the BTT and the space for rehearsals and adjacent workshop transformed the possibilities and offered significantly greater numbers of Carthusians the opportunity to take part in drama. The BTT saw 100 plays in the first six years.

The introduction in 1989 of the Poetry Festival was an important highlight of the period. Poetry took centre stage. The first festival was chaired by George Macbeth with contributions from many key figures – for example, Carol Ann Duffy, Wendy Cope, Vernon Scannell, Blake Morrison, Jon Stallworthy, Edwin Morgan, Peter Porter and Alan Jenkins. This was principally the initiative of Harvey Hallsmith and Ian Blake. I understand that it was initially quite a daunting prospect for some of the contributors, but hugely enjoyed by them in the event – and many of the poets were only too happy to return the following year. After the second festival the BBC took an interest and based a series of programmes on Radio 3, A Time for Verse, on readings from the festival. The BBC showed continued interest, and by the time I left was to sponsor a prize of £500 at the fifth Poetry Festival in 1993.

Peter Attenborough

In the early 1980s Roger Smeeton formed a jazz band specializing in music of the Glenn Miller era. The Band Show came into being in the Ben Travers Theatre, an annual variety show featuring the band but also including sketches and for many years the wonderful magician Andrew Wilson. The band performed on *Blue Peter*, appeared frequently at charity receptions at places like the Mansion House and Goldsmiths Hall, played on a float in the Lord Mayor's Show and was a warm-up at Wintershall for a rock concert featuring Phil Collins and Eric Clapton. Foreign tours included trips to Paris, Budapest, Vienna, Malta and Atlanta, USA.

The Ben Travers Theatre was also the location of another addition to the cultural calendar, the Poetry Festival:

Other facilities in the School were also improved and increased in Peter Attenborough's time. The science department, which, with its old-fashioned lecture theatres and demonstration benches, almost predated its building in spirit, required modern facilities to make sure that science teaching could be delivered effectively. This need was recognised by the School, and the difficult question of whether a new science department should be built or the existing one refurbished had to be addressed. After careful deliberations, the Governing Body opted for the second option, partly because this could be carried out in phases. It was eventually opened officially by Lord Wakeham in 1991. Peter Attenborough views the Governing Body's attitude to the development programme as a whole very positively:

One of the features of the development programme was the timely decisions made by the Governing Body: just as one stage was drawing to a close, decisions were published about the next, creating a sense of a successful community going from strength to strength and always looking ahead with confidence. As the decision to complete the second phase of the RVW was announced, plans were also made public for the refurbishment of the Science block and lecture theatre.

The sporting facilities were also enhanced, The golf course was opened on OC Day in July 1988, Chetwynd, the new all-weather tennis and hockey area, followed in 1991 and, in 1996, the Sir Greville Spratt athletics track. The sports centre was planned earlier, but came into use in 1996 and was officially opened by HM The Queen in 1997.

I would like to conclude this broad overview with a contribution from a former colleague, Ian Blake, against himself, hingeing around a custom that has since been abandoned:

Act I Scene 1
Late November. Dark outside.
Room 32, sixth hash (17.00) with a Fourth Form has just ended, next and last of the day is a very bright Second Year Specialists division.
I realise that I need a few more photocopies of a poem I want them to discuss and so follow the Fourth Form out to go to Brooke Hall to make them, waving the poem at my Specialists coming in. As often happens, the photocopier jams. By the time I have unjammed it and get back, I find Room 32 empty: my division has observed the custom that decrees that if the 'beak' is not there when the quarter strikes they can go back to House.

Scene 2
Room 32 the following day. Second Year Specialists.
Enter IMB v. grumpy
IMB: Why didn't you wait for me? I was making copies for you.
Voice: When the quarter struck, Sir, you weren't here.
IMB [irate]: But you saw me rushing out as you came in!
Voice: We didn't know where you were going, Sir.
IMB [v. irate]: Why didn't you ask me where I was going?
Tense pause
Eedle (D) (quietly): Well, Sir, I expect we thought you knew.
Collapse of stout party, as they used to say in *Punch*.

At work in the chemistry laboratory.

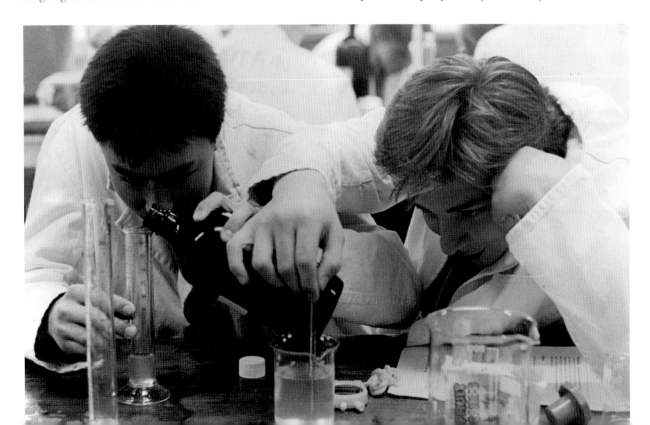

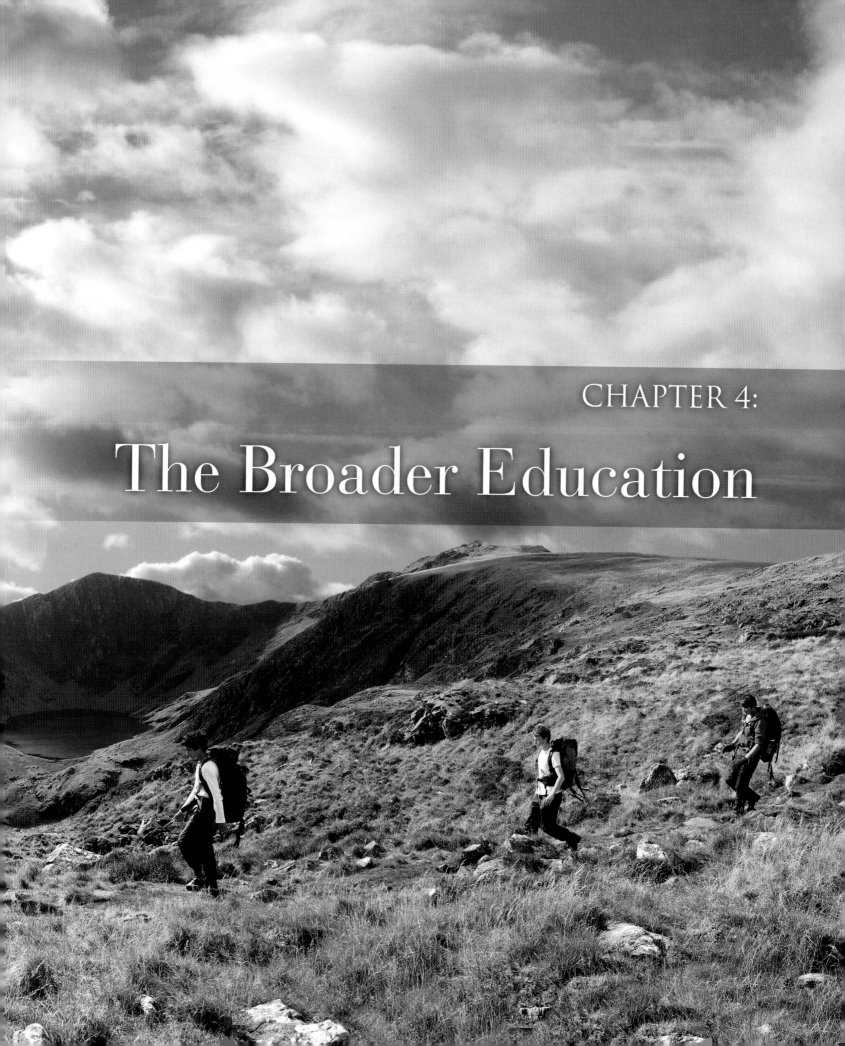

CHAPTER 4:

The Broader Education

Music

ROBIN WELLS, BROOKE HALL, 1965–2003, (DIRECTOR OF MUSIC FROM 1987)

In 1626 Benjamin Cosyn was appointed organist of the Charterhouse. The organist's duties were 'to attend divine service every Sunday, holiday and holiday eve and to bring up the Schollars to musicke'. It is likely that one of Cosyn's earliest charges was Christopher Gibbons (son of Orlando), who was nominated for a scholarship in 1627 and in time was to become organist of Westminster Abbey. He could be regarded as the first of the school's many composers.

The position of organist of the Charterhouse was to become a very desirable position, and many eminent and influential musicians held the post over the next 400 years, often in harness with another appointment. John Jones was also organist of St Paul's Cathedral, while Richard Stevens was also organist of the Temple Church. Another organist was John Pepusch, who arranged the tunes and wrote the overture to *The Beggar's Opera*. The Restoration saw the installation of a new organ in the chapel by John Hingston, 'Keeper and Repairer of His Majesties Organs'. Hingston's assistant in tuning and repairing instruments was Henry Purcell, and so it is most likely that Hingston introduced Purcell to the Charterhouse. Purcell composed several pieces for the Charterhouse, including an anthem, *Blessed is the Man*, for Founder's Day.

In the 19th century John Hullah, one of the most important figures in English musical education, held the post of organist. Hullah was a huge advocate of singing in schools and was appointed to the Charterhouse particularly to teach singing. In 1846 he established the annual concert at the School, at which an important feature was the singing of the *Carmen Carthusianum* composed by his predecessor William Horsley, a custom that continued for many years.

The removal of the School to Godalming in 1872 was beneficial in every way. One great advantage over the small London site was space to expand activities outside the classroom. Haig Brown records that music benefited especially, and shortly after the arrival on the new site there were three bands, a choir, a military band, a string band and an orchestra selected from these ensembles. The brass band quickly became established and gave its first

concert on 11 October to all staff and the whole School. As a mark of appreciation a half-holiday was granted.

An editorial in *The Carthusian* of November 1872 refers to the increasing vigour with which pursuits were being taken up since the move to Godalming, especially in music. The brass band was very popular, as was the choir. The editorial ends: 'We may fairly congratulate ourselves on the improvement and advancement of the musical taste in the School, and we trust this is not a mere temporary liking which has sprung up, but rather that music, now a beginning has been made, will continue to receive the attention it deserves.'

Musical performances in the School from 1872, which were largely described as entertainments, took place on Saturday evenings. These were largely performances by

Previous page: Mallory Group on Cader Idris, 2009.

Left: The Epicure Society was set up by pupils in 1864 to poke fun at the more serious public-school clubs of the time. This page from the Epicure Society minute book shows Society members performing in a school concert.

Below: The School band, 1882.

Above: Joseph Dando, violin teacher at Charterhouse from 1875–94.

Above right: Arthur Becker, music master 1881–1903, caricatured by Beerbohm.

music staff: Robinson (the organist), Dando (the string teacher) and Becker (a pianist and brass player). Friends and other members of Brooke Hall, such as Bode, Stewart, Marshall and Girdlestone, performed with great regularity, and in time more boys began to take part. Many seeds were

sown in these early days in Godalming that were to bear fruit and become the foundation of the School's music throughout the 20th century. There had been an annual concert since 1846, and after the move it expanded to include solos, vocal items, ensembles, the string band and the orchestra, which included pupils and staff. Charity concerts also featured, and in 1883 a concert by Carthusians at London's Victoria Hall raised £60. Eminent professional musicians of the day also gave performances at the School.

The early years in Godalming produced several figures who acquired national recognition as composers. The first of these was Basil Harwood (G 1876), who was to make his name in the world of cathedral music as an organist and composer, being known especially for his two hymn tunes, 'Thy Hand O God hath guided' and 'Let all the world in every corner sing'. Lionel Monckton (P 1879) was famous for writing musicals, his best known being *The Quaker Girl*.

Henry Balfour Gardiner (H 1894) set out as a composer, but after writing one or two established pieces, such as his anthem *Evening Hymn*, which is still sung

widely in cathedrals and churches, he gave up composition and turned to other interests. Nevertheless, he became a great musical philanthropist and, being a man of means, promoted concerts of new music that might otherwise not have reached the public. One such work was Holst's *The Planets*. He also promoted the compositions of Vaughan Williams, his senior by five years, and enabled Frederick Delius to continue to live in France by buying his house at Grez-sur-Loing.

In 1901 Edward Rendall was appointed director of music and continued the expansion of music that Robinson had initiated. One of his appointments was Arthur Trew, a pianist, cellist, composer and conductor, who was to teach for 43 years, during which time he became a much loved local figure. The orchestra consisted of pupils and staff, friends and professionals, who were an inspiration to the younger generation. The most significant musical event during Rendall's time was the Charterhouse Masque, which was designed to celebrate the School's tercentenary in 1911. Episodes depicting the history of the foundation with music by choir and orchestra composed by Rendell involved the whole school. The intention was that it should be produced every five years, but because of the First World War it was not revived until 1922.

Reginald Thatcher succeeded Rendall in 1919. House choirs developed after the move to Godalming, and in 1874 a House choir competition was won by Gownboys. In 1921 Thatcher introduced an instrumental competition,

which was judged by Vaughan Williams. Was there a hint of favouritism in his decision to place Robinites, his old house, first? Composer Philip Radcliffe featured in the Hodgsonite programme. On leaving Charterhouse he went to King's College, Cambridge, where he remained as a lecturer in music until his death in 1986. These two competitions ran in tandem until they were amalgamated in the 1980s to create the House Music Festival. Thatcher's obituary in *The Carthusian* states: 'The musical foundations which Reginald Thatcher laid at Charterhouse are sound and permanent.'

Top left: Page from 1911 programme showing music written by Edward Rendall.

Above: Masque orchestra, 1950.

Thatcher moved on to Harrow in 1928, then to the BBC and finally ended his career as principal of the Royal Academy of Music. He was knighted for his work in music education. He was followed by Thomas Fielden, a most accomplished pianist and teacher, whose piano recitals became legendary among Carthusians of that time.

Fielden built on Thatcher's foundations as more boys were encouraged to take up an instrument and facilities were expanded with the conversion of the old chapel into the music school, which was opened by Vaughan Williams in 1940. To celebrate the occasion he played the cuckoo in the *Toy Symphony*, which was conducted by the Headmaster Robert Birley.

In 1938 the Choral Society met its toughest challenge to date when Fielden conducted the Brahms *Requiem*. The following year there was a Vaughan Williams concert, which included his one-act opera *The Shepherds of the Delectable Mountain*. The composer was in attendance and afterwards congratulated the performers, describing the performance as 'really remarkable'. One of Fielden's inspired appointments was George Draper in 1942. An ex-guardsman, Draper was a superb clarinettist but capable of playing every wind and brass instrument as well as the violin. He was responsible for the huge

Above: Sketches of Carthusian musicians, The Greyfriar *1929.*

Top right: John Wilson conducting the choir.

Ian Wallace

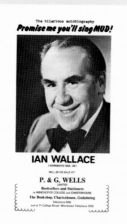

The notable opera singer Ian Wallace OBE (G 1933–8) made regular appearances at Glyndebourne and the Edinburgh Festival. While still at Charterhouse he became a popular jester, performing comic turns in concerts and plays. He became a household name as a radio and TV singer, most notably as a regular panellist on *My Music*. For many years Wallace performed with the piano accompanist David Money (S 1930) in a highly entertaining double act entitled 'An Evening with Ian Wallace'.

development of wind and brass playing in the school.

John Wilson succeeded Fielden in LQ (spring term) 1947. Having been Fielden's assistant since 1932, he was familiar with the School and its music, although during the war years he taught physics. He developed orchestral playing in the School, and more boys became involved. The standard improved, and the repertoire became more adventurous with boys playing concertos. One of his ambitions was to revive the Charterhouse Masque, which had again lapsed during the war years. To this end he asked Vaughan Williams to compose the music for the final scene. Vaughan Williams agreed, provided he could incorporate the Carmen, which he did to great effect.

On the retirement of John Wilson in 1965, William (Bill) Llewellyn, who had been an assistant since 1950, took over. Again continuity was maintained, but what followed was a period of great expansion in every way. The first music scholar was appointed in Wilson's time, and now the number of music scholarships increased and much fine musical talent began to enter the school, while at the top end many singers and organists began to take up Oxbridge choral and organ scholarships.

The number of pupils taking music lessons increased sharply, until by the end of the century the number of lessons being given weekly was getting on for 500. Consequently, an increase in the number of visiting staff was necessary, and eventually the facilities of the music school became stretched to the limit. Lessons were being given in the small practice cells, in the cloister and in Founders' Chapel.

It was due to the generosity of the Vaughan Williams Trust, helped by the School's appeal, that the financial base was laid for the building of the Ralph Vaughan Williams Centre. The foundation stone was laid by Ursula Vaughan Williams in 1979. An error in the spelling of the composer's name caused wry amusement, and the builder promised to turn the stone over and engrave it correctly on the reverse. The centre was built in two phases, and on completion the building was officially opened by the composer's widow on 13 October 1984. Yehudi Menuhin agreed to be the patron. The occasion was celebrated with a big concert in Hall of music by Vaughan Williams, performed by pupils, OCs, friends and staff conducted by Sir David Willcocks. The RVW Centre was never intended to replace the old music school, which was still perfectly serviceable, but to add much needed additional accommodation for the department.

Bill Llewellyn was a man of ideas and initiatives, and he took music in the School to new heights and set standards that other schools were to follow. He served twice as president of the Music Masters' Association and as president of the Incorporated Society of Musicians, an honour bestowed only on the most highly respected members of the music profession. For his services to music education he was awarded the MBE on his retirement in 1987. It was his mission to make Charterhouse a musical centre for the area, and many local societies and organisations were made welcome to rehearsals, concerts and functions at the School. The building of the RVW Centre had the local community very much in mind when local funding was sought.

Music and drama combined under the dual leadership of Bill Llewellyn and Geoffrey Ford, who had been appointed to teach strings in succession to David Stone in LQ (spring term) 1956. There was everything from Brooke Hall extravaganzas (*Havahavana*, 1967) to grand opera (*The Pilgrim's Progress*, 1972). 1980 saw the collaboration with the Headmaster Brian Rees in a production of his musical *The Birds*. The biggest challenge of all was *King of Macedon* (1979), a three-act opera by composer-in-residence Roger Steptoe.

Bill Llewellyn

Perhaps I didn't appreciate then how lucky we were. Bill Llewellyn was a fireball of energy. Every Saturday morning, instead of morning service, we had congregational practice, and Bill would stride up and down the whole length of the chapel, cajoling 700-odd sulky teenagers into singing. It was a magnificent performance.

The first major work we did in my time was Walton's *Belshazzar's Feast*. It was fiendishly hard — I can remember how Bill would coax us through what felt like only a few bars in a whole rehearsal — and I detested the music for most of the two terms we did it. Then came the day of the concert and the orchestral rehearsal. I had never heard anything quite like it before, and the concert was one of the most thrilling moments of my life to date. I was hooked on choral singing for life.

Robin Darwall-Smith (G 1981)

Bill Llewellyn conducting The Kingdom, *1970.*

Ralph Vaughan Williams

Charterhouse's most famous composer, Ralph Vaughan Williams, was a pupil in Saunderites and then Robinites from 1887 to 1890. He studied violin and viola while at school and organised a concert in 1888, which included one of his own compositions, a piano trio. His family regarded his passion for music as a harmless schoolboy hobby that would lead to nothing. He went on to the Royal College of Music, where he was taught by Hubert Parry and the organist, Walter Parratt, and then to Trinity College, Cambridge.

Vaughan Williams was a prolific and versatile composer, writing everything from hymn tunes to film scores, from opera to full orchestral works, and he is recognised as a seminal figure in the development of 20th-century British music, particularly for his use of English folk music to inspire his compositions. He continued to take an interest in Charterhouse throughout his life. He was commissioned to write music to accompany the Charterhouse Masque in 1950, and the Vaughan Williams Music Centre was opened by his widow, Ursula, in 1980.

Vaughan Williams (right) as a pupil in Saunderites, 1888.

Above: Sculpture of Vaughan Williams by Jacob Epstein.

Right: Ralph and Ursula Vaughan Williams.

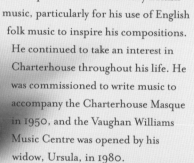

Original score for Vaughan Williams' music for the Charterhouse Masque, hand-written and amended by the composer.

Pupil composing.

The introduction of music prizes for all instruments added impetus and goals for pupils to work towards. On a more public stage the school orchestra, consisting of 38 boys and one girl (and no adults), won the Schools Orchestra Competition at Fairfield Hall in 1967; the prize was a presentation sword given by the sponsor Wilkinsons, together with a cheque for £75, which was used to start the appeal for the School harpsichord. A performance of Mozart's Clarinet Quintet won the top prize in the Schools Chamber Music Competition in 1981 and, as chamber music developed in the 1990s, the School regularly featured in the finals at St John's, Smith Square. In 1992 composer James Webb (V 1992) won the BBC Composer of the Year Award, and in 1995 Philip Scriven (V 1998) won the Royal College of Organists Performer of the Year Award.

Other initiatives at this time include the establishment in 1975 of the highly successful Charterhouse Summer School of Music. In 1976 the Vaughan Williams Trust began to fund the composer-in-residence scheme, which flourished for 25 years. In recognition of the help the trust had given to the School over the years, the Carthusian Trust established in 1985 the RVW US Fellowship. This enabled an American postgraduate scholar to stay at the school for six weeks while researching the music of Vaughan Williams. In 2003 much of this research was published in *Vaughan Williams Essays* edited by Byron Adams (the first holder of the award) and the present writer.

The centenary of the School's removal to Godalming coincided with the centenary of the birth of Ralph Vaughan Williams. He is unquestionably one of the greatest Old Carthusians and one of England's greatest composers, so 1972 called for a double celebration. Musical events of that year began in March with a performance of RVW's *A Sea Symphony*. In the summer the chapel choir led a service in Westminster Abbey devoted to his hymns, followed by the production of a gramophone recording of School music in general and a photographic exhibition devoted to Vaughan Williams. A concert was given in Down Ampney church, where RVW's father had been vicar and where RVW was born, during which Peter Oundjian played *The Lark Ascending*. Finally, in October there was a most memorable production of his opera *The Pilgrim's Progress* by the School in collaboration with the Godalming Operatic Society. Such a work was ideal for a school production, offering many small solo parts for Carthusians as well as a good sing for the chorus.

Right: Ralph Vaughan Williams with score of The Pilgrim's Progress at the Royal Opera House production of 1951.

Below: The choir rehearsing in Chapel.

Haig Brown regarded chapel as the centre of School life, for only in chapel did the whole School meet as a body. That is still the same today, and the music in chapel is something that remains with many Carthusians for the rest of their lives, particularly the congregational singing. The acoustics and the support of a fine and powerful organ enhance the sound of the School in full voice. Charterhouse has been blessed with a number of composers who have written some of the finest hymn tunes in modern use, including 'For all the Saints' and 'Come down O love divine' of Vaughan Williams and 'Thy Hand O God hast guided' and 'Let all the world in every corner sing' of Harwood. In addition, there are fine tunes by directors of music – Robinson's tune to Haig Brown's words, 'O God whose wisdom made the sky', which was written for the dedication of the chapel in 1874 and sung annually on Founder's Day, was followed by further memorable tunes by Thatcher, Fielden, Wilson and Llewellyn.

Peter Oundjian

Currently the musical director of the Toronto Symphony Orchestra, Peter Oundjian studied violin from the age of seven and was offered a place at the Yehudi Menuhin School. He chose Charterhouse instead because the sports facilities were better! Even as a schoolboy he was a dedicated musician who seemed destined for a solo violin career: 'In two minutes I could go from where I slept in Saunderites to what was then music school. I would practise the violin from 6.30 to 7.30 every morning before anyone else was awake, then have breakfast, and then practice for another good half hour before chapel. I'd then go to hashes, but I was allowed to miss a couple of subjects, one of which was biology. I think the other one was geography – so, basically I didn't know where anything was in the body or in the world, but at least I was practising the violin. Then in no time at all I'd be changed and on the soccer field for training and matches. There was no time-wasting.'

After Charterhouse, Oundjian went to the Royal College of Music and then the Juilliard School, New York, studying with Ivan Galamian, Itzhak Perlman and Dorothy Delay. In 1980 he won first prize in the Vina del Mar International Violin Competition and became first violinist of the Tokyo String Quartet. In 1994, however, Oundjian's glittering career as a violinist was cut short by repetitive strain injury. With support

Left: Peter Oundjian at Charterhouse.

Below: Peter Oundjian conducting the Toronto Symphony Orchestra.

from André Previn, Oundjian was able to shift his musical focus to conducting and has never looked back. He has appeared as guest conductor for orchestras across the world, he was artistic director of the Nieuw Sinfonietta Amsterdam from 1998 to 2003 and has been musical director of the Toronto Symphony Orchestra since 2004.

The composer Herbert Howells is one of the most revered composers of church music in the 20th century. Although not a Carthusian, he was commissioned by Thomas Fielden to write tunes for the Clarendon Hymn Book and by John Wilson for Hymns for Church and School. Of those he wrote, 'A Hymn tune for Charterhouse', written instantly at the breakfast table as he opened Fielden's letter, has achieved worldwide fame as one of the finest 20th-century tunes. Better known to the words 'All my hope on God is founded', it can justifiably be regarded on a par with the Carmen as 'our tune'.

Successive directors of music since Fielden have been responsible for editing hymn books for use in chapel.

The chapel choir was the nucleus of the Choral Society, which included Brooke Hall and masters' wives. The first recorded performance, in 1875, was of Spohr's oratorio *The Last Judgement*. Succeeding years featured Bach's Passion music, Handel's *Messiah*, Haydn's *The Creation* and Beethoven's *Mass* in C. Despite a few gaps, the annual choral concert has continued, becoming ever more ambitious and including in recent years Elgar's *Dream of Gerontius* and *The Kingdom*, Bach's *Passions* and the

Carthusian musicians.

Rachel Portman OBE

The first woman composer to win an Oscar in the category of Best Original Score, for the film adaptation of Jane Austen's *Emma* in 1996, Rachel Portman has fond memories of her days at Charterhouse (P 1976–8), particularly of the music department. In an interview for *The Carthusian* she commented, 'I am incredibly grateful to Robin Wells for his superb harmony and counterpoint tuition' and described Roger Steptoe, Charterhouse's first composer-in-residence, as 'the best composition teacher I ever had'.

Rachel Portman was nominated for an Academy Award for her scores for *The Cider House Rules* (1999) and *Chocolat* (2000). She has composed the scores for dozens of other feature films and for television series, including Jim Henson's *The Storyteller* and two episodes of *The Jim Henson Hour* ('Monster Maker' and 'Living with Dinosaurs'). Other works include a children's opera, *The Little Prince*, and a musical based on the *Little House on the Prairie* books by Laura Ingalls Wilder. In 2007 she was commissioned to write a piece of choral music for the BBC Proms, and she was awarded an OBE in the 2010 New Year's Honours.

B Minor Mass, Verdi's *Requiem* and Walton's *Belshazzar's Feast*. Solo parts have been carried by professional soloists, OCs, Brooke Hall and, where appropriate, current Carthusians, who have had the opportunity of singing solos alongside eminent professional singers. It must be acknowledged here that the admission of girls to the sixth form was an enormous boost to the school's music and especially to the chapel choir and Choral Society.

The 'entertainment' that featured in the early days at Godalming developed through the years in different forms, and performances by professional musicians continue to the present time. In 1967 a series of subscription concerts was established very much on the initiative of John Blatchly, then head of science. This series put professional concerts onto a firm footing, and there was good support from the local community. A huge array of the world's most famous artists featured, including Heinz Holliger, James Galway, Alfred Brendel, Dame Janet Baker, Paul Tortelier, Igor Oistrakh, the Amadeus String Quartet and Simon Rattle. But at the same time the up-and-coming

Genesis

Ask members of the general public to name famous Old Carthusians, and many will say 'Genesis'. Four members of this rock band were educated at the School in the mid-1960s, Peter Gabriel, Tony Banks, Anthony Phillips (all in Girdlestoneites) and Mike Rutherford (Lockites). The original band also included a fifth Carthusian, Chris Stewart, but he parted company from the group before they achieved fame.

While the group may have benefited from the classical music training provided by Charterhouse, pop music was not encouraged, and the disciplined, traditional school structure was not entirely conducive to contemporary creativity. Peter Gabriel recalls sneaking into the dining room of Duckites to compose on the piano, prepared for a quick exit via the serving hatch if necessary. Nevertheless, a number of schoolboy bands flourished informally in the School, performing at House events; Gabriel and Banks were founder members of the Garden Wall, Anthony Phillips was a member of Anon, while Mike Rutherford was in the Climax.

Genesis was formed in 1967 and performed some of their earliest music at Charterhouse. The band's first album, *From Genesis to Revelation*, was released by Decca in March 1969. Genesis are among the top 30 highest selling recording artists of all time, having sold more than 150 million albums worldwide.

Above: A performance in Duckites, 1964, with Peter Gabriel on drums.

Right: Peter Gabriel, was interviewed by Jonathan Opstad and Jocelyne Saunders for The Carthusian *magazine, 2001.*

generation was not overlooked, and many BBC Young Musicians of the Year appeared.

The musical foundations that Thatcher laid have certainly developed into a very strong aspect of School life as may be witnessed by the large number of Carthusians who have gone into the music profession. Many have performed at the highest level, none more so perhaps than Peter Oundjian, who led the Tokyo String Quartet, one of the top three quartets in the world, before turning to conducting; he is now musical director of the Toronto Symphony Orchestra.

Guy Hamilton (G 1974) conducted Welsh Opera, and Andrew West (D 1980) has carved out a successful career as a concert pianist. On the more academic side Robin Langley (L 1960) was a distinguished music editor with Oxford University Press and music publisher to Novello & Co., while Jeremy Thurlow (W 1985) is director of music at Robinson College, Cambridge. More recently Leo McFall (S 1997) has conducted Glyndebourne Touring Opera. Ryan Wigglesworth (S 1997) made his debut conducting the BBC Symphony Orchestra at the Barbican in 2009, as well as having a BBC commission performed at the Proms in 2009. Composer Mark Blatchly has had commissions from the Three Choirs Festival, and Rachel Portman won an Oscar for her music for the film *Emma*.

Rock and pop music has been performed in the School for the past 40 years. Genesis reached the top of that particular tree with music that was original and ahead of its time, and guitarist Dominic Miller (D 1976) has worked for many years with the singer Sting.

On a personal note it has been difficult to know who to include in this brief history. It has not been possible to mention many of the distinguished beaks, musicians, teachers, OCs *et al*, who have been an integral and vital part of the School's music, and for that I apologise. All have played their part alongside the life-blood of the school, which is always the present generation of boys and girls. It is to be hoped that all Carthusians, from the humblest to the most brilliant musicians, whether merely singing a hymn in chapel or playing a concerto with the orchestra, will have gained something from the music at Charterhouse.

Art

HELEN PINKNEY

Art at Charterhouse has always enjoyed an excellent and exciting reputation. Having researched the history of the teachers, pupils and atmosphere of the various places where art has been taught, the reasons for its success are clear. Creativity and self-expression through drawing, painting and making things are an intrinsic part of any young person, and the challenge of teaching art is to encourage individual expression and skills to help interpret our experience of the world around us. During my investigation of art at Charterhouse, I was struck by the many similarities in the characters of the 'drawing masters' and in the work they encouraged. It seems that art at Charterhouse represents a refuge from a larger school environment, allowing students to express their thoughts and ideas freely in a medium that most suits them. The most inspiring part of this research has been the drawings and scribblings of ex-students. This has helped to build a picture of how art has been taught over the years at Charterhouse.

'Charterhouse suspended' by Peter Monkman, Head of Art and winner of the 2009 BP National Portrait Award.

Illustrations from Owen Jones' Grammar of Ornament, *published in 1856 and still in print today. Owen Jones was the interior designer for the Great Exhibition.*

Picture of stagecoach and horses, believed to have been drawn by John Leech at the age of six.

I began my research by looking at the various 'drawing masters', as they were then known. Although there is mention of a drawing master in the 1760s, the first name I encountered is that of Henry William (H.W.) Burgess, who taught from 1823 to 1840. He was a landscape painter, who presumably came to the London Charterhouse for a limited number of hours a week to give drawing instruction. From a family of British artists, he was the son of portraitist William Burgess. Between 1809 and 1844 he exhibited a large number of works at the Royal Academy and the New Water-colour Society in London. He also served as landscape painter to William IV from 1826. He is particularly noted for his set of pastoral landscapes, each featuring different species of large trees. Burgess was among the earliest practitioners of lithography in England, and the attention to the qualities of light exhibited in his prints links him to his contemporaries Constable and Turner. Burgess is known to have given John Leech the very few drawing lessons he ever received and, looking at the work of Burgess, it is easy to see how he might have inspired Leech through his discipline of animated drawing and observation. John Leech is said to have drawn as rapidly as thought itself: 'The idea was thrown upon the paper and seldom saw much change.'

The early works of John Leech in the Archives, including the sketch shown here, make clear that his vigour and maturity were evident from an early age. Leech began a tradition of cartoonists at Charterhouse, including William Makepeace Thackeray (see page 29) and Max Beerbohm. Osbert Lancaster was cartoonist for the *Daily Express*, and more recently Charles Peattie has continued this tradition as cartoonist for the *Daily Telegraph* and *Private Eye*.

Cartoonists

Henry Maximilian Beerbohm

The famous caricaturist and writer (1872–1956) was educated at Charterhouse between 1885 and 1890. He spent his first year in Robinites before moving to Girdlestoneites. His school career was undistinguished. He never won any prizes, was awarded no colours, and he disliked French, algebra and science, although he enjoyed Latin and English literature. He had a natural

Beerbohm as a schoolboy, c. 1885.

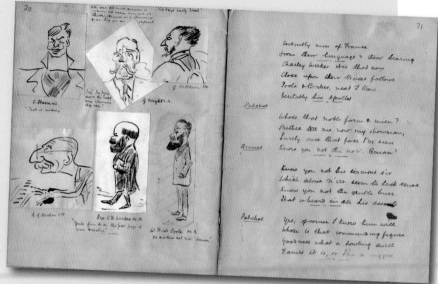

antipathy to sport of any kind and boasted that after his first year no one ever saw his bare knees. He was known to have been rather solitary and did not make many close friends. However, he did have a talent as an artist, particularly as a cartoonist and, to their great credit, the masters encouraged this, even allowing him to draw comic cartoons of themselves. Max contributed some of his 'Carthusian types' to the school magazine, *The Greyfriar*, and found a ready

market for his cartoons among his contemporaries.

According to N.A. Parsons: 'As a young child Max dreamt of being a dandy; and at Charterhouse it was his pleasure to set up as one. He wore short jackets and Eton collars. No one in the school wore an Eton collar so fashionably broad and dazzlingly bright as Max. His trousers were of great concern to him, and it was said that the check was so pronounced that it was possible to

Page from The Epic of Hades, *a poem describing Charterhouse beaks processing to hell, written by Lockites Head Monitor, R.W.H.M. Palk, and illustrated by Max Beerbohm during his final year at Charterhouse. The text and the drawings provided an entertaining parody of the mannerisms and expressions of the Charterhouse beaks of 1890.*

play chess on them. Max's hair was an object of particular attention: it is known that, for fear of ruffling it, he never pulled his school cap full on his head, but pinned it with a hairpin to the back.'

Sir Osbert Lancaster

Osbert Lancaster (1908–86) belongs to a long tradition of OC cartoonists. His autobiography, *With an Eye to the Future* (1973), describes his dismay on arriving at Charterhouse in 1922 to find petty rules governing every aspect of daily life: 'First-year boys had to have all three buttons of their jackets permanently fastened and to wear plain black socks; in our second year we could undo the top button and were allowed coloured socks; one section of pavement was reserved exclusively for those who had their House colours, while only School Bloods could walk on the road itself; ordinary speech was rendered almost impossible by the fact that so many

things, places and activities had to be referred to by special traditionally hallowed names that were, in most cases, as misleadingly inexpressive as they were philologically uninteresting.' Lancaster survived Charterhouse, going on to Lincoln College, Oxford, and then the Slade School of Art. For 36 years he was a cartoonist for the *Daily Express* and is best remembered for his witty and astute pictorial comments on British life, but he was also an acclaimed writer, stage designer and graphic historian of architecture.

Cartoon of Housemaster T.E. Page drawn by Sir Osbert Lancaster.

Above: The art studio, 1882.

Right: Page from The Greyfriar minutes, 1884.

father and son teaching art at Charterhouse was close to 70 years. Throughout Robinson's time at Charterhouse, drawing was entirely voluntary – it was noted as an 'extra' on the School bill. Robinson taught for 23 years at Charterhouse in London, and after the move to Godalming he travelled on Wednesdays and Saturdays for half-days to give drawing instruction. His love of the School and his teaching inspired him to build at his own expense what later became known as the 'drawing shed', which was a lofty shed-like structure at the top of Girdlestonite steps. He was never happier than when in the shed or out on a painting expedition. An artist in his own right, he exhibited regularly at the Royal Academy.

During his time at Charterhouse the School's illustrated paper, *The Greyfriar*, was conceived. Its full title was *A Chronicle in Black and White by Carthusians*, and the first edition was issued in August 1884. It contained etchings and reproductions of charcoal, pen-and-ink and sepia work. Each edition contained two full-page illustrations and many smaller ones. The first page of *The Greyfriar* minutes, which are preserved in an illustrated book held in the Charterhouse Archives, states: 'At a Boule holden at Girdlestonites at 12.45 pm on Monday April 14th 1884 it was resolved to try to start an illustrated paper next

Another influential 'drawing master' was Struan Robinson, appointed in 1856. He acted as assistant to his father, who held office before him and whose tenure reached back as far as Burgess; the combined tenure of

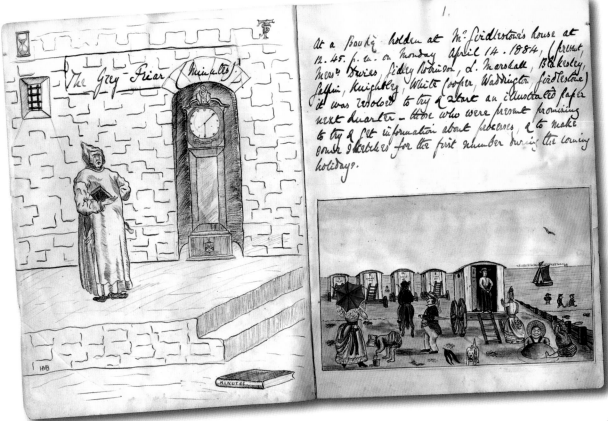

Above: Art department, c. 1930s.

Below: Studio under construction, 1958.

Seasons', is pasted into the book. At the end of each meeting, at the bottom of the page, a note is made to conclude the mood of the Boule – for example, the first meeting ends with 'Conclusion Tea and Teacakes' and the meeting on 2 April 1892 ends with 'Prosperity everywhere'. A meeting in May was described as 'jovial', in October 1893 the group was 'small and select', while a Saturday meeting in December 1893 ends with 'that dreadful flu'. These simple notes and the accompanying illustrations help make you feel part of those meetings, and the subjects, techniques and concerns they discussed are still comparable with those of today in Studio.

Struan Robinson retired in 1902, and C.W. Johnson took over. He became known as 'Purple' Johnson, and of the various explanations for this nickname the one which seems to go with his character is that if a boy's work lacked something, he would say, 'Why don't you add some purple?'

By this period, drawing featured in School work as well as School amusements. Tod says that much sketching was done from live animals, and summer sketching excursions were arranged for most half-holidays. All boys who joined the lessons also had permission to use bicycles. Johnson appears to have loved Charterhouse, and, as with previous drawing masters, he was renowned both for his own

Quarter.' Those who were present promised to get information about processes and to make sketches for the first number. A page from 1886 mentions the meeting held in Robinson's room and notes that Max Beerbohm was present. A full-page cartoon by Beerbohm, entitled 'The

HM The Queen touring Studio with Michael Woods, 1972.

stimulating work, painting and, in later years, aquatints, and for his influence as a teacher. He liked to experiment with new techniques, and his strength was encouraging the individual work of his pupils. He never dictated and was particularly successful in training candidates for the scholarship offered by the Architectural Association. He retired in 1937 and, sadly, died within a week of leaving.

Alexander Barclay-Russell arrived in LQ (spring term) 1938 but left to serve as a captain in the Royal Engineers during the Second World War. He later rejoined, leaving Charterhouse again in 1947 to become an inspector of art education; he was a key figure in the development of art education in Britain, founding the Art Teachers' Guild, which amalgamated to form the Society for Art in 1940.

Fleming Williams was appointed art master at Charterhouse in 1947. He recruited some gifted young assistants, including Howard Hodgkin in 1954–6. Williams was a wonderful teacher, both in informal tutorials and in his memorable epidiascope lectures. The rather cumbersome epidiascope lay at rest in Studio until recently. His rare flashes of temper earned him the nickname 'Flaming Onions', but mostly he was a benign, white-overalled figure radiating calm with never any signs of oppression. He supervised the building of a new studio at the School, working closely with the architect James Dartford, who had worked with Marcel Breuer for two years. The design is said to have evolved from a discussion during which a matchbox was placed on top of a cigarette box. Pevsner commented: 'The latest addition to Charterhouse and a much more hopeful one, is the crisp, two-storyed art school in 1958.' Pevsner then notes in the back of his book: 'The art school has recently been spoilt by infilling under the projecting upper storey.

In 1957, under Fleming Williams, the Beerbohm Society was born, with members paying a subscription and raising additional funds from the winter sale of studio pottery and Brooke Hall art classes. The money was used to purchase art directly from artists and London galleries, the idea being to acquire works for comparatively small sums of money by artists who might later be well known. It also allowed Carthusians to be confronted with works by young professional painters and sculptors, including David Hockney and Allen Jones. The society also held lectures and organised trips.

Fleming Williams retired early in 1970 at the age of 56 to pursue his interest in English landscape art. He moved to London to work closely with the Tate Gallery's resident Constable scholar, writing many books on the subject.

Michael Woods had worked alongside Fleming Williams, arriving at Charterhouse in 1957, and he took over as director of art in 1970, running Studio until 1994. He was known as 'Potty' Woods because he taught pottery, but he was just as talented with paint as with clay. Peter Attenborough wrote of him in his farewell in *The Carthusian*: 'He can with his brush convey the mood of Norfolk coasts or rivers, for example, or produce heavenly pots from a hunk of clay.' His pots are still drawn in the Studio as part of still lives, and three books he wrote on teaching art can be found in the library to continue to inspire others.

I arrived at Charterhouse to take over the teaching of ceramics in 1994, and Brian Souter took over as director of art. I remember Brian for the well-organised trips, 'Souter Tours', he took to Italy every year, which were of great benefit to many students. He was also a dedicated editor of *The Carthusian* for many years and a fine photographer and footballer.

Peter Monkman, the current director of art, is an inspirational painter who finds time both to run the department and to enjoy a successful painting career. He has recently won the BP Portrait Award, a prestigious achievement and inspiring for the students and teachers in the Studio.

All the drawing masters have been exceptional individuals who have been practitioners as well as teachers. Because of them and the congenial atmosphere in the various art rooms at Charterhouse, numerous students have been inspired to go on and find their own success in

Below: Sir Anthony Caro with Headmaster, John Witheridge, and art teacher, Helen Pinkney, at his studio in France.

Right: Pupil in the Art Department.

the arts. It would be impossible to name all of the great artists from Charterhouse, but William Pye (L 1956) should be noted for his remarkable sculptures which interpret the natural world through water, metal and stone. It would also be unforgivable if I did not give a final mention to Sir Anthony Alfred Caro (G 1942), unquestionably the most important sculptor in Britain. As a successful artist and teacher, Caro taught at St Martin's School of Art, London, from 1953 to 1981. He says: 'It is no good teaching what you know, you have to teach what you don't know or feel comfortable with.' He leads by example, and his declared aim 'to expand the language of sculpture' has always involved 'pushing at the boundaries to see where it gives'. Recently Sir Anthony revisited Charterhouse and shared many memories about the School and his early interest in art. He also invited a group of Carthusian artists to his vast studio in Camden so that they could try their hand at welding. He believes that all artists are in some form optimists, and what he says about his own optimism sums up how I feel about teaching at Charterhouse: 'There is too much left to do in the studio. That is the source as well as the place for my optimism.'

My own optimism for the future is that many more budding artists will enter Charterhouse and leave amazing legacies in the art world.

Theatre at Charterhouse, a personal memory 1956–92

GEOFFREY FORD

Dramatic entertainment has always been a feature of Carthusian life. By the mid-19th century the school was putting on a theatrical performance at the end of every OQ and, after the move to Godalming, home-grown Saturday evening entertainments also became a regular feature. Notable thespians during the 20th century have included Richard Goolden (S 1914), best known as Mole in the perennial London production of *Toad of Toad Hall*, Robert Eddison (P 1927), Geoffrey Toone (H 1929) and the playwright Ben Travers (D 1904), after whom the School theatre is named. Among numerous current OC actors are Nicky Henson (H 1961), Graham Seed (W 1968), whose voice is known throughout the land as Nigel Pargetter in *The Archers*, Christopher Ravenscroft (V 1964), best known as DI Mike Burden in ITV's adaptations of Ruth Rendell's Inspector Wexford mysteries, Daisy Bates (G 1992), Adrian Schiller (G 1981), Giles Henderson (B 1997; stage name Fergus March), Christopher Hollis (G 1978), George Asprey (V 1985), whose many roles include the wicked Scar in the West End production of *The Lion King*, Gerald Avvakoum (g 1992; stage name Gerald Kyd), Rupert Vansittart (R 1975) and writer and director Toby Gough (V 1988).

I arrived in 1956 to teach the violin, but even then I had at the back of my mind the hope that perhaps this school 'did plays', and so I wondered if there would ever be the possibility of involvement in theatre and perhaps directing a few plays.

All plays in those days were done in Hall. The school play – one a year and no girls, of course – was performed at the end of LQ. The other regular annual drama event was the Brooke Hall play (the masters' play) and this traditionally took place at the end of OQ.

Hall was very difficult for putting on plays. It was most unsuitable as a theatre: too big, with a primitive and

Geoffrey Ford during a rehearsal for Thark.

Joyce Conwy Evans with Judy Macdonald, preparing costumes for The King of Macedon.

totally inadequate lighting system, virtually no heating and no sound system. The seating was uncomfortable, and there was no black-out facility. Audibility was always a problem too. Oddly enough, however, in spite of these serious shortcomings, I recall some extraordinary achievements – Peter Gardiner's production of Ibsen's *Peer Gynt* is still a vivid memory.

Later on I did some variety shows, either in the summer, or the end of OQ. I recall a group of boys in the Remove applying to appear in the show. They were remarkable and became Genesis. Nicky Henson was another discovery. He was in a Christmas show, being very funny in a comedy musical number, and a parent, Richard Stone, a well-known theatrical agent, happened to be in the audience. After the show he signed Nicky up on the spot, and Nicky is still with the Stone agency.

Above: On the Razzle.

Below: Pilgrim's Progress, *1972.*

Two other large-scale theatrical performances were done in Hall – *King of Macedon* (1979), an opera by composer-in-residence Roger Steptoe (see page 90), and in 1972 Vaughan Williams's *The Pilgrim's Progress*, to celebrate the centenary of RVW's birth and the move from London to Godalming. These two operas were extremely difficult to stage successfully, given the limitations of Hall as a theatre. Lighting for these ambitious productions was helped immeasurably by two OCs, Dominic Allen and Robert Bittlestone, who had designed and built a lighting system, way ahead of its time, before they left. Dominic and Robert continued to help us at a distance from their respective universities, and they also supervised and operated the lighting for *The Pilgrim's Progress* from their own console. These operas were rehearsed without a black-out facility, and there was no technical rehearsal, which is unthinkable. I don't know how we managed. In spite of everything, the Charterhouse production of *The Pilgrim's Progress* now occupies a significant position of importance when the history of that particular RVW opera is considered.

The costumes for *King of Macedon* and *The Pilgrim's Progress* were designed by Joyce Conwy Evans and expertly made by Judy Macdonald, Helen van Oss and the legendary Lorna Polunin. Lorna's contribution was enormous. She started a 'wardrobe', a cupboard containing a motley collection of clothes (most of which she made) in the 1940s, and this grew and grew, ultimately filling several cupboards, then a large room, then a larger room and finally the whole lot moved into the Ben Travers Theatre. She also gave extremely lively performances in most of the Brooke Hall plays.

Costume designs by Joyce Conwy Evans for The Mikado, *1985.*

THE FRENCH PLAY

This series started somewhat uncertainly in 1967 with Cocteau's *La Machine Infernale*, a difficult play. I was called in at a rather late stage to 'give them a hand', but it turned out to be a rather larger job. However, the important thing was that, although this was a hesitant start, it spawned an interest in French drama and as a result developed into a rather distinguished annual event, attended by a surprisingly large number of Carthusians, but also enthusiastically visited by various universities. After all, if you wanted to see a French play in England, where else would you go? We did mostly classics and A-level texts, but there was the occasional attempt to do more modern plays, such as those by Labiche, Anouilh and Giraudoux. In most of these productions Robin Totton and Frank Wiseman dealt with interpretation and text, while I was mostly responsible for the staging. We used Hall, Lecture Theatre and, ultimately, the Ben Travers Theatre. German and Spanish plays also featured from time to time.

From a purely selfish point of view, the rehearsal and work on these French plays – 15 of them in all – were, for me, some of the happiest hours 'doing plays' during my 36 years at Charterhouse.

THE 'OXBRIDGE' FARCE

Another theatrical event that gave me particular pleasure was the so-called 'Oxbridge Farce'. This dates back to the days when Carthusians hoping to go to Oxbridge stayed on for an extra term in the sixth form. At the end of that term they took the exam, and then there was just a week or so to fill before the end of the quarter and their school careers. Thus was born the Oxbridge farce. The breakneck timetable went like this:

Friday evening: into Hall; blocking
   the moves of the whole play;
   learning lines during the day
Saturday evening: rehearsal of Act I
Sunday evening: rehearsal of Act II
Monday evening: rehearsal of Act III
Tuesday evening: whole play
Wednesday evening: whole play
Thursday: dress rehearsal
Friday: performance
Saturday: performance

It was very hard work for all, but the greatest, greatest fun.

Oxbridge Farce, December 1984, The Importance of Being Ernest.

The 1961 Masque.

THE MASQUE

I think I must also include in these memories something on the Masque of Charterhouse. It wasn't really a Masque – more like a pageant – which was first performed in 1911. It was performed outdoors in Founder's Court (we insured against rain) and contained scenes from the School's history: the eviction of the monks, a famous governors' meeting featuring Judge Jeffries; and a scene with the Jacobean poet, Richard Lovelace. Later additions included Thackeray and, newest of all, Baden-Powell. The music to accompany the opening scene, the monks' eviction, was written by Edward Rendall, the director of music in 1911. There was other music for a St Bartholomew's Fair scene, and for the 1951 production Vaughan Williams was asked to write special music, incorporating that of Rendall and, at Vaughan Williams' insistence, the Carmen (School song) (see page 106). The final performance of the Masque was in CQ 1961, and it was clear that it would have to be the last one. Times had changed. Apart from the costs, which had become prohibitive, it was no longer possible to justify the enormous amount of time taken up with the preparations, let alone the three performances right at the end of term. A levels suddenly mattered. The Masque, it had to be admitted, belonged to another era, and that era was sadly over.

The Masque

It is almost impossible to convey what strong emotion was given rise to by the whole performance [of the Masque] ... The 1929 performance in which I took part in the choir, remains as my most vivid memory of five years at the School.

Hugh Bayley (H 1933)

At one of the performances old Mr Russell (classics beak), who was playing Judge Jeffreys, suffered a heart attack after his final tirade: 'I tell you the king hath the dispensing power.' He slumped down into his chair, and I could see his foot twitching under the table. The other cast members of the scene carried him out to South African Cloister where he died. A local journalist wrote: 'We thought we were seeing part of the play.' That evening I met Collingwood (S) who had been recording the performance from a window in upper cubes, which looked out on to Founder's Court. I said, 'I suppose you recorded the scene where Sniffy Russell died.' 'I did,' he said, 'and I have deleted it. It would be morbid to keep it.'

Apart from that event it was a good Masque. Dimbleby (g) rides in on a large grey to announce to the brethren of the Charterhouse that their house is to be closed by order of the king. If they go quietly, 'well. But if ye are stubborn, and will not bend, ye shall be *broken*, and that – *utterly*.' Exit Dimbleby on horse left. The monks, led by the school chaplain Henry Bettenson ('Rev Bet'), sang the lugubrious 'De Profundis' in a plainsong arrangement possibly by RVW. Usborne (B) was an excellent Prologue, and Dill-Russell (D) did some fantastic juggling and fire-eating in the St Bartholomew's Fair scene.

Anthony Hippisley (S 1956)

THE MASQUE OF CHARTERHOUSE

1956

At a particular moment I had to put down my violin and position myself on a rostrum at St Bartholomew's Fair ... all sorts of things were going on, David Dimbleby was riding a horse, Tim Dill-Russell was juggling, there were stall holders shouting their wares, singers, a wrestler, a thief, a stilt walker, a bear and beggars. Dressed in a medieval costume with cloak, I called out for clients, and a drunken 'boy' was brought on in a wheelbarrow. I inserted a massive tooth extractor into his mouth and squeezed the jaws shut. I pulled hard and noticed the awful expression on the boy's face, a fine piece of acting I thought. I removed the tooth and held it high with a flourish and the audience cheered. Looking down I saw blood on my victim's mouth, I think his name was Evans, and I hope I said sorry to him afterwards because in my enthusiasm I had caught his lip with the tooth extractor.

Peter Creswell (D 1958)

Scenes from the Masque.

Ben Travers on the site of the Ben Travers Theatre (BTT). Sadly he died before its completion in 1984.

Sandy Attenborough and Richard Smith (P 1984) in Thark, *1984.*

THE BEN TRAVERS THEATRE

In 1973 Brian Rees became Headmaster, and he asked Harvey Hallsmith, head of English, if the department needed anything. Harvey promptly said, 'a theatre!' It took quite a long time to get it off the ground. Who was to design it? Where would it be sited? Where would the money come from? And so on.

Richard Scott, the architect who did so much at Charterhouse – the new Houses, for instance – worked with a theatre specialist, Michael Way of Theatretech, and a design finally emerged.

The theatre was named after Ben Travers, an OC and a famous writer of farces, and I will never forget the foundation stone ceremony on OC day 1980, with the minute figure of Ben Travers standing on a mound of rough grass in the middle of the site, invoking the spirit of Aristophanes. It was an important moment.

The Ben Travers Theatre (BTT) opened with a production of the famous Travers farce, *Thark*. The cast was recruited from OCs, members of Brooke Hall, wives and contemporary Carthusians. The Headmaster's wife, Sandy Attenborough, made a sensational appearance as Mrs Frush.

The BTT became a place of remarkable activity with perhaps two major productions a year, but much more important was the appetite for 'boy-run' productions – that is, plays chosen, directed and cast entirely by Carthusians. And such was the enthusiasm that I was to see, during my time at Charterhouse, the number of plays grow from one a year to, at one time, a production every two weeks. Of course the quality was uneven, but it launched the BTT as a place of fantastic activity and available to all. The BTT was a success and a haven for many Carthusians.

I continued to be director, a job I took on to find out what the demands really were, and I soon realised that it was a full-time job. I wrote to the Headmaster recommending that a new post should be created, and eventually Julian Freeman was appointed. He is looking after things as they should be, and BTT flourishes.

I have always believed strongly in the value of rehearsing and presenting a play. A play is about human behaviour and the best plays delve deep into character. This delving I believe to be a valuable exercise, and the ultimate performance demands and requires the very highest standards of physical and mental discipline. There is no better team game. The only way one got anywhere near understanding a play when I was at school was 'reading round the class', but this was always of little use. The only way to understand a play is to do it. A play is not a novel.

Many people thought of this new theatre as a luxury, a plaything, but this was certainly not so. It has proved to be a valuable enrichment to the School.

Theatre at Charterhouse since 1992

JULIAN FREEMAN

When Geoffrey Ford retired in 1992, Alastair MacNaughton took over from him until he left in 1996. From 1996 to 1999 Hammy Sparks was the director of the BTT. He did a great deal to encourage junior drama, especially in the Fourth Form. Brian Robinson took over from him until he handed over to David and Irene Wright in 2001. Under their guidance the theatre continued to mount a variety of productions, which involved pupils from all year groups. The new millennium saw a spectacular production of David Edgar's adaptation of *Nicholas Nickleby*, directed by Emily Fox. Both staff and pupils took part, as did the Headmaster. Other notable successes during this period were *Return to the Forbidden Planet* and *Les Misérables*. Both productions exploited the exceptional musical abilities of the pupils alongside their dramatic talents.

At this point A-level theatre studies was introduced, offering Carthusians with a particular interest in theatre the opportunity to study the subject in the curriculum. Under the tutelage of Emily Fox and Joanna Bratten, the subject proved increasingly popular. Many students now go on to read drama at university, while a few gain direct entry into some of the top drama schools in the country. A number of Carthusians have also won places in the prestigious National Youth Theatre.

Above: Kes.

Below left: The Wind in the Willows.

In September 2004 Julian Freeman was appointed as the first director of drama with specific responsibility for the running of the theatre, for overseeing drama throughout the school and for teaching theatre studies. He has mounted or overseen a diverse range of productions including *Find Me, Our Country's Good, City of Angels, Alarms and Excursions, Oliver Twist* (the play), *The Trial, The Government Inspector, On the Razzle, Kes, A Lie of the Mind, No Exit, Tartuffe, Oedipus* and *Oh! What a Lovely War*, to name but a few. During this period the school was also fortunate to collaborate with Tim Rice on a restaging of his musical *Blondel*.

There have also been numerous drama festivals in which the pupils are encouraged to mount their own productions either of existing plays or of plays that they have written. Under School pupils have twice entered the School's Shakespeare Festival with productions of *Julius Caesar* and *Henry V*, which played to great critical acclaim at the Yvonne Arnaud Theatre in Guildford and the Maltings in Farnham.

Freeman has established strong links with many Ivy League prep schools on the east coast of America and on two occasions has taken productions to these schools. For

example, a production of *The Country Wife* was taken to five such schools, including Phillips Exeter and the Hill School in 2006. He returned in 2008, but on this occasion to conduct collaborative workshops with American pupils at Phillips Academy and Middlesex School. This trip included visits to the Yale Drama Department and to some outstanding theatre productions in New York. Several of these American schools have since made return visits to present their productions here and take part in the School's workshops.

LAMDA speech and drama lessons for individual pupils have also been added to the drama programme and are taught by Helen Freeman, and over 50 pupils each year have achieved the highest grades in either acting or public speaking.

One of the most successful innovations of recent years has been the annual Shakespeare production, which has proved to be popular with Carthusians and the hundreds of prep school pupils who attend the matinée performances. The first of these productions was *Macbeth*, and in 2009 the choice was *A Midsummer Night's Dream*. A significant feature of these productions has been the way in which they have made use of the versatile stage formations in the

BTT, from theatre 'in the round' to traverse, while also making use of the gantry, green room and foyer.

As we look to the future of drama and theatre at Charterhouse, we can be confident that the success in this area of the School will inspire future generations to achieve greatness in this vibrant and essential art form.

Above: Blondel.

Below: Oh, What a Lovely War!

Sport

ROBERT NOBLE

The public schools were the cradle for organised sport, and Charterhouse has played its part in the nurturing and development of most of today's more popular sports. Whether as innovators, law-makers, administrators, participants or commentators, Carthusians have featured and continue to feature strongly in almost every sphere.

It is a popularly held misconception that Charterhouse wrote the rules for association football, the country's favourite game. This is not strictly true. Carthusian B.F. Hartshorne (G 1863), the captain of the XI, was present at the first meeting of the Football Association in 1863, and at that meeting, in the Freemasons' Tavern in London the newly printed Charterhouse rules were taken along as a guideline. A comparison between the Charterhouse rules and those adopted by the FA shows many similarities.

The Association struggled for recognition and barely grew for some time after that meeting, and it was only when, in 1868, it adopted a more liberal interpretation of the offside rule as used by Charterhouse and Westminster that things took off. The secretary of the time wrote to every football club in Britain inviting membership, and 'the response was gratifying, particularly in the adhesion of the two important public schools, Westminster and Charterhouse'. By then the annual match between Charterhouse and Westminster had become established in the calendar. With its known origins dating back to 1863 it is the oldest extant football fixture in the world.

Charterhouse's own alternative version of the game, known as the 'cloister game', was played throughout the School's time in London. The cloister was originally a covered walkway leading from the old Duke of Norfolk's mansion to his tennis court. When Charterhouse became a school, it ran from Gownboys to the Gownboys dining hall. According to Eardley Wilmot, it was 'a species of tunnel paved with smooth flagstones but roughly constructed with sharp, jagged flint at its sides'. The goals were not at the ends of the pitch but at the side a little way short of the ends: they were the door to Gownboys at the north end and the door opening on to Green at the other.

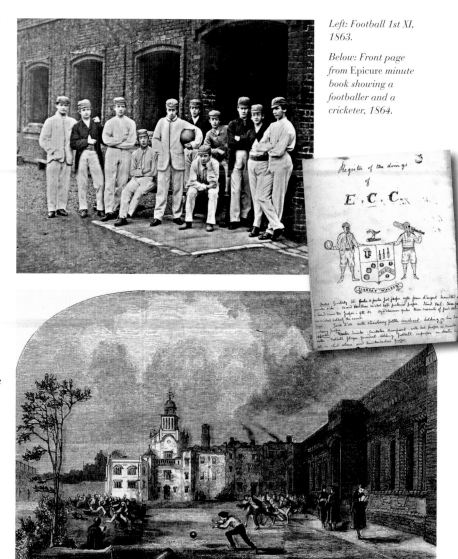

Left: Football 1st XI, 1863.

Below: Front page from Epicure minute book showing a footballer and a cricketer, 1864.

Any number could play and often did, the result being lengthy periods of stalemate, with the ball buried beneath a surging mass of participants, followed by a sudden dash forward when the ball somehow miraculously emerged. It was best played, however, in teams limited to six, nine or, naturally, eleven players; this made for a much more open and more satisfactory game.

Illustrated London News drawing of football at Charterhouse, 1858.

The School 1st XI of 1891–2 with a 'dream-team' of Old Carthusian international players. The School players were photographed individually before another OC v. School match in March 1892; the OCs 'sat' for their portraits in London and the artist devised this imaginary scene.

Games of football at the London Charterhouse were played indoors or out depending on the weather, and on a number of occasions the match between the School and the Old Carthusians took place half on Green and half in cloisters. Incidentally, when the ball disappeared through an open window, which it frequently did, the first player to touch it was the one to bring it back into play. It is thought that this is the derivation of the modern term 'touch'.

In these embryonic days of football the public schools ruled the roost, and Charterhouse was at the forefront. The Old Carthusians won the FA Cup in 1881, beating Old Etonians 3–0 in the final, and several Carthusians also played in FA Cup finals with other teams – Thomas Hooman (V 1868), for example, earned a winner's medal in the first FA Cup final in 1872 playing for the Wanderers. Between 1872 and 1900 Charterhouse excelled by releasing to the world 56 football Blues and 14 players who went on to play for England, as well as one Scottish and one Welsh player. Between them they earned 74 international caps in a period when almost the only

international matches played were against the other home nations, so that the most caps one could acquire in any one year was likely to be three. Between 1885 and 1890 over one-sixth of all England football caps awarded went to Carthusians. There was at least one Carthusian in the 'Varsity match every year from 1881 to 1900 and often many more. The Oxford and Cambridge teams between

Left: FA Cup Winner's Medal, 1894.

Below: Old Carthusian team, winners of 1881 FA Cup.

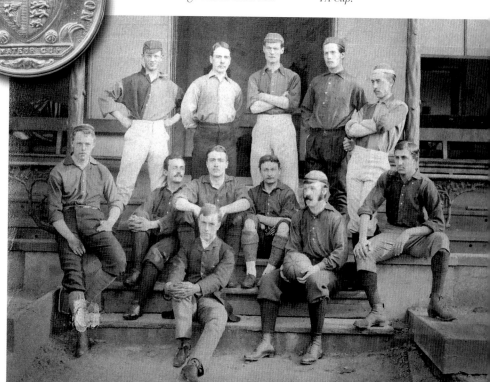

them contained six Carthusians on no fewer than five occasions, and in 1897 the Oxford team alone had six Carthusians playing for it, while Cambridge fielded three in the same match.

Among these stars two deserve special mention: W.N. Cobbold (V 1882) and G.O. Smith (H 1892). Cobbold was an outstanding athlete. Known as 'the prince of dribblers', he played nine times for England and scored six goals. G.O. Smith was simply the best. Known universally by his initials, G.O. was as famous in his time as W.G. (Grace). He played 20 times for England and was captain on at least 14 occasions, registering 11 goals. He went on to play for the Corinthians and scored 125 goals in 131 matches for them. As if that were not enough, he still holds the School record for the number of runs scored in one innings with 229 against Westminster in 1892.

Cricket at Charterhouse goes back even further than football: there was a match between the 'City of London' and the 'City of Westminster' in 1795, which was Charterhouse against Westminster in all but name. Prints of cricket at Charterhouse date from 1775, and a portrait of a Carthusian, William Wheatley, dated 1786, hangs in the pavilion at Lord's. The records show Carthusians playing for the Gentlemen versus the Players in 1827, and in the 'Varsity match in 1829. Carthusians were also among the founders of the Free Foresters and I Zingari, and the School also produced its share of Test cricketers in the late 1800s, including two, Frederick Fane (RW) and Aubrey Smith (UG), the film star, who captained their country.

Another Carthusian, Teddy Wynyard (g 1877), probably should have captained England – he actually captained an MCC tour to New Zealand and an amateur MCC tour to America, and twice had to decline the chance to tour Australia. What made Wynyard special and at the same time typical of his era was his ability as an all-rounder. Not only did he play in the last match in which W.G. Grace led England to victory over the Australians, but he also scored one of the goals in the Old Carthusians' victory in the FA Cup final. As a rugby player he was 'a glorious three-quarter and, had he not gone into the army, he would have reached the top in rugby'.

Another great Carthusian of this era was Richard Webster (S 1861), who was to become Lord Alverstone. Primarily an athlete, he was said to have been one of the best runners over a distance of ground that the School or Cambridge afterwards has ever produced. He won the mile and two miles against Oxford and also gained a cricket Blue while at Cambridge. In later life he was president of

Top left: Cobbold (on the ground, to the left) with the 1881 1st XI Football team.

Centre: G.O. Smith, 1891.

Above: Teddy Wynyard, a glorious all-rounder who excelled in cricket, football and rugby.

Below: Engraving from the Illustrated London News *showing cricket and hockey (far right) being played at Charterhouse, 1861.*

THE GREAT SCHOOLS OF ENGLAND.—CHARTERHOUSE FROM THE GREEN

Right: Lord Ellenborough, Edward Law (S), laid down a set of rules for 'hoops'.

Below: Hoops being played at Charterhouse.

the MCC, Surrey CCC, the Amateur Athletics Association and the Royal Society for good measure. He was also a founder member of Guildford Golf Club. He achieved all this while carrying out duties as Master of the Rolls and, later, Lord Chief Justice.

Another Lord Chief Justice, Lord Ellenborough, Edward Law (S), formalised a set of rules for the game of 'hoops' while at Charterhouse. This involved the seemingly simple task of propelling a hoop around the quadrangle of Green using a stick. The task under Edward Law's rules was made considerably more difficult by demanding that two and sometimes four hoops should be propelled simultaneously around the cobbles surrounding Green. The course of the race ran from Middle Briars, a bulge halfway along the cloisters, to a finish drawn on the wall on the far

side of Green. Here Law had written the word 'Crown' along with a drawing of a crown. The crown represented a public house of the same name, which stood on the other side of the wall and from which the London coach would leave for Oxford. When the School moved to Godalming the name moved with it, and Crown was initially stationed on the side of the pavilion on Green; it now resides on the edge of Under Green.

The game of hoops has long since died its death, but the game of golf, at least as far as competitive golf is concerned, was just in its infancy then. As with football and cricket, the early pace was set by a Carthusian: During his brief time at Charterhouse H.G. Hutchinson (G 1873) won the first two amateur golf championships and went on to become the first 'voice of golf', a highly knowledgeable author and commentator. He was succeeded in this some years later by the great Henry Longhurst (S 1927), the man who brought golf into our living rooms in the 1960s.

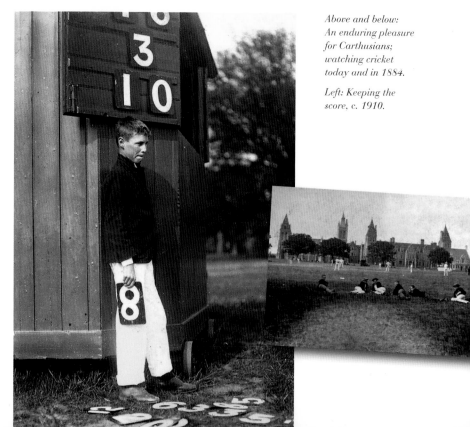

Above and below: An enduring pleasure for Carthusians; watching cricket today and in 1884.

Left: Keeping the score, c. 1910.

The transfer of power in football from amateur to professional happened very quickly. The Old Carthusians won the FA Cup in 1881, reached the semi-final in 1883 and again in 1885 and were beaten in the sixth round in 1886 and 1887. By 1893 they had stopped entering the competition. The legalisation of professionalism in

keeping with their traditions, the Old Carthusians contested the first final. They drew with Old Salopians, drew the replay and ended up sharing the trophy. One hundred years later the two schools met in the centenary final, and this time the Old Salopians emerged victorious. Since its inception the Old Carthusians have won the Arthur Dunn Cup 22 times, a record unmatched by any other school.

Unlike football, the amateur element of other sports retained its prestige for much longer, and in these Charterhouse excelled. In racquets the School entered the first public schools' championships at the Queen's Club in 1868, despite having no racquets court at the London Charterhouse. They did not win, but by the turn of the century they had found an outstanding racquets champion in Francis Dames Longworth (P 1881), who was not only amateur singles champion in 1892, 1893 and 1901 and doubles champion in 1895, 1901, 1906 and

1885 was clearly a significant landmark, but it would not be too fanciful to mark the hand-over of power with a single date – 2 March 1887. On that day the Old Carthusians played out an epic quarter-final against the Invincibles of Preston North End at Kennington Oval in front of a crowd of over 5,000. The Old Carthusians came close to defeating the northern professionals, but went down by the odd goal in three after extra time. The *Preston Guardian* described the game as 'about the hardest the North End have played this season'.

It is rare for a Carthusian to have gone on to play sport professionally, though a good number have made a living from it as commentators, journalists or even nowadays as players' agents. For a long time through the 20th century there was room and recognition for the good amateur.

The football team won the first FA Amateur Cup in 1894. They repeated the feat in 1897. In 1903 the Arthur Dunn Cup was first played. This was a trophy played exclusively between Old Boys' teams, and, entirely in

1908, but was also to develop the burgeoning talents of many Carthusians as a member of Brooke Hall. Of his brood Vane Pennell (g 1894) went on to become amateur doubles champion in 1901 and 1908 (partnering Dames Longworth) and also won the Olympic gold medal in 1908. Pride of place, however, must go to H.W. Leatham (g 1910), who won the amateur singles title twice either side of the First World War and picked off the amateur doubles title on no fewer than seven occasions. In 1930 he went on a trip to the USA and won the US and Canadian doubles titles to go with the British one he had won that year. Only Charles Swallow (V 1956) has come anywhere near that record subsequently. He won the amateur singles championship in 1964, 1968 and 1979.

Pennell excelled at tennis, too, and won the amateur singles title in 1904. In this sport – decried as pat-ball for many years and not allowed minor sport status at the School until 1978 – Pennell had considerable competition for the title of best School player. Noel Turnbull (g 1908) played a number of Davis Cup matches and won the doubles gold medal in the Olympic Games of 1920. Ten years later Raymond Tuckey (g 1928) won the men's doubles at Wimbledon and was a member of the last British team to win the Davis Cup.

Pennell and Turnbull are not the only Olympic champions to come out of Charterhouse. In what was to remain the last bastion of amateurism for many years, the Olympics has been the site of success for two other Carthusians, while many more have taken part. Perhaps the most interesting story is that of Wyndham Halswelle (g 1899). He had come second in the Olympic 400 metres in Athens in 1906 and was determined to go one better in London two years later.

Halswelle reached the final of the 400 metres with the fastest qualifying time (an Olympic record 48.4 seconds). Pictures of the race indicate that Carpenter blocked Halswelle. While blocking was allowed under US rules at the time, the Olympic race was conducted under stricter, British rules that did not allow this. The race was ordered to be rerun in lanes two days later without Carpenter, but the other two US runners refused to compete. Although reluctant, Halswelle ran the race by himself to win the gold in a time of 50.2 seconds. It is the only occasion in Olympic

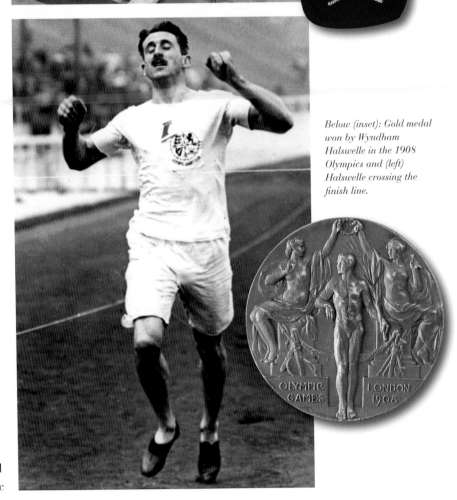

Racquets champions: Vane Pennell (seated) and Ernest Garnett (P 1894), winners of the Public Schools Racquets Challenge Cup in 1893. Pennell went on to win an Olympic gold medal.

Inset: Francis Dames Longworth (P) who joined Brooke Hall and brought on many Carthusian sportsmen.

Below: Racquets blazer badge, 1900.

Below (inset): Gold medal won by Wyndham Halswelle in the 1908 Olympics and (left) Halswelle crossing the finish line.

Telegraph called him 'one of the century's most distinguished sailors'. He won the Prince of Wales Cup a record 12 times and was a great administrator, serving on the RYA Council for many years and serving as president from 1980 to 1983.

But if it is administrators you seek, then look no further than Charles Wreford-Brown (G 1885). A highly gifted sportsman himself, Wreford-Brown gained four international caps at football, played for Gloucestershire at cricket and represented Great Britain at chess in the 1924 Olympic Games. Despite little concrete evidence, it is he who is accredited with first using the term 'soccer', and he played for the Corinthians on over 100 occasions, captaining tours to South Africa, Sweden and the USA and Canada. Stories about Charles Wreford-Brown are legion. On a South African tour in 1903, the referee adjudged one of the Corinthians to have committed a foul in the penalty area. As captain, Wreford-Brown ordered his goalkeeper to stand aside and allow the opposition a free shot at goal. Later on the same tour, when awarded a penalty, he intentionally shot wide.

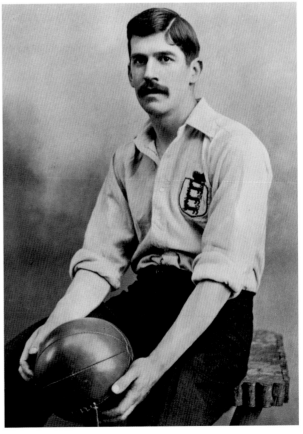

Charles Wreford-Brown.

history where the final was a walkover. As a result of the controversy, from the next Olympics in 1912 onwards all 400 metre races were run in lanes, and the International Amateur Athletic Federation was founded to establish uniform worldwide rules for athletics.

The School's other Olympic champion was Stewart Morris (g 1927). He claimed the Swallows class in the sailing events of the 1948 Olympics in Torbay. While his medal was less contentious than that of Halswelle, it was hard earned. In a rising wind and a roughish sea, he had to come fourth in the last race to secure his medal. Everyone told him to start carefully. He did and was next to last at the first mark. He gradually climbed up and was fifth at the final mark. He got his fourth – but by a margin of only 14 seconds. It was no fluke. In his obituary the *Daily*

If anything, however, his range as an administrator was even greater than that as a player. He was instrumental in the founding and organisation of the Arthur Dunn Cup, was responsible for the formation of the Amateur Football Association of which he became chairman, was a member of the FA Council and vice-president from 1941 until his death, managed tours to Canada and Australia, attended the first meeting of the Athenian League and was chairman of the international selection committee for England within the FA. He managed the British Olympic soccer team in the 1936 Olympics in Germany and famously forbade them to give the Nazi salute. Wreford-Brown's contribution to the development of 'soccer' was considerable and should not be underestimated. In his book *Corinthians and Cricketers* Edward Grayson claims with some justification that: 'When he died in 1951, a link was broken which had bound the International Selection Committee to the Golden Age and international experience on the field of play.'

The tradition of the great all-rounder was carried on well into the 20th century by an almost constant stream of talented sportsmen. It is quite impossible to list them all here, but one of the greatest stars was John Morrison (W 1911), whose career began at Cambridge University where he gained Blues for football and cricket and, remarkably, captained the side both before and after the First World War. He once scored 233 not out in 2¾ hours against the MCC, and went on to play cricket for Somerset and football for Sunderland FC and the Corinthians, gaining an amateur international cap against Wales in 1920. When the best of his playing days were over, he turned his attention to golf, at which he won a Blue in

1919, and played for England against Ireland in 1930, the same year that he won the Belgian Amateur Championship.

This was a golden period for Charterhouse golf, and perhaps 1930 was the greatest year of all. In addition to Morrison's successes, T.A. Bourn (W 1921) won the English amateur championship (he was famous enough to appear on a series of cigarette cards along with all the golfing greats of the day). John Beck (V 1917), already a Walker Cup player and soon to be the first Walker Cup captain to defeat the Americans in that competition, also played for England. H. Wesley Smith (L 1911) won the Argentine amateur championship, and there were five Carthusians in the 'Varsity match that year. The following year Longhurst (G 1927) and J.P. Marston (L 1927) captained the respective teams. It was no surprise that the Old Carthusians, with Bourn, Beck, Morrison and Marston in the team, won the Halford Hewitt competition, named after the Old Carthusian who put up the trophy, for the first time.

Charterhouse almost owned the trophy throughout the 1930s, failing to win it only twice in the decade. In addition to those mentioned, the team was bolstered by another international, E.M. Prain (G 1927), and by Charles Hooman (g 1906), who played in the first Walker Cup match. We have already seen that Hooman's father, Thomas, won a winner's medal in the first FA Cup final (see page 133). He also played in the winning Old Carthusian team in 1881, played in four pre-official internationals against Scotland, ran the sprint for England in 1872, rowed in the grand final at Henley and headed the school batting averages in 1867 and 1868. His son, Charles,

Left: 1st XI Cricket team, with Morrison (seated in the centre), 1911.

Above: Tommy Garnett (seated in centre) as Captain of 1933 1st XI cricket team.

Below: Front covers of The Greyfriar.

Above: John Middleton, 1929.

Right: John Lomas, 1937.

the first batsman to score over 1,000 runs in a season in 1933 with 1,023 runs at an average of 93. Garnett won the British amateur doubles at fives and had a brief spell with Somerset before setting off on an illustrious career in education. The other great cricketer of the time was R.C. 'Crusoe' Robertson-Glasgow (L 1919). He had a much longer spell with Somerset, picking up 464 first class wickets, and then went on to grace the pages of Fleet Street as a journalist.

Apart from C. Middleton (B 1930), who in 1930 scored the only other double century made by a School batsman, the other great of the period was John Lomas (g 1937). Known by his contemporaries as the Great Lomas, his was a brief but dazzling career. A sickly and weak boy, he nevertheless managed to score four goals in a match for the 1st XI five times in the 1936–7 season. In cricket he scored over 2,000 runs in his time in the 1st XI and went on to play for Oxford University, where his average of 45.4 placed him 14th in the first class averages in 1938. He was captain of the Charterhouse XI that in 1936 ended Eton's run of almost 18 years unbeaten by another school at cricket.

inherited a good deal of his father's talent, since he was also a racquets champion, played cricket for Devon and Kent and lost the US amateur title to Cyril Tolley in 1922. As with the Arthur Dunn Cup, the Old Carthusians have the best record in the Halford Hewitt competition, with 16 wins since the competition began in 1924.

The period between the world wars saw a number of landmarks for the School and the blossoming of talents beyond the golf course. Tommy Garnett (P 1933) became

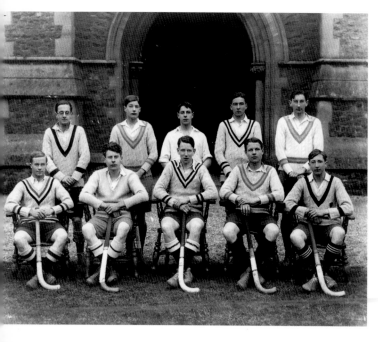

The period between the wars also saw the beginning of hockey as a main (though not major) sport in the School. The season ran initially from after the football match with Winchester until the end of LQ (spring term). There had been hockey at the London Charterhouse, though it was spurned as 'a game for the younger boys', and a team played four matches in 1876, although the records do not show any repeat until 1930. Thereafter things slowly took off, but hockey did not achieve major sport status until 1970.

The period immediately before the Second World War saw the first tours by School teams. The football team went to Paris in 1937 to play a couple of games and cement the *entente cordiale* and that same year entertained a team from Germany. The hockey team went to Germany twice, in 1936 and again in 1938, when they were in Nuremburg at the time of the famous rallies. Despite reports of great conviviality and hospitality, the efforts of the Carthusians were not enough to prevent the inevitable.

Left: Hockey team, 1935.

Peter May

I remember Peter May (S 1947) who was a new boy in 1942. I tried to get him to join our House cricket team, with at first no success. Our Housemaster, Robert Birley, was also Headmaster, and he told me not to push Peter as his only interest was football. Peter was very shy. He hated parties and in some ways was a loner.

The following year I did persuade Peter to play cricket, but instead of the normal hard ball we substituted a tennis ball. Wow! It soon turned out that Peter was a natural at cricket. His classmate friend, John Perry, who was in Verites, came to watch. He could not believe that Peter never missed hitting the ball. Later in the nets, now with a normal cricket ball, Peter hit the ball every time. Robert Birley told us to lay off pushing Peter into joining the House team, pointing out that Peter had no background playing cricket and had been ill and had to build up his strength.

But he did join the House team, then the School team. Peter did his two years National Service in the Royal Navy. After attending Pembroke College he went into insurance and later became an insurance broker. He played cricket for Surrey, Cambridge University and in 1951 was selected for the England team, becoming captain. He was well respected and was often described as 'the perfect English gentleman'.

Ian Parker (S 1944)

Above: Peter May (on the right) playing in an OC match.

Right: Richard Gilliat and Peter May, 1967.

Below: Cricket at Charterhouse, 1960.

The early-July Old Carthusian two-day match was probably the most anticipated match at Charterhouse in decades, for in the OC team was the recently retired England and Surrey captain, Peter May, one of England's greatest ever batsmen. On the first day, Friday, May scored a glorious century. That innings was particularly memorable to me, who was opening the bowling. When May was in the 30s and I was bowling, his partner, Joe Ullman, hit a return catch back at me, which hit my hands and bounced on to the non-striking end stumps. May was out of his ground as the bails came off, clearly run out. I looked at the umpire, ex-cricket master John Marriot, and then at skipper Richard Gilliat, who was fielding at mid-off. Seconds passed and no appeal came. So May survived and went on to score a century, at which time I returned to the attack. During one over I overheard Marriot and Ullman mentioning that May was delighted with his century but rather tired by now. I thought a fast, straight yorker would do him. And indeed it did. I had in the end got May's wicket.

To have played in that XI was a privilege and one that has given me a lifetime of memories. We were a great school side, capable of large scores batting as we did down to No. 9, and also capable of blowing sides away – Winchester 27–7 and Harrow 17–7 were two particularly good examples of that.

Michael Coulson (W 1963)

Towards the end of the war and immediately after it came another golden period for Charterhouse sport. The centrepiece was a cricket team which an article in *The Times* some years later vaunted as the best side from any school in the previous 50 years. With a bowling attack spearheaded by R.L. Whitby (H 1947), Tony Rimell (W 1945) and Simon Kimmins (R 1948) and a batting line-up that could boast Oliver Popplewell (R 1946) as well as Peter May, it was a team to be feared. All went on to play first class cricket, and May's career was quite the stuff of legend. He was in the 1st XI for hockey, was unbeaten in three years partnering his brother at fives, including winning the Kinnaird Cup, and captained Cambridge University at football; but all this pales into insignificance when compared to his cricket career.

May played for England 66 times, 41 of them as captain and, until Michael Vaughan overtook him recently, he was England's most successful captain ever. He retired from top-class cricket at the remarkably young age of just 32, with an impressive test average of 46.77. His love of cricket never diminished, however. He did a brief spell as a test referee, was a test selector from 1965 to 1968, was president of MCC in 1980–81 and his career culminated in his being made chairman of selectors from 1982 to 1988. His record at Charterhouse was a good indication of what was to come. He never quite achieved 1,000 runs in a season but totalled 1,794 in four years in the first XI. In all he made eight centuries for the 1st XI and seemed to reserve his best performances for the School's keenest rivals: 108 against Harrow as a 15-year-old and 101 not out in his final year; 106 not out against Wellington; 105 not out against Cranleigh; 115 not out against Bradfield; 109 not out and 145 not out against the Old Carthusians; and a magnificent 185 not out against Eton. In all his innings against school opposition May averaged a staggering 91.85. Richie Benaud, perhaps his most formidable opponent, called him not merely the greatest English batsman to emerge since the war, which is the conventional judgement, but the only great one.

The cricketers were by no means the only successes, however. John Tanner (P 1940) was the last Carthusian to play international football for England, representing the England Amateur XI against Ireland in 1947. Nor did his feats stop there. Having captained the Oxford University team to a thrilling 5–4 victory over Cambridge in the 1948 'Varsity match, he went on to play for the famous Pegasus team that won the FA Amateur Cup in 1951, scoring the

John Tanner beating L.T. Farrer in the Amateur Cup Final of 1951, when Pegasus defeated Bishop Auckland 2-1, before a record crowd of 100,000 at Wembley.

decisive goal against Bishop Auckland in front of 100,000 people. He also played for Huddersfield Town in the old first division. His greatest asset was his lightning speed, and he was followed closely in almost every respect by David Miller (D 1948). Miller gained his Blue at Cambridge and went on to play for Pegasus, Sussex, Portsmouth reserves and a host of other teams in the mid-1950s. He was selected to play for an England Amateur XI against Queen's Park Rangers in 1956, and he came close to representing his country in the 1956 Olympics as a sprinter, but was injured in the build-up. Miller subsequently became a sports journalist of note with the *Daily Telegraph*. He followed Brian Glanville (B 1949), who spent 30 years writing for, among other newspapers, the *Sunday Times*. Both were regarded as authoritative voices on football for many years, and Glanville was particularly known for his outspoken views and once described the Premier League as the 'Greed is Good' league.

The third great journalist of the time (though he began rather earlier) was Peter O'Sullevan (D 1935), who was racing correspondent for the Press Association and for the *Daily Express* and who gave some of the earliest television commentaries on any sport in the late 1940s. He also did many radio commentaries in his earlier years (including the Grand National before it was televised for the first time in 1960). On television his was the voice that guided viewers through many of the biggest events of the racing year, from the Cheltenham Festival (until 1994) to the Grand National at Aintree and Epsom Derby (until 1979), Royal Ascot and Glorious Goodwood. During his career he

Below: Pontifex race: 'The prefects ran all sports and participation was obligatory. I was forced to jog around the Pontifex course and take part. On the day I just kept running and overtaking everyone finishing sixth to everyone's surprise. Cellan-Jones (captain) asked me to join the school team. The Saturday away fixtures and my colours, allowing me to use Crown, were a wonderful relief.'

Jervis Whiteley (R 1947)

called about 30 renewals of the Prix de l'Arc de Triomphe and commentated on racing from America, Ireland and Rome during the 1960s. If Longhurst was the voice of golf then Peter O'Sullevan was known as the voice of racing. In a television interview before his 50th and last Grand National in 1997 he revealed that his commentary binoculars came from a German submarine. He was knighted the same year, the only sports broadcaster at the time to have been granted that honour.

One athlete who did feature in the British squads of the 1950s was Paul Vine (R 1946). He won a bronze medal in the 110 metre hurdles at the World Student Games in Dortmund in 1953, the AAA 220 yards hurdles in 1955 and 1956 and had the distinction of winning the race (the low hurdles) before Roger Bannister's four-

minute mile run at Iffley Road in 1954. Vine held the British and European record for the 202 yards hurdles for 20 years from 1955 to 1975.

Meanwhile, in the 1950s golfers continued to proliferate. Graham Pratt (G 1954) reached the semi-final of the British Boys' Championship at Dunbar in 1953, and, five years later, Richard Braddon (G 1959) went better still by winning the tournament at Moortown. Braddon was a youth international in 1959 and 1960 and reached the quarter-final of the English amateur championship in 1965. This was another great time for Charterhouse golf, with Martin Christmas (G 1957) playing in the 1961 Walker Cup team (where he won Great Britain and Ireland's only point against a team that included Jack Nicklaus) and again in 1963. Peter Benka

(R 1964) was another to make the side in 1969. Benka
was a great servant to golf, both as a player and later as
an administrator: he served on the Surrey county
committee for 25 years, was on the championship
committee of the English Golf Union and was chairman
of selectors from 1994 to 1998.

If the cricket team of 1946 was considered great, the
side of 1963 might stand fair comparison. Captained by
Richard Gilliat (G 1963), the team contained two others
who would go on to play first class cricket in Andrew
Barker (S 1963) and Mike Hooper (G 1965). It had
strength in depth, which saw them sweep all before them,
defeating Bradfield by 84, Eton by 184, Winchester by
149 and Westminster by 7 wickets. Only rain saved
Harrow, who were teetering on 48–7 and chasing a
distant 216 for victory.

The late 1950s and early 1960s were a rich time for
Charterhouse, particularly on the cricket field. Eddie
Craig (R 1960) scored over 1,000 runs twice in
consecutive seasons for the 1st XI and went on to play for
Cambridge University and briefly for Lancashire. His
brilliant academic career took him in that direction when
a shining career in cricket beckoned, but he still managed
to turn out for the Cricketer Cup side to considerable
effect, scoring 85 not out in the final against Oundle when
the Friars took the trophy for the first time in 1978. The
House match final of 1959 bears mention: Weekites, led
by Joe Ullman (W 1959), scored 334, of which Ullman
made 229. They lost to Robinites by the small matter of
82 runs, Craig having scored 250.

Richard Gilliat may be the last in the line of great all-
round sportsman to come out of Charterhouse and make
an impact on a national level. His grandfather, Walter

(G 1888), had played once for England at football,
scoring a hat trick against Ireland in 1893, and his uncle,
Ivor, scored 65 goals for the 1st XI in the 1919 season, a
record unlikely ever to be surpassed. Richard captained
Oxford University at football, won a Blue for fives and
was the key member of the Charterhouse tennis team that
reached the Youll Cup final twice in succession. Indeed, so
good was Gilliat's tennis that he played Junior Wimbledon
and might well have gone on to a career in this sport had
it not been for a comment from the doyen of British
tennis at the time, Dan Maskell. Gilliat had a double-
handed backhand at a time when such a technique was
unfashionable, and Maskell pronounced that he would
never make it as a top player while he employed such a
stroke. Tennis's loss was cricket's gain, and Gilliat went
on to captain Hampshire to the County Championship for
only the second time in its history in 1973.

The last great all-rounder? I fear so. With the advent
of television and strong commercial interest in sport many
more see professional sport as a lucrative future.
Carthusians are, by and large, still of the amateur,
Corinthian persuasion, and the ethos of the School
continues to be one of producing good all-rounders rather
than players who are outstanding in one particular sport.

However, such is the level of competition in sport nowadays that, even in the amateur game, a 'professional' approach is required. No one makes a name in more than one sport nowadays, and yet Carthusians are encouraged to participate in as many as possible and to be good at all of them. As a result, while the School has seen a few who have played county cricket since 1970 – Nick Wisdom (R 1971), Gregor Macmillan (V 1988), James Bovill (V 1989), James Hamblin (g 1996) – and one or two who have gone on to play football for minor league clubs, including Alan Stewart (S 1972), who had trials with Leeds United, the days of the gentleman sportsman are long over.

This is not to say that the School has stopped seeing sporting talent. In fact, teams of recent years have produced records to match those of any era, but few have gone on to greater things. Instead, the Old Carthusians' sides have been strengthened and, particularly in football, golf and cricket, the OCs are a force to be reckoned with on their respective circuits. The footballers won the Arthurian League and Cup double in consecutive years in 2008 and 2009, but the ultimate was achieved in the spring of 1982. It was then that the Old Carthusians, already holders of the Cricketer Cup, won the Arthur Dunn Cup and the Halford Hewitt to be in possession of all three at the same time.

Below: The winning OCFC Dunn squad, 2007–8.

Above and right: Old Carthusian football and cricket.

There have been a number of significant changes within the School since the 1970s, including the introduction of girls. Naturally, the girls wish to take part in sport as much as the boys do, and they have had their share of success. Lacrosse and netball teams have had unbeaten seasons at times, and in Lucy Tomlinson (G 1991) and Lindsay Dart (V 1994) the school had junior lacrosse internationals in successive years in the mid-1990s. Louise Baner (D 1993) followed them a few years later. In 2003 Anne-Marie Brewer (D 2004) played against Fay Dalby (R 2003) for their respective universities in the 'Varsity tennis match and, perhaps the most remarkable for a school where the girls all start their cricket from scratch, a Carthusian, Isabelle Duncan (S 1992), was one of the first women to be elected to membership of the MCC.

Football tour to Sweden for Gothia Cup, 1999.

The 1970s also witnessed the start of touring, and Andrew Morrison took a cricket team to New Zealand and John Peters took the footballers to Jamaica. The Headmaster, Brian Rees, also went on the football tour and, no doubt feeling that he should show willing, joined the first practice. He pulled up lame almost immediately and was not seen in training kit again. In the 1990s, trips to Australia and South Africa for cricket, to Malaysia for hockey and to Sweden for the Gothia Cup for football, became regular events. These and other tours established many links with schools abroad, where boys have subsequently worked in their gap years.

Perhaps the biggest shift over the past 30 years or so, however, has been the change in competition. In the past traditional rivalry was enough to give a game its meaning, and the football and cricket teams in particular would regularly play against men's sides like the Liverpool Ramblers and the Corinthian Casuals at football and MCC, I Zingari, Grasshoppers and Butterflies at cricket. The ISFA Cup, the Southern Independent Schools' League, the Cowdrey Cup, the Southern League, the Boarding Schools' Cup for hockey and as many other county, regional and national competitions in a wide variety of sports are of much greater importance now. This is reflected in the much larger number of minor sports in the School. Carthusians now compete against other schools at badminton, basketball, canoeing, fencing, judo, karate, rowing, squash, tennis and water polo.

In national competitions the School measures up pretty well. In football Charterhouse reached the first ISFA Cup final played at Craven Cottage and lost on penalties to a Forest side which included Quinton Fortune, who went on to play for Manchester United and South Africa. They reached the final again in 2000 only to lose to Shrewsbury by the only goal of the match. In 2007 they were in the final again, this time losing to Hampton, once more on penalties. In 2008 Charterhouse finally won the competition, beating Millfield – on penalties, of course. Apart from Millfield, no school has

contested more finals. The season of 2007–8 is on record as the School's most successful season since 1881–2, when the 1st XI won every match. Anthony Beddows' (G 2008) team went unbeaten in 20 games and conceded only five goals all season. They were runners up in the ISFA six-a-side competition at the start of the season, and, in addition to the ISFA Cup, they also won the Southern Independent Schools' League.

There have been successes in hockey, too. The 2004 vintage reached the semi-final of the national championships, beating Millfield in an unforgettable quarter-final along the way. The 2009 team won the Surrey Cup and the Southwest Regional championship and were knocked out of the national championships at the quarter-final stage by Millfield. That same year they reached the first final of the Boarding Schools Cup and, in Charlie Jamieson (W 2009), had the leading goal-scorer of all time with 36 goals in the season.

The under-15 cricket team of 1998 reached the final of the Lord's Taverners' Trophy, and a wonderful day was had by all at Trent Bridge. In the past few years the 1st XI has recorded more wins in a season than almost any of its great forebears (though this is due in very large part to the 50-over format, which has largely replaced declaration cricket). They have yet to win the Cowdrey Cup but came within a whisker in 2009. Meanwhile, the Friars are a close fourth in the all-time standings for the Cricketer Cup and have won the trophy as often as all but Malvern and Tonbridge. In 2007 James Hamblin (g 1996) and James Wood (g 2004) broke all records for the competition with an opening stand of 415 against Stowe. With 235 and 207 not out, respectively, they also stand at the top of the league for highest individual scores.

When the School moved to Godalming the boys swam races in the river Wey initially and then quite soon afterwards in one of the earliest indoor baths in the country; but they never produced a swimming champion. Recently the swimming team has had some excellent seasons. They converted their ability in the pool to very good effect as National Regional under-16 water polo champions in 2006 and as the under-18 champions two years later.

Carthusians excel as able amateurs rather than as committed and sharply honed professionals, as their varying degrees of success in tennis, badminton, karate, fencing or the squash team reaching the national quarter final in 2009, demonstrate.

Outdoor Education

JIM FREEMAN

In 1873 the War Office granted the School leave to raise a company-strength Rifle Corps to be attached to the Queen's West Surrey Volunteer Regiment, and on 10 November Lieutenant Colonel Deane Shute (Adjutant of the 3rd Battalion) arrived at Charterhouse to inspect a hundred boys who had volunteered. *The Carthusian* of that time welcomed the institution of the Corps:

We hope that all in the Corps will practise so readily and steadily, that at some future date the band may have the glory of crashing forth 'The Conquering Hero' as the Rifle Corps march up hill triumphantly bearing the Ashburton Shield, a trophy of their powers, to hang up in some hall in Charterhouse.

The Asburton Shield was the prize in Britain's premier shooting competition for schools, and it is clear that shooting and drill were the principal elements in the Corps' training programme, as an early instruction enjoins:

Recruits on joining the Corps must learn their drill, and that thoroughly, both the Manual and Firing Exercise, also the Bayonet Exercise and Position Drill. No recruit will be allowed to fire at the target till he has passed in the above Exercises before the Captain.

Such attention to rifle drill paid off, and the hopes of *The Carthusian* were realised in 1882, and perhaps surpassed in the years 1889 to 1892, when Charterhouse won four successive victories. Furthermore, in 1904 Charterhouse was the first British school to win the Schools of the Empire competition.

In 1908 the Corps was merged with the nationally organised Officer Training Corps (OTC), although it retained the name of the Rifle Corps until 1914. In that year of the outbreak of the First World War, all pupils were enrolled in the OTC as cadets, and 687 Old Carthusians gave their lives in that conflict. The Memorial Chapel, the largest war memorial in Britain, was built in their memory. A further 339 Old Carthusians died in the Second World War, including

Shooting team: above, 1931, and right, 2007.

Right: Adventure training in Snowdonia.

the leader of the Chindits, Major-General O.C. Wingate DSO (see page 76).

Some Carthusian military leaders were less illustrious. Colonel Smart (Brooke Hall 1904–32) was famous for issuing some strange orders on parade. On one occasion, while marching to entrain in Godalming, he threatened: 'If the marching doesn't improve I will make you mark time all the way to the station.' On another occasion, drilling cadets in Founder's Court, he ordered them to advance and walked backwards himself. He forgot the School fountain into which he disappeared except for his feet. It is recorded that the discipline of the cadets was 'not quite equal to the occasion'.

Below: CCF on exercise.

In January 1941 the name was again changed to the Junior Training Corps, and from 1951 it became known as the Combined Cadet Force (CCF). The army section now wears the cap badge of the Parachute Regiment and is joined by Royal Navy and Royal Air Force sections and also a Royal Marines (RM) detachment. Approximately half the pupils join as Fourth Formers, and all these remain members for their Under School career. NCOs continue their service as Specialists. Training extends far beyond the original remit of drill and shooting and includes first aid, navigation, command tasks and adventurous training, such as mountaineering, sailing and canoeing.

The current Charterhouse CCF continues its forebears' tradition of winning prestigious prizes. The RM detachment won the coveted Pringle Trophy (a military skills competition run at Commando Training Centre for all schools with a RM detachment) in 2007 and 2008.

The change in emphasis in training attracted Roger Smeeton (BH from 1971). Employed originally to teach music, Roger developed an interest in photography, and his first mountaineering trip was a walk up Snowdon, in jeans and suede shoes, to photograph the CCF in action. His enthusiasm for mountain walking was born, and he joined the CCF in order to run Adventurous Training, the highlights of which were the camps in Easter and summer holidays in the Brecon Beacons, the Peak District and the Cairngorms.

In partnership with the Old Carthusian CCF at that time, Bob Noble (BH from 1977) and with the support of School Staff Instructor Mick Nash, Roger devised a weekly programme of Adventurous Training for the removes in

the CCF, who had previously been mainly occupied with drill for the year. This programme also formed the basis of the present syllabus for the pioneers, first run by Peter Poolton (BH 1989–95) until his tragic death. This delivers training in self-reliance, leadership and skills in outdoor pursuits to those who choose not to join the CCF.

He also initiated a three-day expedition for removes during the field day weekend in CQ (summer term). This expedition had its origin in weekends, being spent by removes in the CCF finding 'treasure' buried on Exmoor the previous Easter holiday by Roger and Peter Reeves (BH 1984–2006). All removes, members of the CCF and pioneers still take part in the annual three-day expedition at the end of the CQ. They complete a 30-mile route around West Sussex in groups of four to six, finding their own way, spending two nights under canvas and carrying their own food and shelter. At each camp site they complete a command task, which might be 'defusing' a nuclear bomb or creating a work of art. The three-day expedition is used as a practice silver expedition for those taking part in the Duke of Edinburgh's Award Scheme. The Award Scheme has been run at Charterhouse since 1957, and its certificates make clear what might be expected of every Carthusian: participating in a physical activity, developing a non-physical skill, planning and executing an expedition, and service to the School or local community. In 2002 Fay Dalby (R) became Charterhouse's first winner of the Gold Award while still at school.

Charterhouse formed its Scout Troop in 1927, coinciding with the arrival of Baden-Powell's son, Peter (S 1930), at the school. It is perhaps surprising that Charterhouse had not formed its own troop sooner, but

the assumption was that public school boys were already enjoying most of the benefits of Scouting under their school regime. The Scout Troop provided outdoor activity for those boys who were too young to join the Corps, teaching the universal Scouting skills of camping, cooking, map and compass work, and practical construction skills. Baden-Powell took a keen interest in the troop, presenting a troop flag and, in 1938, donating an inter-patrol trophy that he had made himself – a

Above left: Camping at Cwm Cywarch.

Above: A snow hole.

Below, clockwise from left: David Loader at scout camp, 1935; Baden-Powell with Charterhouse scouts, 1928; Scouts, c. 1930.

bronze bust of Captain John Smith, founder of Virginia. By 1939 the troop had 60 members and divided into two, 1st and 2nd Charterhouse. During the Second World War the annual Charterhouse Scout camp took on a more serious role as a farming camp, to help bring in the harvest at Forde Abbey Farm in Chard, Somerset. During the 1950s the Senior Scouts (later re-formed as a mixed Venture Scout Unit) were established as a separate entity, led for some years by Wilfrid Noyce (W 1936, BH 1950–61). A national reception for Queen's Scouts was held at the School in 1953, and a South African Scout contingent stayed at Charterhouse following the 1957 World Jamboree. The School hosted celebrations of the 75th anniversary of Scouting in 1982, and of its centenary in 2007. Distinguished visitors on these and similar occasions have included at least three Chief Scouts and HM the King of Sweden as Chairman of the World Scout Foundation. The Foundation kindly contributed to the restoration of the statuette of a Scout created by W. Goscombe John, sculptor of the statue of Thomas Sutton. The Charterhouse Scout Group is no longer active, but Charterhouse continues to promote Baden-Powell's Scouting values of service to others, self-reliance and enjoyment of active challenges.

Stephen Venables advising a Carthusian climbing novice.

George Mallory

Mallory (BH 1910–21) became an assistant master at Charterhouse in 1910, teaching English, history and French. A quiet, shy man, he had difficulty controlling his classes – Robert Graves commented that 'he tried to treat his class in a friendly way, which puzzled and offended them' – but he was at his best outside the classroom, taking boys on mountaineering trips and encouraging the debating society. He was killed in June 1924 while attempting to make the first ascent to the summit of Mount Everest.

The Mallory Group commemorates the most famous name in a long tradition of distinguished mountaineering at Charterhouse: George Mallory was lost on Everest in 1924. Wilfrid Noyce played a part in the successful 1953 Everest expedition. Through Tom Peacocke's (BH 1970–6) membership of the elite Climbers' Club, Carthusians have been able to use Climbers' Club huts throughout Britain, and Stephen Venables (G 1971) was the first Briton to climb Everest without carrying oxygen.

The group was started in 1955, and the first log book contains this entry:

Small parties of Senior Scouts had been going climbing under the leadership of Mr Noyce in Snowdonia and on the sandstone outcrops in the Tunbridge Wells area [Harrison's Rocks]. However, after a very successful meet in Wales in April 1955 which, although it had started as a Scout enterprise, consisted mainly of non-Scouts and many non-Carthusians, it was decided to form a Mountaineering Club in the School.

Wilfrid Noyce

A scholar at Charterhouse between 1931 and 1936, Wilfrid Noyce became Head of School. A distinguished author and poet, he returned to Charterhouse to teach between 1950 and 1961, but he is remembered above all for his extraordinary skill as a mountaineer. When he was young he startled Alpine circles by the breakneck speeds at which he and Armand Charlet achieved difficult climbs, and he achieved similar fast times with Hans Brantschen. Twenty years later he was leading intimidating north faces. In spite of a serious accident when a turf ledge gave way on Scafell East Buttress, he was one of the best climbers on British rock before the war and 25 years later was still leading routes of good Very Severe standard. Not only fast and tough, he seemed tireless. He climbed Pauhunri (23,385 feet) in just over a fortnight from Darjeeling and reached the top of Trivor (25,370 feet) in a day of 14 hours with a sick companion. His part in the successful ascent of Everest in 1953 gets less than its due in Hunt's book.

He was killed when the ice on the ridge slid away with him and Roger Smith after ascending Garmo Peak (about 22,000 feet) in the Pamirs.

Mrs E. Freake, Librarian (BH 1969–85)

Wilfrid Noyce's son, Jeremy (R 1971), returned to the Pamirs in 2009 to visit his father's memorial. Pictured here (centre) with Stewart Hawkins (R 1956) and Peter Norton (V 1957).

On Wednesday 11 May a meeting was held in Mr Noyce's hashroom, and the Charterhouse Mountaineering Club was founded with Mr Noyce as President and R.L. Hills (R) and S.J. Hawkins (R) as joint secretaries. The names of 40 were taken, and afterwards it was decided to limit active membership to those over 16 on account of the risks involved. This rule, though, could be overlooked in certain cases. There was also to be no entrance fee or terminal subscription.

Graham Howlett (BH 1964–2001) was the last to lead regular outdoor rock-climbing trips. On his retirement from climbing, Roger Smeeton, having now left the CCF, took over the name of Mallory Group and has led many Fifth Formers and Specialists on mountain walking expeditions to Cornwall and Snowdonia on Activities Weekends (as Field Day weekends are now called), sometimes camping, sometimes staying in huts or bunk houses. Another common destination was the Peak

District, where the group often employed the services of freelance mountaineering instructor Ken Dibble (universally known as Ken D). When the group went on night hikes to visit the wreck of a Second World War bomber on High Shelf, Ken would secrete himself in the wreck and test the nerve of the mountaineers by pretending to be the ghost of the dead pilot.

Some of Roger's most ambitious trips were to India between 1983 and 2000, to trek at high altitude in Kashmir and Ladakh. Stories from these trips are legion. Once the expedition arrived at a camp at 19,000 feet to find the local population in a state of alarm as a snow leopard had slaughtered many of their flock. Later that day some boys spotted this rare animal, and all at the camp immediately gave chase – the locals with sticks and stones, the Carthusians with cameras. Carthusians also played cricket against a local team at the world's highest cricket ground at Leh, where a century partnership

The rare snow leopard.

between Al-Fareed Rehman (G 2000) and Robert Bogdan (BH from 1975) proved decisive in Charterhouse's favour.

The inclusion of an indoor climbing wall in the Queen's Sports Centre has revived interest in climbing at Charterhouse, and Richard Crowsley (BH from 1973) has taken Carthusians climbing at Harrison's Rocks again.

Charterhouse acquired the abandoned grammar school at Tideswell in the Peak District in 1975. It was used for field trips for academic departments, the CCF and the Mallory Group and, in the tenure of Andrew Morrison (BH 1973–81, 1994–7) as Master of the Under School, Fourth Forms were schooled there for a week and took advantage of the area to visit coal mines, factories,

Above right: Expedition to Himalayas.

Right: Cricket at Leh.

Jodrell Bank and Chatsworth House. However, the School calendar became more crowded, the number of trips decreased and the discovery of dry rot in the roof led to the closure of the centre at the end of 2003.

Fourth Form expeditions are now run on a House basis, and Roger Smeeton again started the trend. He ran a trip to Tideswell for yearlings in Robinites where he was House tutor under Ian Blake (BH 1968–94). This group went to paint at Chatsworth, but later the weekends were spent walking and camping when Roger again teamed up with Bob Noble as tutors in Pageites. As he moved between Houses, Roger took the idea of these weekends for yearlings with him, and other Houses followed his lead. Such weekends, providing boys new to the school with valuable shared experience beyond the confines of Charterhouse, are now almost universal.

In 1963 four men, inspired by President J.F. Kennedy's suggestion that well-trained marines should be able to hike 50 miles in 14 hours, took up the challenge and finished in 13 hours 10 minutes. It may be that R.M.M. Flowerdew (B 1965) was, in turn, inspired by this feat to organise what became known as the Fifty-Mile Walk. The first such walk took place on 7 March 1964, when 11 runners and 21 walkers set out to complete in 20 hours three laps of a loop from Charterhouse to Runfold, Tilford, Hindhead, Milford and back to Charterhouse. One who didn't finish, writing in *The Carthusian* of June of that year, salutes those 'who battled on against eight

Above: Pupils exploring Bagshawe cavern near Tideswell.

Left: Phoning home before the advent of mobile phones.

Below: Fourths' expedition.

156

Above: A team participating in the Fifty-Mile Walk, 2010.

Right: A team at the end of the 50 miles.

degrees (F) of frost on a black and windy night, against aching muscles and sore, sore feet, against the same ups and downs between Runfold and Hindhead, against the undulating monotony of the A3 back to Milford, and then up the final stretch to the "Squirrel" and home, cursing, swearing, no doubt, but each determined "to get back if it kills me"'. Now nearly all first year Specialists take up the challenge to walk the 50 miles from the outskirts of Brighton back to Charterhouse in under 24 hours during the last week of CQ (summer term). They start in the afternoon and walk through the night, past checkpoints manned by beaks and matrons. Blisters and stories of endurance and hallucination from fatigue are paraded as badges of honour, and the tie awarded to successful finishers as they pass under Brooke Hall arch is worn with pride. Anyone seeing them at the finish would echo the words of that correspondent in *The Carthusian*: 'What a sense of achievement – of personal triumph – shined in each exhausted competitor as he struggled in.'

CHAPTER 5:

Old Carthusians

CHAPTER 5:

Old Carthusians

HIGHER EDUCATION AND CAREERS
Angela Bailey

Every year, at least since 1614, when there are records of scholars at Charterhouse, a cohort of Carthusians has set out on diverse career paths that reflect not only their own aptitudes and abilities but also the state of the nation as a whole.

In the 17th and 18th centuries the guiding principles for these paths were based on class and family tradition. The parental backgrounds of only six of the original scholars are known – they were from the professional classes, including a surgeon, an attorney and a clergyman. A hundred years later scholars came from broadly similar backgrounds.

Each year scholars leaving the School competed in Greek and Latin for one of 24 exhibitions of eight years' duration at a Cambridge or Oxford college. In 1627 each exhibition was worth £16 a year, giving the scholar the opportunity to get a university degree and the Church preferment that normally went with it. University study was limited to classics and divinity for the most part.

A long line of Carthusians returning from university to the School for a teaching career stretches from William Middleton, who became Schoolmaster in 1626, to Michael Gillespie, who left Robinites in 1998 and joined Brooke Hall in 2002. Brooke Hall is, in fact, named in memory of Robert Brooke OC, who followed William Middleton as Schoolmaster in 1628. The vast majority of Carthusians going to university in the 17th and 18th centuries, however, found a career in the Church. The Charterhouse livings were virtually reserved for Carthusians, and five

English sees – Chester, Chichester, Ely, Gloucester and Norwich – were occupied at some point in the 18th century by bishops who had been foundation scholars at Charterhouse. Pupils not considered fit for further learning were 'bound apprentice', and as the School was in the city there were many opportunities. The 'city' it seems has always been a career destination for Carthusians.

There was a marked change in the career paths of those not going to university by the 18th century. Carthusians were apprenticed to surgeons, apothecaries and attorneys rather than tradesmen, but more

OC Bishops at the Lambeth Conference of 1920: (back row l–r) W.L. Vyvyan (Zululand), L.H. Burrows (Sheffield), H.K. Southwell (Lewis), H.L. Wild (Newcastle)

(Seated l–r) B. Pollock (Norwich), E.S. Talbot (Winchester), E.C.S. Gibson (Gloucester).

significantly Britain's maritime expansion needed mariners and soldiers, and the East India Company became a significant employer of Carthusians as cadets and writers.

Examples of Carthusians achieving distinction in their careers in the 17th century are Joseph Henshaw, who became Bishop of Peterborough, and Isaac Barrow, Professor of Mathematics at Cambridge, who resigned his chair to his pupil Isaac Newton. At the turn of the century

Right: Joseph Addison OC: essayist, playwright, conversationalist and hymn writer, 1672–1719.

Below: The Tatler *was started in 1709 by OC Richard Steele writing under the pseudonym of Isaac Bickerstaff. It covered politics and popular topics such as fashion, entertainment and gossip from London's clubs and coffee houses. Steele was later joined by Joseph Addison, who steered the newspaper towards cultural and moral issues and literary criticism. In 1711, the two men launched* The Spectator *which proved to be hugely successful.*

Joseph Addison and Richard Steele, both writers and politicians, broke new ground in British journalism with *The Tatler*, *The Guardian* and *The Spectator*, and during the 18th century John Wesley, as a tutor at Lincoln College, Oxford, set demanding standards in requiring to see his pupils once a day, including Sundays. Sir William Blackstone did become a lawyer, although he retained a distinguished teaching post as the first Vinerian Professor of Law at Oxford.

The early 19th century witnessed a Carthusian prime minister, Lord Liverpool, a Carthusian Archbishop of Canterbury, Manners Sutton, and, until 1818, a Carthusian Lord Chief Justice, Lord Ellenborough.

With the Industrial Revolution – the age of steam, technology and, most importantly, empire – Britain was turning into a more urban, industrial and commercial society. The binding of the 'colonies' to the motherland became stronger as distance had effectively been abolished by steamship and the telegraph, and this bond required many men to support it especially those educated in the public schools. The rise of Charterhouse at this time reflects the success of its clientele, who tended to be from clerical, professional and trading families rather than the landed gentry. The curriculum widened to include more English, mathematics, history and geography, a foreign language, one of the natural sciences and music or drawing – in fact, the curriculum was not far removed from that of today.

Although the majority of Carthusian graduates still went into the Church, the empire provided many Carthusians with careers, particularly in the armed forces and the Indian Civil Service. Two notable Carthusian judges in India were Sir Henry Russell and Sir Joseph Arnold. Employees in the Indian Civil Service were generally exceptionally hard working, conscientious and dedicated to British imperial ideals. Carthusians, as others educated in Victorian public schools, had imbibed through their education a true sense of patriotism and a vocation as guardians of the empire. It was believed that the best proof of a man's fitness to rule India was to have been good at games at school. The Carthusian example of this ideal is Sir Elliot Graham Colvin. He played 1st X1 football in 1878, won a Blue at Cambridge in 1881 and played in the Old Carthusian FA Cup winning side the same year. In 1882 he passed the examination for entry into the Indian Civil Service and worked there tirelessly for the next 36 years.

Of the 225 boys who entered Charterhouse in 1872 and 1873 (the first two years of the School in Godalming), 33 went to Oxford and 23 to Cambridge. Eventually 30 went into the army, 23 into the Church, 17 became solicitors and five barristers. In the list of Carthusian distinctions for 1894–5 there are 11 awards at Oxford, nine at Cambridge, 12 in the army and four in the Indian Civil Service.

During 1902 and 1903 the Army had become more prominent, accounting for 60 careers among the 300 who left the School. The Church had declined to six. Twenty became solicitors and five barristers while medicine had grown from five to 14 and engineers from six to 19. The biggest increase was in those proceeding to university, with 42 entering Oxford and 67 going to Cambridge.

Major changes in higher education and careers began in the years following the Second World War. In the more egalitarian atmosphere of postwar Britain, examinations became much more important as a means of regulating entry into university and careers. The professions demanded first A levels and then degrees. Practically all boys at Charterhouse now stayed on to study for A levels, but increased competition for places at Oxford and Cambridge meant that other universities came into the reckoning for the first time. In 1958 about a third of leavers achieved places at Oxford or Cambridge, and others went to other established universities, Durham, Bristol, Exeter and Southampton being most in demand. The most popular choices of career in the 1950s were commerce and industry (18 per cent), accountancy (8 per cent) law, medicine and engineering (all 7 per cent) and the armed services (5 per cent).

I have a careers encyclopedia published in 1952, rubber-stamped 'Hodgsonites House Library', which I keep to remind myself how rapidly the nature of careers changed in the late 20th century. The traditional graduate career path of a Carthusian in 1952 is still recognisable today – a 'good' university degree followed by entry into one of the established professions such as law, accountancy, banking, medicine, journalism, science and engineering. In the postwar years Charterhouse has produced distinguished judges, doctors, academics, writers, cabinet ministers, a chief of defence staff, an editor of *The Times* and a chairman of the CBI, but the big changes have been in the career opportunities outside the traditional male graduate labour market. Emigration to the 'dominions of Australia, New Zealand, Canada,

Football 1st XI team of 1878 with E.G. Colvin seated in the centre.

South Africa and Southern Rhodesia' was a favoured path for many Carthusians in the postwar era. The 1952 careers encyclopedia has a special section for women, albeit added at the end. It makes the point that almost all responsible positions in 1952 were held by men and the list of suitable professions for women contained in the appendix omits key careers such as banking, law, the Church, engineering and business.

The advertisements of this period show the inequality of career opportunities at this time and must seem almost unbelievable to the Carthusienne of today. Since girls were admitted to Charterhouse in 1971 they have competed equally for places at university (indeed they prove slightly more successful than boys in gaining places at Oxford and Cambridge), and they have forged ahead in career areas previously thought unsuitable for women. A role model is Natalie Davies, who left Charterhouse in 2001 to read engineering at Selwyn College, Cambridge. Having obtained her Masters degree she joined Shell to work as a project engineer, and she has been based in the Netherlands, dealing with the restructuring of the gas

processing infrastructure on the Groningen field to make gas supply more efficient and environmentally friendly.

In recent times the UK higher education system has undergone a major transformation from being one where a small number of universities catered for an elite group of entrants (about 5 per cent of an age cohort in 1960) to one where a much larger set of institutions aims to provide higher education to half the national population as well as a number of international students. Male full-time undergraduate numbers were 241,000 in 1970, and this figure had more than doubled by 2000 to 511,000. For female undergraduates the increase is three-fold, from 173,000 in 1970 to 602,000 in 2000.

Given the scale of this expansion, university application has become a more complex decision-making process, especially as competition for courses at the best universities becomes ever more fierce. Perhaps not surprisingly, many Carthusians decide to take a gap year on leaving school so that they can apply to university when their examination results are known. 1994 seems to have been the high point for gap years. Of the 98 per cent of leavers who went on to a degree course, 75 per cent of them did so after a gap year. 22 per cent went to Oxford or Cambridge that year (a figure that has been typical for the last 20 years or so). Almost half applied to humanities and social science courses, and 16 per cent to science and engineering. The recent appearance of US universities as destinations for our leavers is something that seems likely to grow.

Practically all leavers in 2008 went on to higher education, the majority to their first choice of university, and about 48 per cent after taking a gap year. A total of 96 per cent went to universities in the UK, with the remainder going to the USA or Hong Kong. There were 11 Oxford and 11 Cambridge places (12 per cent) in this year group; the next most popular universities were Edinburgh (16), Bristol, Durham, Newcastle (12), Leeds, Nottingham (11), Exeter (8), Imperial College, Manchester (6), LSE and UCL (5). In the leavers 2008 year group the most popular courses were engineering, maths and sciences (27 per cent); social sciences (20 per cent), including economics, politics and human geography; humanities (20 per cent), including history, English, philosophy, theology and classics; arts (9 per cent), including music, art and theatre studies; modern languages (8 per cent); medicine (6 per cent); and business and management (6 per cent). Carthusians were admitted to over 100 different courses.

The graduate of the 21st century is much less likely to follow a straightforward career path in a traditional graduate job. Graduate occupations have opened up in new professions and new employment niches, particularly in management, finance, information technology and creative areas of the media. More Carthusians are now becoming software engineers, computer programmers, advertising executives, hedge fund managers and property developers – doing a huge variety of jobs that take them all over the world. Setting up a business is still an aspiration for many. Brett Akker left Charterhouse in 1993. Ahead of the game in thinking about a low-carbon economy, in 2004 he launched the car club Streetcar in London. Starting with eight vehicles in 2004, the club now has over 70,000 members and operates from 1,000 locations across seven UK cities.

The career paths of Carthusians may vary, but I hope that the education, advice and guidance given at the School will continue to provide them with a decent map and compass to help them on their way.

A Career in the Bank

Never before have opportunities for young people been as promising as they are today in Barclays Bank. Here is a brief outline of the career that awaits you there.

The Bank wants young men of character and integrity, with a good standard of general education. Given these qualifications and an aptitude for the job, there is no reason why you should not find yourself a Branch Manager in your thirties, with a salary upwards of £1,300, and the chance of doubling your pay by the time you are 50. Looking right ahead you could even be one of those Managers whose salary exceeds £3,000 a year—a man with a big job, full of interest and responsibility. A goal worth striving for: and those who reach it will have a pension at 65 (without any contributions on their part) of £2,000 a year or more.

Moreover, the biggest jobs in the Bank are open to all. In the meantime, your salary at the beginning of your career will be keeping pace with changing times. If you come into the Bank at 16 you will start at £260 a year. By 20 you will be getting £340, by 26 £620 and by 31 £800. All this is for normal work and responsibility; many young men in the Bank are earning salaries well over these figures. Moreover, if you come in later, with G.C.E. at advanced level, you will have a year's seniority on the salary scale; coming in later still, from the University, three years' seniority.

CARTHUSIANS IN ACADEMIA

Charterhouse can boast a number of eminent academics, including the historians Hugh Trevor-Roper and Lawrence Stone. Isaac Barrow, Professor of Greek and Mathematics at Cambridge, was mentor to Sir Isaac Newton.

Henry George Liddell

Best known as the co-author of Liddell and Scott's Greek Lexicon, familiar to generations of schoolboys and still the standard dictionary for scholars of Ancient Greek, Liddell was the son of a Durham clergyman and was educated at Charterhouse in London between 1823 and 1829, boarding in Watkinson's house. He went up to Christ Church, Oxford, in 1830 and remained there, as undergraduate and then student (don), until 1846. Liddell was headmaster of Westminster School between 1846 and 1855, before returning to Oxford as Dean of Christ Church. His other claim to fame is that his daughter, Alice, was the original namesake for Lewis Carroll's *Alice in Wonderland*.

John Sinclair Morrison

A Bodeite Junior and Senior Scholar from 1926 to 1932, Morrison was also Head of School. He won a scholarship to Trinity College, Cambridge, and embarked on a prestigious career as a classicist and author. He was Professor of Greek and head of classics at Durham University from 1945 to 1950, tutor at Trinity College, Cambridge, and then vice-master of Churchill College from 1960 to 1965. He was an expert on the Greek trireme, and his work led to the reconstruction of an Athenian trireme. He became the first president of Wolfson College, Cambridge, in 1966. He was a governor of Charterhouse for 25 years, dying at the age of 87 in October 2000.

Michael Prestwich OBE

Michael Prestwich (R 1961) began his academic career at St Andrews, before moving to Durham University as Professor of History and, in later years, Pro-Vice Chancellor. He has written extensively on 13th-and 14th-century history, perhaps most notably in his biography of Edward I and his volume of the New Oxford History of England, *Plantagenet England 1225–1360*.

Lawrence Stone

Robert Birley recognised Lawrence Stone's potential and coached him for a history scholarship to Christ Church, Oxford. As an undergraduate, Stone was greatly influenced by another famous Old Carthusian historian, the medievalist Michael Prestwich. Stone began his academic career in Oxford after the Second World War as a lecturer at University College, but he moved to

Michael Prestwich sliding down a refectory table in Robinites watched by friends, c. 1958. Photo courtesy of Hugh Marsden (R 1960) who remarked: 'It shows one of our more honourable pastimes before TV encroached on us!'

Left: H.G. Liddell, Dean of Christchurch, from Vanity Fair, 1875.

Princeton in 1960. A prolific writer, Stone's greatest impact was in the area of social and economic history in the 16th and 17th centuries.

Hugh Trevor-Roper, Lord Dacre

Hugh Trevor-Roper joined Daviesites in 1927 as a scholar and rose rapidly in academic terms. His younger brother, Patrick, also came to Charterhouse and pursued a distinguished medical career. A solitary, self-reliant boy, Hugh Trevor-Roper nevertheless thrived at Charterhouse, becoming head monitor of Daviesites and editor of *The Carthusian*. While not a natural sportsman, he commanded the Daviesite platoon of the OTC, and it was accepted that he did not wish to take part in school team sports, preferring long-distance running and studying butterflies. Trevor-Roper announced to his headmaster, Frank Fletcher, that he wished to study mathematics as a Sixth Form Specialist, only to be told that this was not possible because 'clever boys read classics'.

Trevor-Roper won a classics scholarship to Christ Church, Oxford, but lost enthusiasm and switched to history. He became a research fellow at Merton in 1937 and published his first book, a biography of Archbishop William Laud, in 1937. During the Second World War he was recruited by the Radio Security Service, a branch of the SIS, as a code breaker, later transferring to MI6. In November 1945 he was asked to investigate the circumstances of Hitler's death, leading to his acclaimed publication *The Last Days of Hitler* (1947).

Trevor-Roper returned to teach history at Christ Church from 1946 to 1957, becoming Regius Professor of Modern History in 1957. He was created Baron Dacre of Glanton in 1979 and was appointed as Master of Peterhouse, Cambridge, in 1980. Sadly, he was among those academics who were deceived into believing that the bogus 'Hitler Diaries' were genuine. This much-publicised controversy in 1983 dented his academic standing.

Left: Dr Leonard Noon (V 1896) with John Freeman carried out ground-breaking research into the treatment of allergies. In 1911 they published their findings in The Lancet *describing the first successful treatment of hayfever. Their work is viewed as a forerunner of modern-day immunotherapy.*

Above: The new Hunt Health Centre opened in 2009 is named after Lord Hunt of Fawley (S 1924), who was instrumental in setting up the Royal College of General Practitioners.

Left: Medical trunk belonging to Dr Clarence Haig Brown, School Doctor from 1886 to 1929.

MEDICINE AND SCIENCE

Brooke Hall science teachers have often included eminent specialists, such as the botanist Oleg Polunin and the biologist Oswald Latter, and their passion for their subjects has inspired many Carthusian medics and scientists. The earliest recorded Carthusian doctor was Henry Levett, born in 1668, who was elected physician to St Bartholomew's Hospital in 1707 and became physician to Charterhouse in 1713. Later examples of eminent medical men include Sir George Paget (P 1827), who became Regius Professor of Physic at Cambridge and President of the GMC, and Sir Edward Buzzard (G 1890), who was Regius Professor of Medicine at Oxford and Physician Extraordinary to the King. Arthur Farre (day boy 1821–7), a Professor of Obstetrics, was also physician to the monarch; and Sir Edward Tuckwell (S 1929) was surgeon to Queen Elizabeth II. Sir Harold Ridley (P 1925) and Patrick Trevor-Roper (D 1934) were both eminent ophthalmologists.

Among many famous scientists are Gregory Bateson (R 1922), a renowned anthropologist and communications theorist, and pathologists Leonard Noon and John Freeman, who undertook joint research at St Mary's Paddington.

The new Charterhouse Medical Centre is named after Lord Hunt of Fawley (S 1924), who was co-founder of the Royal College of General Practitioners.

THE MEDIA

Don Cupitt

The theologian, writer and broadcaster was born in 1934 and won a junior scholarship to Charterhouse in 1947, joining Bodeites. Cupitt was an exhibitioner at Trinity Hall, Cambridge, and then trained for the Anglican priesthood at Westcott House, Cambridge, being ordained deacon in 1959 and priest in 1960. After a curacy Cupitt returned briefly to Westcott House as vice-principal before being appointed Dean of Emmanuel College, a post that he retained until 1996, in addition to teaching the philosophy of religion at Cambridge.

Cupitt's work began to be published in the 1970s, but it was his participation in the controversial 'Myth of God Incarnate' symposium in 1977 that first attracted hostile attention from the media. Cupitt was involved in a series of thought-provoking programmes for the BBC during the 1970s, in which he challenged comfortable, established Christian thinking and encouraged the faithful to explore their doubts and question what they really believed. Cupitt's book *Taking Leave of God* (1980) provoked an outcry from traditionalists and caused the press to brand him an atheist, although the then Archbishop of Canterbury and the Master of Emmanuel defended his right to express his ideas. Cupitt ceased officiating at public worship in the early 1990s but continued teaching and writing, developing his ideas in a long series of books and encouraging a new approach to philosophy and religion.

David and Jonathan Dimbleby

These two luminaries of the media world were both Duckites. David Dimbleby was at Charterhouse from 1952 to 1956, going on to study politics, philosophy and economics at Christ Church, Oxford, where he also edited *Isis* and was a member of the Bullingdon Club. He then embarked on a highly successful career as a journalist with the BBC. He is a major presenter of BBC television current affairs programmes and documentaries such as his series on the history of Britain. He has chaired flagship programmes, including *Panorama* and *Question Time* and has acted as commentator for many national events, such as the funeral of Diana, Princess of Wales in 1997 and the Queen's Golden Jubilee celebrations in 2002. He is regularly the anchor man for coverage of national and international political events, such as the general election and the US presidential election.

Jonathan Dimbleby was educated at Charterhouse from 1958 to 1962, and studied philosophy at University College, London, before following his brother into a career as a television and radio reporter. Jonathan has been a regular political presenter for ITV since 1972, mirroring his brother's role with the BBC. His programmes have included *This Week*, the Jonathan Dimbleby in Evidence series and *First Tuesday*. He currently presents ITV's weekly flagship political programme, *Jonathan Dimbleby*. Jonathan has chaired BBC Radio 4's *Any Questions?* since 1987 and began presenting *Any Answers?* in the following year. In 1994 he wrote and presented a documentary on the Prince of Wales, *Charles, the Private Man, the Public Role*, and published his book, *The Prince of Wales: a Biography*. In 1997 the BBC screened *The Last Governor*, his series on the final five years of British rule in Hong Kong, with an accompanying book. Recently he wrote and presented series on Russia and Africa. Jonathan Dimbleby is President of the Soil Association and a trustee of the Richard Dimbleby Cancer Care Fund and the One World Broadcasting Trust.

Left: Jonathan Dimbleby being interviewed for the School magazine, 2000.

Above: Max Hastings.

Below: David Dimbleby.

Above: Sir Christopher Walford (G 1954), Lord Mayor of London, 1994.

Above right: Lord Rees-Mogg.

Sir Max Hastings

A prolific journalist, author and broadcaster, Max Hastings was a foundation scholar in Bodeites from 1959 to 1963 and won an exhibition to University College, Oxford. However, he left after one year to pursue a career in journalism. He became a foreign correspondent for the BBC and the London *Evening Standard*, reporting from more than 60 countries and 11 wars, including the Falklands War. Max Hastings then became editor and editor-in-chief of the *Daily Telegraph* before moving back to the London *Evening Standard* as editor in 1996. He retired in 2001 but continues to write. He was knighted in 2002.

Gerald Priestland

Another example of the many Old Carthusians who have followed successful media careers, Gerald Priestland joined Daviesites as a junior scholar in 1940 and went on to New College, Oxford, in 1945. He was a writer and broadcaster for BBC radio and television, first as a foreign correspondent, and then as BBC religious affairs correspondent.

Frederic Raphael

A well-known screenwriter, novelist and journalist, Raphael was in Lockites from 1945 to 1949. His most acclaimed screenplays include *Darling* (which won him an Oscar in 1965), *Two for the Road* (nominated for an Oscar in 1967), the 1967 film adaptation of Hardy's *Far from the Madding Crowd*, and *Eyes Wide Shut*, written in collaboration with Stanley Kubrick. Raphael has also written more than 20 novels, the best known of which is the semi-autobiographical *Glittering Prizes*; he has also published several history books and writes regularly for a variety of newspapers and magazines, including the *Los Angeles Times* and *The Daily Telegraph*.

Lord Rees-Mogg

A leading political editor, Lord William Rees-Mogg (V 1945) is the former editor-in-chief of *The Times* and a member of the House of Lords. His writings on political issues are always insightful and influential – his comments in the *Sunday Times* were said to have convinced Alec Douglas-Home to resign as Tory leader, making way for Edward Heath in 1965 – and he has been credited with accurately forecasting glasnost and the fall of the Berlin Wall, as well as the 1987 economic crash. Rees-Mogg has also been a member of the BBC Board of Governors and chairman of the Arts Council.

Sir Ronald Millar

An actor, playwright and speech writer to three prime ministers, including Margaret Thatcher, Sir Ronald's unique talent for words rendered his speeches unforgettable and his phrases, such as 'the lady's not for turning', have entered political history. He joined Saunderites as a junior scholar in 1933 and went on to King's College, Cambridge, in 1938. Following wartime service with the RNVR, he embarked on a career as an actor, appearing in many West End productions, including *Waiting for Gillian*, *The Bride and the Bachelor* and *The Affair*. He also wrote plays for the London stage and many Hollywood film scenarios, including *The Miniver Story* and *Rose Marie*. Sir Ronald died in 1998, leaving a generous bequest that enabled the Charterhouse Library to be refurbished. His papers are held in the School Archive.

POLITICS

Throughout its history, Charterhouse has produced politicians and statesmen who have influenced national events. Childhood friends Sir Richard Steele and Joseph Addison both became MPs, but are best remembered for their collaborative efforts to produce *The Tatler* and *The Spectator*. Charles Jenkinson, 1st Earl of Liverpool, became the first President of the Board of Trade in 1786

167

and was known as the King's Secret Adviser; his son, Robert, 2nd Lord Liverpool, holds the record as the longest serving Prime Minister apart from Margaret Thatcher. More recently Lord Wakeham has had a distinguished career in the House of Commons and, since 1992, in the House of Lords. Despite the tragic death of his wife in the Brighton bombing of 1984 and sustaining serious injury himself, Lord Wakeham went on to be Leader of the House of Commons and House of Lords, and Secretary of State for Energy.

James Prior had an equally impressive political career, holding a number of ministerial posts, including Minister of Agriculture, Secretary of State for Employment and Secretary of State for Northern Ireland, as well as a stint as Leader of the House of Commons. Jim Prior showed early signs of entrepreneurial flair and interest in agriculture while he was still at Charterhouse, organizing a successful business scheme to raise pigs and offering fellow pupils shares in the project. He was created a life peer in 1987.

In 2005 Jeremy Hunt (W) was elected MP for southwest Surrey, the School's constituency, and in 2010 he was appointed Culture Secretary.

LORD BEVERIDGE

William Beveridge, 1896.

The social reformer and economist was a junior and senior scholar and exhibitioner in Girdlestoneites between 1892 and 1897 where, despite a lack of talent at sport, he was appointed Head Monitor. Beveridge excelled in both classics and mathematics. Leonard Huxley coached him in chess and also had a profound influence on his political views. Beveridge won an exhibition to Balliol College, Oxford, where he gained first class honours. He went on to study law and looked set for a glittering legal career when, to his parents' horror, he gave up law in favour of studying social reform. Beveridge joined campaigners calling for old age pensions, free school meals and help for the unemployed. In 1906 he became a leader writer on social problems for the *Morning Post*, and in 1908 Winston Churchill invited him to join the Board of Trade. In 1916 Beveridge drafted a new Unemployment Insurance Act, but he was widely opposed and found himself excluded from the new Ministry of

Labour and sidelined instead to the Ministry of Food. In 1919 he became director of the London School of Economics, and in 1937 he was appointed Master of University College, Oxford, and was also elected a Fellow of the British Academy.

During the Second World War, Ernest Bevin asked Beveridge to chair an inquiry into the coordination of social services, which Beveridge initially saw as an insignificant task; but he soon realised that his recommendations could radically improve British society. He carried out a detailed survey of the failings of the social services, focusing particularly on unemployment, health care and poverty among children and the elderly. The Beveridge Report of 1942, recommending a free national health service, family allowances, strategies to maintain full employment and social security for all, met with an enthusiastic response from the general public but little enthusiasm from the government. In 1943, however, parliament forced the government to accept Beveridge's main proposals, which were then implemented by the welfare state legislation of 1944 to 1948. In 1946 Beveridge was made 1st Baron Beveridge of Tuggal and he eventually became leader of the Liberal Party in the House of Lords.

THE OLD CARTHUSIAN CLUB
Joe Ullman (W 1959)

The Old Carthusian Club is the official club for former pupils. Originating in 1874 as the Greyfriars Club, it was renamed five years later as the Old Carthusian Cricket and Football Club, adopting cerise, dark blue and pink as its official colours. In 1922 the name changed again to the current style, and committee membership opened to other sports and activities.

Among the 77 presidents to date are such famous names as Lord Baden-Powell (G 1876), Lord Alverstone (S 1897) and Prince Albert of Schleswig-Holstein (S 1888), a grandson of Queen Victoria. However this ultimate OC honour was refused by some. C. Aubrey Smith (G 1881), the renowned cricketer and actor, declined in 1947, preferring to return to Hollywood to resume his postwar screen career there. Similarly, Ralph Vaughan Williams (R 1890) felt strongly that other commitments would prevent him from being able to take an active share of the work. Four past Headmasters and several long-established members of Brooke Hall have

Old Carthusian Football Club v Arsenal, 22 April 2006.

held the office, as have prominent Old Carthusians from law, medicine, politics, theatre, business and the armed services, with each House being represented at least twice.

Affairs of the club are managed by an elected committee, to support the endeavours of the clubs and societies that operate under its aegis. Old Carthusians have the opportunity to extend and enjoy sporting camaraderie and keep the School name prominent in prestigious competitions. OC Football Club teams and Charterhouse Friars Cricket Club have won distinction in major competitions, such as the Arthur Dunn Cup and Cricketer Cup. The Old Carthusian Golfing Society was a founding member of the Halford Hewitt Cup competition in 1924 and the OC Yacht Club has thrived and competed since 1935, with one member winning a gold medal in the 1948 Olympics. Since the 1930s other OC teams have regularly played fixtures in fives, squash, racquets, hockey, lawn tennis, athletics and cross country, and the Rifle Club has maintained a strong record at Bisley.

In 1978 a club room and bar was created in the Long Room above Crown, overlooking the familiar and virtually unchanged vista of Green with Big Ground beyond, thus providing a base for Carthusian hospitality after matches and other functions. The building has since been renamed the Peter May Pavilion in honour of England test cricketer P.B.H. May (S 1947), who died in 1994.

The OC Medical Society for graduates and students of medicine, dentistry and allied professions has been in existence since 1884. More recently the OC Property Association and OC City Association have been formed, giving an opportunity for those sectors to meet, as does the OC Livery Association for liverymen of other companies.

The remit of the club has broadened to embrace the formation of an Art Society, the revival of the Music Society, an Old Carthusiennes Association representing the strong contingent of girls over 40 years, with future plans for other cultural activities and enthusiasm to develop new initiatives. *The OC* magazine started in 2008 as an annual publication with an Old Carthusian perspective.

Membership of the club is open to all Old Carthusians over the age of 18, normally from the time of leaving School or at a later date on application. Long-serving members of Brooke Hall are elected as honorary members and since 2009 have their own distinctive tie.

Traditionally, Old Carthusians living or serving around the world have met together, often on or around Founder's Day in early December, to share reminiscences of their Charterhouse education and propose the toast 'Floreat!' Possibly the most unusual was a small dinner in 1928 at Gullmang, Kashmir, 'in the clouds' at 9,000 feet. Such gatherings continue today with volunteer ambassadors spanning most of the globe. House associations, too, arrange social functions and support the Houses. Old Carthusian Day (latterly Carthusian Day) takes place annually during CQ when the School is open to Old Carthusians, parents and friends, and reunions are organised for specific year groups.

THE CARTHUSIAN TRUST
David Williams

The Carthusian Trust was created in 1972. It sprang from the desire of a number of Old Carthusians to build up a permanent fund that would enable Charterhouse to maintain its traditional excellence and also help it to meet the demands that the new and challenging developments in education bring to the School.

The Carthusian Trust is a registered charity set up as a permanent fund to promote the active participation of Old Carthusians, parents and friends of Charterhouse. The Trustees operate independently of the Governing Body, although close links exist. Under the terms of the trust, trustees are given extensive powers with regard to their application of capital and income, and their management of the trust. It is their policy to retain and safeguard all monies given or bequeathed, and through investment to provide substantial income that will provide additional bursaries to the School. In addition, the trust assists with financing planned developments of the School.

The Carthusian Trust has been active in raising funds for the Ben Travers Theatre (BTT), the John Derry Technical Centre and the new music school. More recently the trust was a forum for fundraising for the Queen's Sports Centre. The Carthusian Trust continues to play an active role in fundraising, both as a forum to raise money and also as an entity to ensure that money is spent according to donors' wishes. The School has also established a Development Office to coordinate fundraising efforts for the next 400 years.

THE CARTHUSIAN SOCIETY
Margaret Mardall

The Carthusian Society was formed in May 1938 by the committee of the OC Club with three objects: to foster relations between the School and Old Carthusians, to provide amenities for the School that help to enrich life there, for which the Governing Body could not reasonably be expected to pay, and to provide additional finance for the OC Club. Membership is open to all Old Carthusians and to any person interested in Charterhouse or Charterhouse activities.

The society's income derives from the investment of various bequests and other gifts and from members' annual or life subscriptions. The committee meets three times a year, and the term of president normally lasts for five years. Many illustrious OC names have held that office, steering the society forward to its current charitable status.

Grants have been made to support a large variety of sporting and cultural activities, enabling many pupils to benefit during their time at School. Examples range from sleeping bags and tents for Scouts in the 1950s, a telescope for the Astronomical Society in the 1960s, archery bows, arrows and targets in the 1970s, to more recent acquisitions of a coxed four boat, new blades and rowing machines for the Rowing Club and DVD/multimedia equipment for the sixth form club.

Considerable funds have been contributed to the preservation, restoration and digitisation of the many volumes of Mrs Haig Brown's scrapbooks, which are a unique treasury of information in Archives, and to the 2009 publication *From Cloister to Cup Final, a History of Charterhouse Football*, written by Malcolm Bailey.

Several substantial grants have also been made to the Ben Travers Theatre towards furnishing the foyer, lighting and other purposes. Its workshop was built with the help of a bequest to the Society. The Beatson Memorial Garden has recently been created between Fletcherites (formerly Northbrook House) and the Central Dining Hall, thanks to a bequest to the Carthusian Society from Robin Beatson (W 1944).

Sailing

Many Carthusians developed a love of sailing whilst at School, which they have carried on into later life as members of the OC Yacht Club.

Wartime Sailing at Broadwater

Instruction was there none. We learned by our own experience, and probably picked up some bad habits in the process. Paint and varnish were also non-existent – we never thought about what would happen if we had to replace the sails, and replacement rope came from my Lords of the Admiralty via the Naval Section (without their knowing, admittedly).

It was truly messing about in boats. Winds tended to be either too high or almost a calm. There was a bit of racing, but most of us were far too busy getting the boats to go where we wanted to get much involved with that.

Brian Russell OBE (G 1945)

Above: Sailing club, 1949.

Left: Winners of Baden Powell Sailing Trophy, 1952.

Below: Sailing today.

Above: OC Yacht club member, Michael Briggs (B 1962) sailing his yacht, Mikado.

CHAPTER 6:

A Wider Community

CHAPTER 6:

A Wider Community

BEHIND THE SCENES
Catherine Smith

Charterhouse can only function with the support of an army of domestic, administrative and grounds staff, who are an essential part of the School community. There are currently nearly 300 support staff, who make sure that pupils and beaks are fed and housed and that the grounds and buildings are properly maintained. In many cases, support staff choose to stay at Charterhouse for their entire career, and some families have been employed over several generations.

William Veale, for example, worked at Charterhouse all his life, starting as a part-time errand boy in 1885 when he was only 10 years old. Veale's father was the Headmaster's private butler, moving with him from London to Godalming in 1872, and his mother had been Mrs Haig

George Mandeville, Charterhouse carter and odd-job man for over 30 years, and C.B. Lee, House butler, drawn by Art Master C.W. Johnson for The Greyfriar, *April 1903.*

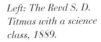

Left: The Revd S. D. Titmas with a science class, 1889.

Brown's housemaid. William Veale left School when he was 14 and became an assistant in the School stationery shop and laboratory technician for the science master, the Revd S.D. Titmas, a somewhat risky occupation. Pupils recalled one of Titmas's favourite phrases: 'This is a very dangerous experiment. Veale, hold the test tube.'

In 1914 Veale and his wife were asked to take over the management of the sports pavilion tuck shop, Crown, and they continued to provide sports lunches, teas and homemade confectionery for over 30 years. Hugh Bayley (H 1933) also remembers obtaining supplies from 'Buttery':

Although we obtained things like ice creams at Crown, the House butler (not meaning Thomson's private butler), an old, much-loved character named Bill Denyer, who presided over 'Buttery', sold biscuits at 6d a time. How well I remember his 'Vandro' and 'Bourbon' biscuits and shouting 'Tizzy Vandro' or 'Tizzy Bourbon, please, Bill' (i.e., 6 pennyworth). He ruled it over two 'Buttery boys' (nastily called 'buttery hops' by us) – two lads from the town who waited on us at table.

Veale published his memories of Charterhouse, *From a New Angle*, in 1957, providing a fascinating insight into the lives of the staff who maintained the school behind the scenes.

More recent managers of the tuck shop, from 1988 until 2003, were Sue Cole and Diana Whitney:

The tuck shop is known to the boys as Crack. This name derives from the slang, half-a-crack (in old money half a crown), which relates to its origins in Crown, a feature of the London Charterhouse. Until its refurbishment in 2003, when management was taken over by the School caterers, the premises, the cash till and the style of the shop were indeed still notably traditional.

A large range of 1p sweets, a long shelf of 10p bars, homemade fudge and much more brought boys into the atmosphere of a social centre. At the busiest times takings were over £1 a minute, at a till which predated the management, from a crowd which 'queued', perhaps three deep, along the length of the counter. They wouldn't otherwise have fitted into a very small room.

The counter was high, bar height; it was essentially a talking shop, almost a dry pub. This was especially valued on Sunday afternoons when very few boys were in School at weekends, and in winter, when the fact that the heating was manually controlled was a bonus. Conversation over the counter was wide and deep ranging; 80 per cent were addressed by name, perhaps making it easier to share events and emotions. So joys (passing a driving test, winning colours) were celebrated; stress (exams, relationships) shared; problems (parental, academic) discussed. One boy described the service as 'counselling'. Another, a frequent visitor, agreed at the end of one term that he hadn't once bought anything. A third suggested that as no one knew him better, perhaps the shop staff would write the reference for his UCCA form. It was a very stimulating atmosphere to work in.

At the end of a pupil's career, if he was taking A levels, he was allowed to go to the head of the 'queue'

Left: Millie and Lou Mann celebrating their retirement from the School Clothing and Sports Shop in 1977, which they ran for more than 28 years, initially with the Tuck Shop as well. Both served on Godalming Town Council, with Millie spending two successive years as Mayor.

Below: 'Young' Mr Dean supervising a swimming class.

when he had done the first exam. A small reward for five years' loyalty.

Mrs Sue Cole

The legendary 'Old Dean' and 'Young Dean' are still remembered fondly by Old Carthusians and by local children whom they taught to swim. Father and son, both named Edward Dean, ran the swimming pool at Charterhouse, while three other children of Mr Dean senior worked as butler, gardener and cook at the School. In total, the Dean family clocked up 146 years of service.

'Old Dean' was originally a stonemason who came to Charterhouse to work temporarily on the Museum building, but when he saved three men from drowning in the river Wey, Dr Haig Brown offered him a job at the new School baths. After his retirement in December 1928 'Young Dean' replaced him in the same job. The Deans are remembered for their character and dedication, and for catchphrases, such as 'You *can't* swim? There's no such word'.

More recently, the Sykes family has maintained a working connection with Charterhouse for over 30 years. Mike Sykes was appointed as head gardener in 1974, and his wife, Gloria, started as a cleaner in Lockites and soon was promoted to be a maintenance clerk. Their children and foster children enjoyed having the entire Charterhouse grounds as their playground and, as teenagers, all benefited from pocket money earned in part-time holiday jobs at the School. Graham Sykes joined the Charterhouse grounds staff as soon as he left school, relishing the opportunity to learn how to maintain one of the finest school sports grounds in the country; he later transferred to the gardens department, following in his father's footsteps. Graham's sister, Elaine Downes, has also worked at the School for many years and was appointed as Daviesites matron in OQ (autumn term) 2009.

Before the days of modern electrical appliances each House had a large team, including a butler, cook, kitchen maids, housemaids, buttery boys and errand boys, usually managed by the Housemaster's wife or the matron. In 1872 the Headmaster's wife, Annie Marion Haig Brown, listed the servants at her new home in Godalming as follows:

I have 16 servants –
Nursery – Bayly, Hannah, Pamela
Kitchen – Stannard, Mrs Norman and Mrs Smith's daughter
Housemaids – Elizabeth Reed and Laura Reed
Pantry – George and a page
Scholars' Pantry – Bayly, Charles and a page
Matron – Mrs Eldridge
We have also Winton, coachman and postman out of doors and Norman Pigman, Cloister cleaner and general fag.

Each Housemaster employed his own staff, so there were no central School records and very little information has survived about most of them. A Girdlestoneite memorandum dated 1900 set out the kitchen maid's daily routine as follows:

6.30 am Must be down in the kitchen
7 o'clock Stove must be cleaned and fire lighted
7.55 Servants' breakfast to be ready
9.15 Young men's beds must be made
10 o'clock Kitchen must be ready, scrubbed and thoroughly dusted
10.30 Servants' coffee ready
12 o'clock Dining room's vegetables to be cleaned and servants' dinner ready – 12.30
3 o'clock Kitchen **must** be cleared
4.30 Tea for drawing room
'Servants' tea
6 o'clock Vegetables to be cleaned <u>ready</u> for dining room dinner
8.45 Servants' supper ready
9.15 To help scullery-maid to clear away
10 o'clock Bed.

Mike Syskes with his children Graham and Elaine.

Domestic staff, probably Saunderites, c. 1872.

Matrons have always provided much-needed maternal care, commonsense advice and practical support for the boys, and generations of Old Carthusians remember their House matron with affection and gratitude. Miss J.C. Young, matron of Daviesites from 1924 to 1940, kept all the correspondence that she received from 'her boys' after she retired. These letters, now in the School Archive, demonstrate the affection and regard in which she was held. Her obituary, published in *The Carthusian* in 1943, records: 'Each boy meant something to her as an individual, and from the time she befriended him as a new boy, cheering him with that stray piece of cake, to the day when he visited her in the dignity of advancing years for coffee and bridge, and was allowed to know something of her ready wit and surprising powers of mimicry, she had his best interest at heart.'

Miss Bland Jameson, matron of Bodeites from 1922 to 1929, recalled her daily routine:

Up early, in order to be on duty in my room before the House began scrambling down the stone stairs, past my door, in haste to be in time for early School and early chapel ... After the boys' breakfast, a number of them always surged up to my room for any regular medicines that I had to give out or to have bandages changed. It was through these daily calls that I got to know the individual boys ... I soon made a habit of watching all the games of cricket and football that I possibly could; I suppose I felt that one could tell a good deal about a boy's character and also spot the scrounger who was asking to be let off School and yet thoroughly enjoyed games, by watching the games. When the House was in School, there was always the linen to sort and keep in repair and the clothes back from the wash to check and mend ... And perhaps more important

than any of these activities, was the habit, that grew out of small beginnings, by which the monitors and elder boys, for whom it was not compulsory to have lights out by any particular hour, stayed on in my room, chatting and arguing – not about who was likely to get his colours, but about the burning questions of the day.

Miss Anna Dodgson, Lockites matron, c. 1930.

Charterhouse cadets parade in Godalming at the proclamation of Edward VIII's succession, 1936.

TOWN AND GOWN
Brian Souter

Eight days after the School's arrival in Godalming, on 26 June 1872, the mayor and Corporation of Godalming paid a ceremonial visit in four open carriages to present an address of welcome to the Headmaster who, after a suitable expression of thanks, conducted the civic dignitaries around the new buildings. Thus began a continuing relationship between town and gown.

With its arrival on Frith Hill, the School became overnight a major source of employment in the town and as T.E. Page was to say at a later mayoral banquet: 'United to Godalming by the deep and dear attachment of a common sewer.'

Page, the founding Housemaster of Pageites, was a classical scholar and notable public speaker, and he and F.K.W. Girdlestone were first elected to the borough council in 1892. Page went on to become an alderman

and a county councillor as well as a JP and freeman of the borough. For reasons best known to himself, Page declined the offer of the mayoralty, but Girdlestone, who was also a alderman and JP, did not and became mayor twice (1893–4, 1898–9).

The next member of Brooke Hall to become mayor of Godalming was P.C. Fletcher, who served three terms (1924–5, 1930–31 and 1936–7). *The Greyfriar* of March 1925 records that during Fletcher's first year as mayor the school presented the town with a badge of office and chain to be worn by the mayoress. Later, in March 1937, *The Carthusian* reported that in recognition of Fletcher's third term as mayor, a silver mace was presented by the governors, members of Brooke Hall and Old Carthusian residents of the borough.

In keeping with this fine tradition, during the mayoralty of B.R. Souter (BH 1970–2004, mayor 1988–9) the Governing Body presented the town with a badge of office and chain for the deputy town mayor.

Coincidentally, Brian Souter served as both a Godalming town councillor (1979–91) and a Waverley borough councillor (1981–9) while living in the same house, Oakhurst, in which Fletcher had lived while mayor. More recently, two former members of Brooke Hall served as successive mayors, R.A. Gordon-Smith (BH 1982–97, mayor 2007–8) and P. Rivers (BH 1976–8, mayor 2008–9).

Other notable contributions to Godalming civic life by members of Brooke Hall were from Everest mountaineer Wilfrid Noyce (BH 1950–61), after whom the Youth and Community Centre in Godalming was renamed, J.R.S. Mash (BH 1961–78) and D.H. Darbishire (BH 1956–85), while J.C. Thomson (BH 1909–47) was a notable county councillor.

For many years the retiring collection from the late-evening carols has been donated to the Godalming Old People's Welfare Association, while the School's buildings and grounds have often been a welcome venue for local events. The Godalming Theatre Group uses the Ben Travers Theatre for three productions each year, while the Godalming Music Festival uses chapel and the Vaughan Williams Music School.

David Wright, the Housemaster of Hodgsonites, has been for some years the musical director of the Godalming town band, while productions of the Godalming Operatic Society meant that for many years J.H. Sparks (BH 1968–2002) appeared at parents' evenings in a variety of theatrical attire and make-up.

The relationship between 'town and gown', which began in 1872, continues to this day and is beneficial to all concerned.

PUBLIC BENEFIT
David Williams

The School provides public benefit through the provision of bursaries, through teaching activities outside the School and by generally opening up its facilities for local and charitable use. In addition, a number of pupils have a long tradition of taking part in charitable activities as well as raising money for specific causes.

Bursaries
Under the terms of the will of Thomas Sutton, the School was set up to provide funds for scholars. The School receives an increasing number of applications for bursary support, and, wherever possible, the bursar attempts to find finance for bursaries. Funds applied to scholarships have reduced from 100 per cent and 50 per cent down to the current 10 per cent of fee level, and the funds saved from this reduction have been applied to the provision of bursaries.

This is a fundamental ethos of the School and continues the long tradition of making the School accessible to a number of pupils whose parents would otherwise be unable to afford the fees. The School has an active policy of raising additional funds for bursaries, and this provision is likely to continue as it reflects the overall ethos of what was originally set up in 1611.

The School opens its facilities for commercial activities during the School holidays. In addition, the School shop operates as a commercial activity. Profits from both these functions are applied on an annual basis to the bursary fund.

Charitable Activities
Charterhouse has many established links with the community through sporting events, regular activities and higher educational courses. A number of our regular links include those with the Godalming Youth Orchestra, Godalming Choral Society and the Godalming Theatre Group, as well as the facilities of the Chapel, Hall and Ben Travers Theatre, which are used continually during the School holidays as venues for a number of organisations. While the School does charge for the hire of these facilities, all profits are applied to the bursary fund.

SCIENCE PUBLIC BENEFIT
Stephen Hearn, Science Public Benefit Coordinator

In common with many independent schools, Charterhouse has a long history of sharing its facilities and resources. This is relatively easy to do.

Charterhouse has, however, become unique among independent schools in the last five years because of our commitment to working with science teacher training institutions. We have, like many independents, also developed significant links with state school science departments.

Over the last six years, I have built links with key institutions, including the Institute of Physics, the Royal Society of Chemistry, the Association of Science Education and the Science Enhancement Programme.

Charterhouse pupils are encouraged to help in the community. This pupil is providing teaching assistance at a local primary school.

These disparate groups now work together with Charterhouse to help deliver a substantial public benefit programme in science based at the School.

The Charterhouse science team has run a free science Easter revision course for the last four years. Local state school children visit the science department for three days' intensive science coaching. Meaningful links are now developing with the science department at Broadwater (a Godalming state school). Last year Charterhouse helped on a weekly basis with a year nine group's study of physics, and this project will be extended this year to help the school deliver separate subject physics at GCSE.

This very local work is building on Charterhouse science projects with King's and Christ's Colleges in Guildford and a six-year project with the Park Community School in Portsmouth. Groups of up to ten Park teachers visit Charterhouse on a regular basis for in-service training in physics. The Park project is well developed now, and teachers and pupils from Park are comfortable when they visit Charterhouse.

After working long and hard to develop links with Southampton, Reading, St Mary's, Roehampton and Brunel Universities, the Charterhouse summer residential course in physics and chemistry is now nationally recognised as excellent. The course attracts over 200 delegates during two weeks in July. The students on the course are going on to take up teacher training posts in the autumn, and they attend to improve their subject knowledge in physics and chemistry. The network naturally established as a result of attendance at the summer school is making a major contribution to supporting the teaching of physics and chemistry in the state system.

The summer course is followed up with two-hour Saturday-morning sessions in the Charterhouse science department, from October through to March. These sessions attract on average 20 students, many of whom attended the summer courses.

Schools like Charterhouse can make a big impact in the state system by such projects. Offering to set up and host such courses as those discussed here will improve subject knowledge and help build support networks that will foster the development of teaching talent in the state system. Because of our work in science over the last six years, we now have several state school teachers and university lecturers who regularly work in partnership with Brooke Hall teachers.

CHARITY WORK
Annie Hardie

The history of charitable work in the School dates back to the foundation by Thomas Sutton. His plans to create the foundation in the latter part of the 15th and early part of the 16th century were described as the greatest philanthropic act of an era, and 'a Phoenix of Charity in our time'. Certainly no single action since has produced such lasting benefit, but over the years both pupils and masters have sought to help those less fortunate than themselves, for with privilege comes responsibility.

Over the last hundred years a variety of fundraising events has taken place, and in School today the charity work continues. The Charity Committee with a member of Brooke Hall and representatives from all the Houses continues to organise events and to select charities to support. Mufti days are always popular and are an easy

way to involve everyone and to raise money. Every House now supports a major charity as well as a smaller local or international one, and money raised from mufti days goes directly to these.

Links with India

In the course of 2008, Charterhouse students raised £25,000 for the Rhema Partnership through a student-led music concert and a dinner for parents followed by an auction. The Rhema Partnership supports the work of the Church in Tamil Nadu, southern India, primarily in the Cumbum valley. And this was the destination of a trip to India in December 2008, led by Richard Lloyd. On our arrival we received a warm welcome from Bishop Samuel and the other members of the Rhema Garden. We were struck by the friendship that was extended to us by all at Rhema, and it helped to make our visit there an unforgettable experience.

The partnership cares for orphaned children, children with disabilities, and it also runs a Bible college. The money Charterhouse raised has been used to build the Charterhouse Ward, providing access to medical facilities to the surrounding 35 villages. We all tried to make a constructive contribution by physically working there – some of us redecorated the

home for disabled children. I set up the roof structure of the medical centre, which opened in 2009. But what made our work there special was the wonderful opportunity to talk to the Indian people, play with the children and discover what they are achieving with such limited material

means. When we returned we had not only witnessed personally how productively the money we had raised was being spent; we had seen how much happiness it was bringing to such a poor area.

Luke Liddle (G 2009)

Opening of the Charterhouse Ward in the Rhema medical mission in February 2009.
l–r: Charles Wallendahl (R 2008), Bishop Gnanaprahasam, Christian Hacking (H 2008), the Revd Richard Lloyd.

Above and above left: Performers at the Lack of Talent show.

Right: The Revd J.G. Curry (right), first Missioner of Charterhouse in Southwark 1885–8, with a colleague.

Below right: The Charterhouse Mission premises in Tabard Street, London.

CHARTERHOUSE IN SOUTHWARK
Shirley Corke

The mission, Charterhouse in Southwark, started in 1885 to help those living in the appalling conditions exposed by the Inquiry, 'The Bitter Cry of Outcast London'. Throughout its life Carthusians (including beaks) have provided donations, members for the general (managing) committee and help in Southwark activities. Owning buildings secured survival. The girls' clubs (1930) faced St Hugh's Church with the clubs for men and boys (1892) in Crosby Row. The original base in four Tabard Street houses, with a church in the basement (1885), was

The Lack of Talent show, now an annual event, was inspired by two girls from Bodeites 12 years ago. It has grown from a one-night show to a three-night spectacular, with music, dancing and sketches, raising thousands of pounds for charity. There are also concerts, as there is never a shortage of musical talent here at School. Large sums were raised to support the move to 'Stop the Traffick', by helping the organisation formed to raise awareness about present-day slavery and people trafficking.

CHAPLAINCY LINKS WITH INDIA
Richard Lloyd

Charterhouse chapel has growing links with missions in southern India through senior chaplain, the Revd Richard Lloyd (W 1994, BH 2004–10). He has established a close relationship with Anglican Bishop Samuel Gnanaprahasam in Theni District, Tamil Nadu, southern India. There have been three chaplaincy trips to Tamil Nadu over the past three years, with over 60 pupils visiting. Six pupils have also spent part of their gap years working at the missions. The chaplaincy trips are designed to give pupils exposure to poverty and the ways in which the Church is serving and meeting the needs of the poor. These missions care for orphans and widows, run two schools for children with disabilities, a rural hospital, countless vocational training and local caring programmes in the 26 communities in which the mission has newly established churches and dedicated pastors. The mission is resourced by its own theological college, which provides certificates, diplomas and degrees in applied theology, and trains over 40 young people annually to lead churches and social projects in order to transform society.

Residents outside a tenement building in Southwark.

these distinctions were to disappear, such bodies would become otiose. He appears to have thought this point had been reached. Nonetheless, he went on to turn 40 Tabard Street into an air raid shelter, from where boys' club members worked stalwartly to help in (or after) air raids.

After the Second World War, the Church began to play less of a role in the borough as socialist legislation, the work of the London County Council (and later the Inner London Education Authority), and the introduction of newly-trained social workers, all contributed to improving conditions for Southwark residents. However, progress was slow as the borough grew in size while its traditional jobs in the docks declined sharply. It became home to many refugees and immigrants and by the 1990s the area was the second most deprived borough in England.

Secularisation could not be avoided. The new employees were expensive, and despite several successful initiatives it became ever harder to fit in visits of boys going in either direction. Professionally qualified staff wished to have more say in what went on. In 1985 Steven Lancaster, a Cambridge social scientist with wide experience of working with and for charities, was appointed to the new post of director, with the specific task of increasing the work of Charterhouse in Southwark. A new statement of objectives was issued, based on the policy of persuading people to help themselves. An endowment appeal was opened (not for the first time), and many successful short-term initiatives were embarked on. The number of both staff and projects increased. All went spectacularly well for a time, and the name of the mission gained a high profile.

Steven was followed in 1995 by directors who found it increasingly difficult to maintain the momentum as all fundraising flagged. New rules about building regulations and the treatment of children appeared. Gradually, more and more of the seats on the managing committee were occupied by Southwark people, many being professionals. Schemes already in progress could not be completed without making inroads into capital assets. Finally, in 2009 the decision was made to cease working with individuals who needed help and instead to become a charity giving grants to organisations engaged in such work. Two of the antiquated buildings should be sold.

The Christian presence in Southwark was there to help individuals without the ability to help themselves. Such people still exist. Where now will they find such another ever-welcoming open door?

rebuilt as no. 40 in 1937. A football pitch in Eltham came in 1933. Carthusians, encouraged by William Haig Brown and aware of the smoke he had rescued them from, did not forget the charitable origin of their own school. Other public schools had outposts in the slums, but probably none has ever equalled the generosity of OCs. Supporting the mission was not obligatory for boys, any more than for masters or even Headmasters.

The mission has always flourished best when the School was most involved. While the Haig Brown family was in Godalming, most of Brooke Hall and their wives and families shared in the Southwark children's Christmas party and the summer expedition to the school. The most memorable of many assiduous workers has to be Leslie Ferguson OC, whose determination to make boys in London clubs feel themselves proper Carthusians enrolled them all – down to the five-years-olds, 'the Smallest Carthusians' – as members of Godalming boys' Houses and created a magazine for the London Boys, *The Ace of Clubs*.

Father P.M. Gedge OC (Missioner 1931–43), who wrote the chapter on the mission in E.M. Jameson's *Charterhouse* (1937), pointed out that school missions enable the privileged to help the unprivileged, but that if

Charterhouse and Hill School pupils compete to build and race radio controlled sailboats.

HILL SCHOOL, POTTSTOWN, USA
Stephen Hearn

When I became interested in developing links with an American boarding school, Tony Bennett suggested that I contact the Headmaster of the Hill, David Doherty, whom he had known for some time. The Hill is a boarding school situated in Pottstown, a steel town in Pennsylvania, which in its heyday produced the steel for the Golden Gate Bridge. While the town has seen hard times, the school flourishes.

I was hoping to establish particularly good links in science, part of which would be an exchange scheme for science students. I visited the school for the first time in 1994, and slowly our relationship grew. Ryck Walbridge was head of science at Hill during my time in that role, and we worked together on many ideas. We have established good links and a working partnership that has seen a regular science trip every year for the last ten years, a theatre trip, choir visits, football matches, a teaching exchange and the Headmasters exchanging houses in the summer.

The science link is the most developed. We started five years ago the annual challenge. Ryck Walbridge of the Hill has this to say about it:

Six years ago, Steve Hearn and I were sitting in my biology classroom talking about ideas of increasing our two schools' activities. For several years Charterhouse with Steve had been bringing his physics classes to the States and using the Hill School as a base of operations. It had been pretty one-sided up until this point. We had both seen a Discovery show on a competition between the US and UK on who could build a better trebuchet. That show struck a chord with us both. and from there the challenge was born. We have competed every year for the last six in competitions ranging from building a trebuchet, building a human-powered light bulb, racing an America's Cup radio-controlled sailboat, to this year a 'robot wars' challenge. Now the Hill School takes an annual trip to Charterhouse and competes in the spring, and Charterhouse reciprocates. This has been a healthy exchange of cultures, and ideas for over ten years.

The annual science trip gives Carthusians a chance to visit Ivy League colleges, world-famous research labs and sometimes meet Nobel prizewinners. We have met three in the last ten years, including the controversial James Watson. At Brookhaven National Lab we are renowned as one of the few high schools outside New York that visits. This lab allows our students to witness world-class science and engineering. Carthusians, of course, get time in New York and Washington.

The important feature of this project is that it encourages interaction between school pupils from different cultures. This has led to pupils from both sides of the Atlantic developing long-term friendships.

The Hill–Charterhouse relationship is not just about science exchanges. Teachers in both schools can make use of others' facilities and resources to develop curriculum materials and educational projects. We all have a unique opportunity because of our partnership.

CHAPTER 7:

Charterhouse Today

ERNST ZILLEKENS

CHAPTER 7:

Charterhouse Today

ERNST ZILLEKENS

At present interest in the School is considerable, and one of the questions prospective parents often ask is: 'What has changed in the School in recent years?'

Where does one begin? The actual physical appearance of the School is an easy starting point. Beginning in reverse chronological order, the most recent addition is a Sixth Form day House, which opened in September 2010 in the refurbished building formerly occupied by the medical centre; medical care has been moved to modern premises, opened in November 2009. The main focus of the preceding building improvements and additions was on the academic side of the School. A new modern languages centre was officially opened in 2007 by Perez de Cuellar, former Secretary General of the United Nations. Its airy rooms benefit from modern technology. Before that, the former shop block was converted and renamed the Beveridge Centre, in memory of the former Old Carthusian politician and economist, to house economics, business studies and politics as well as the careers department.

Modern languages centre, opened in 2007.

To mark the millennium a small chapel for private prayer was created in the northeast end of the Memorial Chapel.

Another building, which was reconstructed and reopened in 2004, is the library, which is now the academic heart of the School, the central resources centre that houses the borrowing stock in all subjects. The architectural changes that were made in the refurbishment are significant. A concrete floor, which had been inserted into the Victorian building in the late 1960s, was removed, bringing the building closer to the Victorian original. Considerable attention was paid to improving the aesthetic quality of the building in the choice of the new design. This has introduced a gallery and mezzanine structure and incorporated all the hashrooms that surround the building. One of them is a seminar room housing the greater part of the Carthusian Collection of authors. But what is more important than these physical changes is the change in perception of the library. It is no longer regarded as somewhere to go and work as a Second Year Specialist in the run-up to A levels, but rather as a welcoming working environment, where all

year groups of the School come and work or sit and read at different times. The Archives, which resided in the Daniel Wray and Gilbert Edgar Rooms in the old library, were housed in their own premises in the cloisters in 2002, in a strong room, work room and search room; they hold an extensive range of records illustrating the rich and varied life of the School.

Above: The refurbished Library.

Charterhouse Chapel today

The chaplaincy at Charterhouse continues to provide spiritual leadership, counsel and nurture. The chaplaincy vision is best expressed in five words beginning with P: praying, preaching, pastoring, philanthropy and preparing.

Praying – leading the community in prayer, worship and praise to God during four compulsory and four voluntary weekly services and praying daily for the needs of Charterhouse and the world.

Preaching – communicating the Christian gospel afresh to this generation in a manner that is contextually relevant and engaging.

Pastoring – providing pastoral support to pupils with the attachment of a chaplain to each

boarding house, with visits during banco once a fortnight and for lunch weekly. The chaplains are always available to meet any member of the community.

Philanthropy – exposing the reality of global poverty during an annual chaplaincy trip to witness the work of Christian missions that care for the poor in southern India. The chaplaincy also seeks to highlight issues of social concern and injustice, engaging with the needs of our local communities.

Preparing – mentoring and equipping future Christian leaders and servants and encouraging young people to take part in acts of service and compassion.

Richard Lloyd

Special attention has also been paid to improving the up-keep of the grounds and the general maintenance of School buildings. A new lighting system was installed in chapel, and the Saunders Room and Hall were refurbished. When the walls were stripped down to the bottom layer, the colour that emerged turned out to be almost identical to the new one that had been chosen!

Significant improvements have also been made to the pastoral provision in the School, especially to the facilities for the girls. The girls' hall, Chetwynd, was built and additional accommodation added in Northridge and Long Meadow, so that the School can now accommodate more than 100 girls.

At the same time the girls continue to be fully integrated into the 11 boarding Houses, where they have an additional study and participate fully in the life and duties within their respective Houses; the sixth form is much more coeducational than in the early days of girls' admission. The new tutor system, which was introduced in 1996, is linked to boarding Houses, where on arrival each pupil is attached to a particular beak who remains the tutor throughout the pupil's time in the School. Tutors can therefore develop a thorough knowledge of their pupils and monitor and aid their progress effectively. Housemasters, whose role is now firmly focused on pastoral matters, continue to make a major contribution to pupils' development overall. The system of pastoral care was rated as outstanding in the 2007 ISI inspection.

The new academic management system consists of deputy Headmaster, assistant Headmaster (academic), assistant Headmaster (pastoral) and Head of Girls. Together with the Headmaster, senior Housemaster and the bursar they form the management team. Its decisions play a pivotal role in the formation and implementation of School policies.

The standards of School discipline were raised and implemented more rigorously, including pupils' appearance. This included the introduction of a uniform

Specialists in the kitchen at Chetwynd.

for girls, thereby ending years of inequality, during which the girls had enjoyed the liberty of choosing their own dress, not always advisedly.

Excellent results at AS and A2 level, which were achieved without repeating parts of the exam at every opportunity, has led to a significant improvement in the School's academic standing, reflected in its position in the league tables. This success has led to the School being in the forefront of the introduction of a new examination devised by the Cambridge International Board and called the Cambridge Pre-U. This examination is an alternative to the new A-level courses that were started in September 2008 and mark in a number of cases a further dilution of academic rigour. The Pre-U, on the other hand, represents the very reverse – that is, it is a demanding set of courses that reflect a synthesis of some of the requirements of A-level specifications, which ended in the summer of 2008, and the traditional A levels of the past before the invention of modular A-level courses. Like the latter, they are two-year courses that offer no opportunity for repeating parts of the examination.

In 2011 the School is hoping to broaden the repertoire of sixth form qualifications further by introducing the International Baccalaureate as an alternative to the Pre-U for those pupils who wish to continue a broader range of subjects rather than specialise in four subjects. This will

lead to further changes in the School's organisational structure, which underwent some adjustments in recent years, such as the introduction of a split banco system with homebill as a break in the middle. The balance between academic and extracurricular commitments was also improved at the same time.

Cultural activities and achievements have gained greater recognition and now enjoy parity with sporting accomplishments. Time is reserved for cultural activities on some afternoons, and they are an integral part of the activities programme for all year groups. House colours are now also awarded for culture.

The range of activities has continued to be as broad as ever. At the top is an elite society, to which pupils can gain access only by invitation, the Headmaster's Essay Society. This was founded by Robert Birley when he arrived as Headmaster in 1935. He had run a similar society at Eton, where he had taught history. Every year the Headmaster selects 12 of the brightest Second Year Specialists to meet 12 times at his house on a Monday evening. A paper is read on any subject, and lively discussion follows over a glass of wine. It has become a well-established institution in the School. The choice of topics has been, and continues to be, rich and varied and the standard of discussion very high, revealing the participants' promising levels of intellectual curiosity and knowledge:

Above left: A pupil at work in his study bedroom.

Above: School Croquet team.

Below: In the chemistry laboratory.

Charterhouse is always autumnal in my memory: dark nights, fires and a group of over-eager 16-year-olds discussing esoteric subjects with a surfeit of enthusiasm in equal measure to our lack of knowledge. This was the Essay Society, where a select group of pupils was invited for discussions of essays they each prepared in turn. I think even in our pimpled ignorance we appreciated this glorious opportunity to explore new subjects, to learn how to argue, to think on our feet. It was helpful not only in preparing for university, but also in aspects of professional life, where a quick-thinking response must be accompanied by a charismatic confidence (however much the insides may be churning). But I shall always remember it as more than that: we were learning a road map for life, absorbing a love for discussion and argument that could (and does) accompany us any place ... and how to appreciate a blazing log fire – that, too.

Victoria Carlisle, née White (g 1996)

Debating and public speaking continue to be important and successful activities in the School, providing excellent opportunities for developing coherent lines of argument and articulating them convincingly in front of an audience. Both junior and senior debating teams participate regularly in English-Speaking Union and Rotary Competitions, often with admirable success. Some of them are selected to form a team representing the School at the Model United Nations in the Hague, where groups of Carthusians have been taking part in the annual meeting for many years. The Inter-House Quiz is a popular contest and often reveals some admirable levels of general knowledge. Competitions between Houses, such as House music and singing or the House art competition, continue to flourish. A wide range of sporting activities continues to be enjoyed by pupils, and some notable successes have been achieved in recent years, such as victory in the Independent Schools Football Association cup final.

Joining Charterhouse from an all-girls school in Ireland was bound to be a change. I certainly played a lot more cricket for one thing. But new sports were not the only opportunities. Academically we were challenged, often being given the freedom to think for ourselves; for example, we spent a whole year learning 'to read' English literature. One particular memory is Eliot's The Waste Land *being vividly brought to life by Dr Holloway (David) shouting it aloud from atop a desk.*

Learning did not stop in the hashroom either; evenings were also a time for thought and discussion, usually with a glass in hand. On Monday nights a group gathered in the Headman's drawing room for the Essay Society. On Sundays it was louche relaxation chez Dr Opland as we tried to decipher William Faulkner against a background of jazz. And, of course, the best debates took place in club, fuelled by stale booze.

Some of us even tested our knowledge rather too publicly on TV's schools quiz edition of 15 to 1, *losing out to the eventual series winners. Its broadcasting during term time allowed the entire School ever so helpfully to ask us our botched questions over and over again outside crack; and I still don't know where the Euphrates flows to!*

Embarrassing TV appearances aside, those two years were a privilege and indeed proper preparation for new horizons around the corner.

Lisa Pugh, née O'Shea (L 1999)

Pupils' participation in shaping the life of the School continues. They can make their views heard in the School's Pupil Council, and they continue to support Housemasters as House monitors and the Headmaster as School monitors, helping with supervisory duties and the enforcement of House and School rules. The School monitors supervise midweek Extra School and Extra Labour.

Akin to many schools, the post of Head of School at Charterhouse is rumoured to come with numerous esoteric rights and privileges, ranging from the right to parade a goat through chapel to smoking a pipe on Green. I am not convinced of the veracity of any of these traditions but, not being a pipe smoker at 18 nor having ready access to a supply of goats, I did not concern myself with them too much when I was appointed in OQ (autumn term) 2000. My concerns were instead focused on the unique position in which the Head of School finds

himself – still a schoolboy but suddenly attending weekly meetings with the Headmaster meant that nervousness and pride came in equal measure. I need not have worried too much, however, as it quickly became apparent that I was in for the best of my five years at School. Along with the team of School monitors, who were all close friends, I was suddenly invited (and expected) to take an interest in every aspect of Charterhouse rather than the niches which I had carved out for myself in the previous four years – a blessing that meant that I came to appreciate quite what a diverse, creative and energetic place the School is before I left rather than, as is often the case, some time after. It is for this reason above all others that, nearly a decade after leaving Charterhouse, I look back on my time as Head of School with fondness and gratitude.

William Samengo-Turner (S 2001)

Lasting impressions

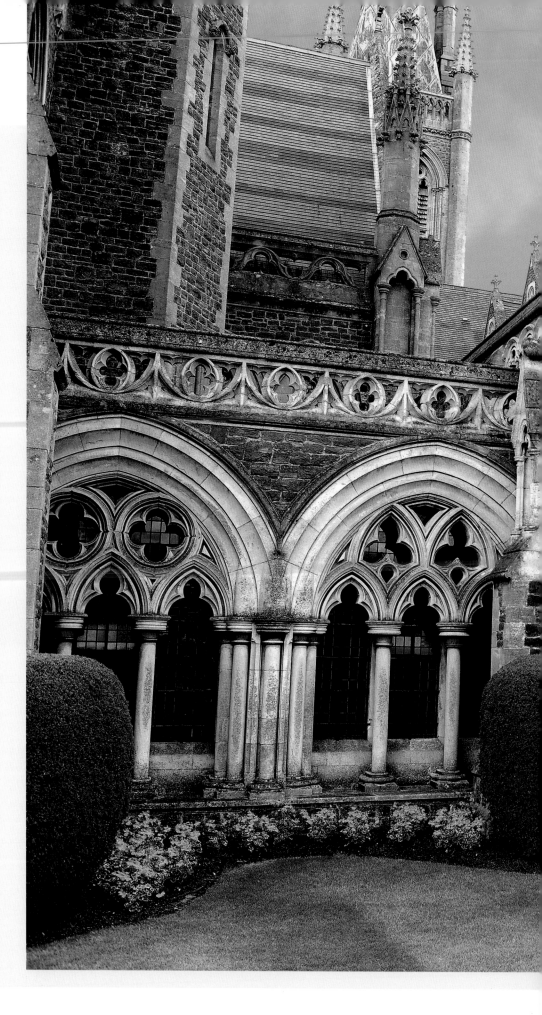

I think many Old Carthusians would agree that Charterhouse goes beyond simply educating the students who enter its gates. On the surface it is clear that the School encourages a strong sense of collective identity and belonging, but less obvious is the strength of its commitment to nurture and shape the individual, to encourage and to involve. The School's clear focus on, and belief in, the abilities of each of its students, together with an awareness of their limitations, enables it to steer them towards their as yet untrodden paths. I left Charterhouse with a strong set of A levels and with a place at a top university firmly on the horizon, but in retrospect those are merely details. Charterhouse brought me great self-assurance, laughter, determination, variety, inspiration and belonging. Perhaps however, what I cherish above all are the deep and lasting friendships that were created during those school years. Those friends are still very much present in my life today and that I owe to Charterhouse.

Amal Brihi (D 1995)

*

I did think that sentimentality would gain the upper hand. The last school lesson; the last exam; the last breakfast, lunch, tea; the last time I would do this and that; and above all the last impressive, sad chapel service and final goodbye.

And so we all file out of chapel with our books underneath our arms, some for the last time. The notes of the organ recede as we emerge into the open air. 'Goodbye, Sir.' 'What, are you leaving too?' 'Yes, Sir, I've got to join up.' 'Well, we shall miss you, especially in the soccer. What are you going into?' 'Rifle Brigade.' 'You'll meet a lot of our fellows there all right. Well, goodbye and the best of luck.' 'Goodbye, Sir and thank you. I'll be coming down sometime.' And so it goes on, quarter after quarter. Little groups outside the chapel. A strain of seriousness underneath the forced laughter.

Rt Hon Sir Geoffrey Johnson Smith PC DL
(g 1942)

*

Wilfrid Walter Timms was undoubtedly the finest teacher I had the privilege to meet. I credit Mr Timms with my life-long ability to learn other languages and even to pass for a 'native' because of my ability to grasp correct diction.

Howard John Knowles (W 1957)

*

I shall always be grateful that my parents chose Charterhouse. There you learned to stand on your own feet and there was always personal encouragement and help to achieve your ambitions. Charterhouse often entered pupils into the local Godalming talent contest, and these entries were generally in the various musical categories. On this occasion in 1956 they entered me as a magician and illusionist in the variety section. As a result of this, which I am happy to say I won, I was asked by a local organisation to appear in a charity performance. As a result I performed my first big escape, having been challenged to escape from regulation handcuffs by the local police when locked in a mailbag and secured in a locally made packing case. This was a great success; I made my escape in 10 minutes and received both national and international headlines, with journalists and others descending on Charterhouse for interviews and photos. What was not publicised, since 'housebreaking' was not on the curriculum, was my special secret on returning to Daviesites after the show: my Housemaster Percy Chapman had promised to sit up and await my return in order to let me in! On arrival I saw the lights on in Percy's study, and Percy could be seen fast asleep in his armchair. Rather than wake him up, I picked the locks to the front door, let myself in, and relocked the door and went to bed.

Tim Dill-Russell (D 1955)

*

Brian Young was a great, if aloof, example to which anyone with an ounce of ambition could aspire. All my life I have admired his one rule: 'At Charterhouse there are few formal rules. But a breach of common sense is likely to be a breach of one of them.'

His final report on me as I left in 1959 read: 'He is not an intellectual, but I am confident he will go far beyond the Charing Cross Road.' On hearing that I had been elected one of the youngest presidents of the chartered surveyors' profession he was reported to have remarked along these lines: 'A triumph for Charterhouse. And a triumph of matter over mind.' And, do you know, I found that very encouraging.

Christopher Jonas (G 1959)

*

It is almost impossible to convey what strong emotion was given rise to by the whole performance [of the Masque] … The 1929 performance, in which I took part in the choir, remains as my most vivid memory of five years at the School.

Hugh Bayley (H 1933)

In retrospect, I feel fortunate and extremely privileged to have been at Charterhouse. For those like myself who were not particularly gifted academically, there were so many other activities to experience and appreciate and from which to benefit, and therein lie many of the reasons why Charterhouse is a great school; as one passes through life it makes one proud to be able to say – 'I was at Charterhouse.'

Francis Monck-Mason (H 1952)

*

My education at Charterhouse kindled an enduring love for the theatre, but it shaped my life in a much more fundamental way, because it was here that Jay Upton inspired my love of the Spanish language and culture. She was such a breath of fresh air: hypnotically eccentric, exquisitely feminine, sartorially unique, highly intellectual and irresistibly committed to all things Hispanic. With her ebullient enthusiasm, her sense of humour and her consummate passion for the Spanish language and culture, especially its literature, she opened doors to a world that I have been exploring ever since. Following a degree and an MA in Spanish, I went on to teach the subject at Dulwich College, and then as head of Spanish at Harrow and now at Eton, where I hope to pass on JHU's baton for many years to come.

Nick Hulme (L 1985)

*

One thing that has stayed with me long after I left the School is the international peer group I met at Charterhouse. Today, as I am writing my PhD at Oxford University, I still visit school friends in foreign countries, and one of the people I am sharing a flat with is a former Carthusian whom I met during one of my first physics hashes, a little over ten years ago. Even though a lot has happened since then, occasionally we still reminisce about the two inspiring years we spent at Charterhouse.

Daniel Schwarz (P 2001)

'He's very proud of being an Old Carthusian.'
Cartoon found in a scrapbook compiled by R.N.H. Simonds (P 1928) whilst serving
with the Royal Tank Regiment in Cairo during the Second World War.

Acknowledgements

PHOTOGRAPHS

The majority of the historic images in this book come from the School Archive and Art Collection. TMI would like to thank Catherine Smith, the Archivist, for her unstinting support and meticulous research throughout the project and The Revd Stanley Underhill for his help with Charterhouse London images. Most of the modern pictures were provided by Roger Smeeton and we are indebted to him for giving us access to such a treasure trove of images. George Titus also contributed by photographing many portraits and artefacts.

Charterhouse and TMI Publishers would also like to thank those listed below for allowing images to be reproduced on the following pages: pp 16, 17, 18 (bottom), 21 (top), 22, 25, 34 Sutton's Hospital; p 19 Bill Price III; p 23 (bottom right) The Granger Collection/Topfoto; p 63 Davey family deposit/Charterhouse Archive; pp 64, 65 Kimber family/Charterhouse Archive; p 76 (bottom) Popperfoto/Getty Images; p 78 Jon Wilkie (W1959); p 80 David Ryder Richardson (S 1962); p 86 Susan Hamilton (G 1976, Mrs Mallet); p 87 (top) Katherine Armitage (D 1978); p 100 BBC Pictures; p 101 Andrew Doran (V 1987); p 112 (bottom) TSO/Hasnain Dattu; p 114 George Burton (g 1964); p 116 Peter Monkman (Brooke Hall); p 122 Helen Pinkney (Brooke Hall); pp 134 (top right), 135 (top left) Mary Evans Picture Library; pp 138 (bottom), 139 (bottom right) Popperfoto/Getty Images, medal photographed with permission of the Halswell family; p 153 (bottom) Stewart Hawkins (R 1956); p 154 (bottom) James Toller; p 157 (top) Mark Blatchly (G 1977 and Brooke Hall), (bottom) Jane Drew (Brooke Hall); p 164 (right) Hugh Marsden (R 1960); p 166–7 (DD) TopFoto/UPP, (MH) Colin McPherson/Corbis, (WRM) Getty Images; p 171 Michael Briggs (B 1972) (Mikado) and club card from Simon Strong (R 1958); p 177 Graham Sykes (Grounds Staff); p 182 Richard Lloyd (W 1994 and Brooke Hall); p 185 Stephen Hearn (Brooke Hall).

For further information please contact the School Archive (archive@charterhouse.org.uk).

CONTRIBUTIONS

Charterhouse and TMI publishers would like to thank the following people for their contributions.

Abbott, Roger (V 2003); Abecasis-Phillips, John (R 1951); Asprey, Edward (V 1962); Attenborough, Peter (Headmaster 1982–93); Austin, William (g 1945); Bailey, Angela (BH 1985–); Bayley, Hugh (H 1933); Beaumont, John (g 1947); Beckles Willson, Tony (H 1946); Blake, Ian (BH 1968–94); Blatchly, Mark (G 1979, BH 1996–); Bonham-Carter, Gerard (G 1948); Brihi, Amal (D 1995, Mrs Riachi); Brooks, Richard (R 1957); Burns, Robin (B 1946); Burrows, D.C. (L 1957); Burton, George (g 1964); Carter, Clive (D 1960, BH 1965–96); Cassidy, Richard (S 1938); Chalkley, David (B 1947); Clegg, Richard (V 1956); Cole, Susan (BH 1988); Corke, Shirley (BH 1988–2008); Coulson, Michael (W 1963); Creswell, Peter (D 1958); Darling, Michael (H 1949); Darwall-Smith, Robin (G 1981); Dehn, Conrad (S 1945); Dill-Russell, Timothy (D 1955); Edwards, Robin (L 1955); Eeley, Nicholas (G 1953); Evans, Norman (BH 1957–91); Fitzherbert, Nick (R 1975); Flower, Bill (W 1947); Ford, Geoffrey (BH 1956–92); Franklin, Richard; Freeman, J.D. (BH 2004–); Freeman, J.P. (BH 1995–); Fricker, Derek (S 1942); Froomberg, Philip (L/B 1943); Galbraith, Simon (g 1990); Gill, Alan (W 1954); Gill, Humphrey (S 1957); Giri, George (B 1941); Goodyear, Richard (G 1940); Haig Brown, Hilda; Hanley-Browne, Mark (BH 1988–97); Hardie, Annie (Matron B 1996–); Hartshorne, Bertram (G 1942); Harvie, Christopher (W 1982); Haynes, Bill (D 1952); Hearn, Stephen (BH 1985–); Hippisley, Anthony (S 1956); Holder, Robert (g 1942); Howard, Shelley (g 1977, Mrs Phillips); Hudson, Christopher (g 1949); Hughes, Christopher (g 1949); Hulme, Nick (L 1985); Jackson, Alan (D 1964); Jameson, David (R 1946); Johnson Smith, Geoffrey (g 1942); Jonas, Christopher (G 1959); Jones, Donald L. (P 1943); Kenyon, Nigel C. (B 1959); Kimmins, Simon (R 1948); Knowles, John (W 1957); Knox, Belinda (B 1978); Larking, Peter (g 1942); Liddle, Luke (G 2009); Lies, Jeffery (P 1946); Lloyd, Richard (W 1994, BH 2004–10); MacAuslan, Alan (g 1939); Mackie, J.C.S. (R 1944); Maidment, David (G 1956); Mann, Michael (S 1948); Mardall, Margaret (Staff 1985–); Marsh, Alan (S 1954); Mawer, Charlie (L 1987); McMillan, Richard (H 1994); Meares, Stan (g 1947); Mellstrom, Juliet (B 1986, Mrs Slot); Mitchell, Janey (L 1983, Mrs Wall); Monck-Mason, Francis (H 1952); Morgan, David Ll. (S 1951); Newman, Cathy (B 1992); Noble, Robert (BH 1977–); Norton, Peter (V 1957); O'Shea, Lisa (L 1999, Mrs Pugh); Page, Nigel (B 1951); Parker, Ian (S 1944); Patterson, Charles (G 1958); Pinkney, Helen (BH 1994–); Porter, Stephen; Ray, Christopher (D 1942, Brooke Hall 1965–85); Rees, Brian (Headmaster 1973–81); Rees-Mogg, Charlotte (L 1982); Rowntree, Andrew (V 1948); Roynon, Gavin (R 1954); Rudebeck, Annabel (V 1995); Russell, Brian (g 1945); Ryder Richardson, David (S 1962); Samengo-Turner, William (S 2001); Schwarz, Daniel (P 2001); Seligman, Michael (H 1956); Silver, Anthony (B 1978); Smith, Catherine (BH 2009–); Souter, Brian (BH 1970–2004); Sowrey, Frederick (V 1940); Spencer, Charles (L 1972); Strong, Simon (R 1958); Temple, William (L 1996); Tennent, Michael (S 1947); Tracey, Andrew (W 1954); Turner, Peter (B 1942); Ullman, Joe (W 1959); Vine, Paul (R 1946); Walker, Alasdair (B 1950); Wells, Robin (BH 1965–2003); White, Victoria (g 1996, Mrs Carlisle); Whiteley, Jervis (R 1948); Wilkie, Jon (W 1959); Williams, David (BH 2006–); Willis, Rebecca (S 1979); Wilson, Brian (D 1942); Winther, John (H 1955); Witheridge, The Revd John (Headmaster 1996–).

Subscribers

This book has been supported by the generosity of the Governing Body and the following subscribers. Names of pupils are listed with House abbreviations (see page 13) and year of leaving. Current pupils appear in italics. Pupils who have yet to enter the School appear without House or year, as do subscribers who have not indicated their connection with the School.

Roger Abbott .... V 2003	Hamish Baker .... P 1975	Andrew R. Best .... g 1979
James Acheson-Gray .... V 1989	M.R. Balfour-Melville .... G 1961	Prateek Bhagchandka .... L 2004
Anthony Adams V	Robert Balihache .... H 1986	J.E.S. Birch .... H 1982
Thomas Ai .... G 2009	Andrew Ball .... R 1973	Christopher Birch .... G 1976
Christopher J.D. Ainsley .... P 1975	Guy Ballantine .... H 1994	Rod Birkett .... D 1979
Frances Ainsley .... P 1981	Sir John Banham DL .... B 1958	Brian Birtwistle .... D 1970
Paul C. Akerhielm .... G 1964	G. Barber .... G 1968	Errol Bishop .... V 1956
Brett Akker .... D 1993	Charles Barber-Lomax .... R 1968	Barnaby Blackburn .... S 2007
Lawrence Alexander .... D 1968	Anthony Barclay .... G 1951	Martin D. Blake .... G 1945
Ali H. Alireza .... G 1979	Andrew H. Barker .... S 1963	Chris Blanchard .... S 1973
Julian Allen .... R 1985	C.W.N. Barker .... S 1964	Guillem Blasco .... Brooke Hall 2009–
Robert Allen .... G 1996	Ted Barker .... V 1953	Andy Blumer .... W 1959
Josh Allen-Back .... g 2002	Pete Barlow	Bruce Blyth .... H 1990
Richard D. Allington .... L 1994	Simon R. Barrow .... V 1953	Tessa Boase .... g 1986
T.J.C. Allom .... W 1964	Max Dyer Bartlett .... W 1975	*Charles Bogard* V
Diana Almazova .... g	Alex Barton .... L 2010	*Dominic A.D. Bolt* .... B
Timur Almazov .... g	Nicholas C.W. Bateman .... P 1971	Leticia Bombieri .... W 2010
Chris Ames .... B 1971	A.W. Bathurst .... L 1980	Sophia Bombieri .... W 2008
Clive Anderson .... V 1964	Robert Bathurst	Annabelle N. Bonham .... V 2010
Giles H.T. Andrews .... g 1959	Hugh Sheppard Bayley .... H 1933	C.E.G. Bonner .... B 1960
Martin Andrews .... g 1960	*Lucy Bayley* .... G	T.P.C. Bonner .... G 1988
Howard Weston Aplin .... L 1950	Caspar Bayliss .... W 2010	Mark Burditt Booth .... V 2008
Alexander M.A. Apponyi .... S 1990	*Charlie Bayliss* .... R	Michael H.G. Boswell .... g 1963
Malcolm Archibald .... S 1948	*Walter Bayliss* .... S	P.A.S. Boxer .... V 1964
John Argent .... W 1981	C.J.L. Bayman .... g 1983	T.K. Boyd .... P 1971
John Arkwright .... R 1948	G.A. Bayman .... g 1948	Sir Henry Boyd-Carpenter KCVO .... R 1958
Hugh Arnold .... S 1962	J.E. Bayman .... g 1950	Amal Brihi .... D 1995
Samuel L. Artigolle .... g	M.L. Bayman .... g 1951	Romanos Brihi .... V 1998
Peter M.C. Ashwell .... g 1969	T.L. Beaumont .... W 1986	C.W. Brinkley .... V 1961
Ben Ashworth .... g	Patrick Bedwell .... R 1957	Cedric Briscoe .... L 1951
Edward Asprey .... V 1962	Jeremy M.G. Bell .... G 1987	Gerald Bristowe .... P 1951
George Asprey .... V 1985	M.J. de H. Bell .... g 1959	M.G. Bristowe .... W 1992
Jonathan Aston .... L 1970	Stuart A. Bell .... R 1976	Oliver Bristowe .... S 2009
Nicholas Aston .... L 1966	Tim Bell .... L 1996	Peter Bristowe .... W 1980
W.D. Aukland .... P 1953	Simon Bellars .... R 1972	Tom Bristowe .... W 1991
Duncan J. Austin .... H 1989	Tony Bennett .... V 1943	David Stopford Brooke .... W 1949
Nicholas Austin .... H 1991	Dr Anthony J. Bennett ..... Brooke Hall 1989–2009	Dr Charles Brookman .... D 1985
W.D. Austin .... g 1945	P. Nicholas Bennett .... g 1951	John A. Brooks .... R 1953
Kalina Babington-Stitt .... S 2010	Naomi F. Bentley .... B 2010	Cameron Peter Brown .... P 2004
Alexander de Bacci .... S 2010	John C.F. Berg .... B 1953	Andrew Bruce .... D 1966
Graham C. Bailey .... V 1981	David Berliand .... H 1953	Tom A. Bruce-Jones CBE .... H 1960
Jonathan Bailey .... D 1968	David Bernhard .... R 2009	Simon M.N. Bryden-Brook .... L 1959
Dr Crispin Baker .... V 1957	Ashley Berns .... P 1987	Matthew Bulley .... D 1995

Miles N.H. Bulloch	W 2005
Christopher Bullock	R 2010
Sue Burden	H 1980
Benedict Burrowes	L
D.C. Burrows	L 1957
Henrietta Emily Burton	V 2004
Isabel Esta Burton	S 1998
Claude Butler	g 1952
F.J. Butterworth	g 1993
D.A.C. Campbell	G 1959
James Alexander Campbell	W 1993
R.A. Campbell	S 1959
Dr S. Campbell-Smith	g 1959
Alexander H. Caplan	W 1998
W.R.C. Carey MBE	W 1962
Steve Carlisle	R 1984
Richard R.F. Cassidy	S 1938
John White Cater	B 1948
Armel Cates	L 1961
Patrick N.R. Cave-Browne	S 1943
David Chalkley	B 1947
Alan Chalmers	W 1960
Jeremy S.K. Chan	S 1995
Sunit Chandaria	B 2002
Keith Chapman	P 1973
Tom V. Chatjaval	G 1977
Simon Chen	P 1989
Kevin Cheng	L 1999
Michael Cheung	g
Suzannah Chick	W 1998
Alexander Chidgey	W
Tim Childs	G 1980
Bryan, Chu Ming Ho	D 2009
The Hon. David Clark	S 1965
Stuart Clark	H 1972
Regina Claros-Bolivar	H 1993
Richard N.B. Clegg	V 1956
Richard Clement	g 1966
James Cobb	V
G.D.R. Cockram	G 1959
Sue Cole	Brooke Hall 1988–
Guy R.W. Coleman	S 1962
Oliver Collin	
Richard Collin	B 1961
William Collin	
Alfie Collins	G
Toby Colliver	G 1991
D.D.S. Comer	H 1958
Carlo Comninos	g 1974
Richard Connell	R 1007
Rupert Connell	L 1972
Patrick G. Constantinides	S 1957
Antony Cooke	Brooke Hall 1966–1990
Rev. D.N. Copeland	D 1957
David Copeman	V 1977
Christopher Corney	g 2009
Francis Cornish CMG LVO	P 1960
Michael Coulson	W 1963
Peter Cowie	W 1958
Dr Nigel Cox	g 1955
I.D. Craddock	V 1950
James Crawford	R 1942
Peter R. Crawford	D 1964

R.H. Crawford	Brooke Hall 1951–1986
George Crawshay	R 1950
S.J.B. Crisford	S 1980
Peter Croft	B 2001
John L. Crosse	B 1990
Matthew P. Crosse	B 1988
John Crossman	D 1942
Richard A. Crowsley	Brooke Hall 1973–
Matthew Cundell	H 1950
The Venerable Dr C.J. Cunliffe	D 1973
Anthony Curl	B 2002
R.M.F. Curry	R 1980
J.G. Curtis	R 1950
Matthew Cushway	g 1997
James Daglish	L 1995
Reverend Martin Dale	L 1972
Jean-Paul Danon	g 1963
Michel Danon	g 1965
Owen Darbishire	V 1983
John Darby	V 1947
Robert Darke	L
Michael L. Darling	H 1949
Robin Darwall-Smith	G 1981
Tasso Dattenberg-Doyle	S
Richard Davey	g 1985
T.R.K. Davey	g 1949
D.G.W. Davis	g 1946
Paul C. Davis	D 1989
Alexander Dawson	L 2007
Annabelle Dawson	H 2006
Jamie Day	G
David M. deFerranti	P 1964
Christopher de Wolff	B 1985
Nicholas de Wolff	B 1988
John G. Deacon	B 1958
John L. Deacon	B 1985
Dr Samantha Deacon (née Negus)	P 1985
Alison Deans	G 1986
Conrad Dehn QC	S 1945
Tom Seymour Dickins	G 1978
J.J. Dickson	B 1952
Alessia Diederich	P
T.D. Dill-Russell	D 1955
Philip Distin	R 1960
D.J.L Dix-Perkin	g 1944
Stephen C. Doble	P 1963
Michael J.R. Dodd	V 1954
John Donaldson	L 1976
Sir John Donne	W 1940
Nigel Donovan	R 1974
Max Downing	R 2010
Nicholas Drake	B 2001
Oliver Drake	B 1998
Chris Drakeford-Lewis	g
Julien Draper	W 2003
Matthew Draper	W 2005
Tim Drayson	V 1994
Jane L. Drew	Brooke Hall 2007–
Daniel J.D. Drury	D 1996
Jason Dunn	P 1990
Michael E.C. Dunn	S 2003
Patrick S.J. Dupont-Liot	H 1993
J.M.E. Dyson	B 1973

Paddy Earp	H 1961
Graham Ede	P 1971
Robert Ede	B 1958
Callum Edge	S 2010
David Edmondson	D 1965
J.R.G. Edwards	L 1955
Nicholas Eeley	G 1953
Derek Elliott	R 1964
David B. Ellis	R 1958
David J. Ellis	P
Benjamin Elsing	H
R.W. Emmerson	G 2000
Martin Ephson	V 1974
Philip N. Erskine	S 1951
Angus Evans	g 2000
David S. Evans	H 1953
Dr John A. Evans	H 1958
John S. Evans	W 1959
Revd Norman C. Evans	Brooke Hall 1957–1991
Peter G. Evans	H 1955
Philip W. Evans	H 1963
Rodney A. Evans	D 1952
M.W. Evans	L 1953
Mark Everett	B 1977
David Ewart-White	V 1961
Fraser Ewart-White	V 1991
Rowan Ewart-White	V 1989
The Very Reverend Richard Eyre	G 1947
Charles Farran	H 1973
Nigel Farrell	B 1974
Michael Fatsis	P 2010
Lucas P.T. Feneberg	L 2002
David B. Fenwick	G 1950
T.R.F. Fenwick	V 1945
Charlie Fergus	P
Fred Fergus	P 2009
Sally Ferguson	S 1993
Joseph E. Fernandes	B 1972
David Fior	D 1985
Robert E.J. Fisher	R 1956
Robert J. FitzGerald	D 1962
Peter Willis Fleming	R 1975
Bill Flower	W 1947
Matthew Fong	R 2004
David Foot	L 1980
Diana Foot	L 1978
Harry Foot	Brooke Hall 1974–1998
Harold Fosker	
Stephen Foot	L 1982
J.J.E. Foster	V 1983
Robin S. Foster-Brown	L 1957
Dr A. Mervyn Fox	V 1954
Victor Murray Fox	V 1949
Robin Fraser	R 1958
Brian Freake	Brooke Hall 1968–86
Karl Frearson	W 1983
Nicholas Freeland	R 1974
Semma Freites	G 2004
Anthony Friend	G 1940
Trevor H.Y. Fung	P 2009
Col S.J. Furness	W 1954
John P. Gabriel	g 1960
Graham B.L. Gale	H 1951

Oliver M.J. Galliford	W 2010	
Thomas Gallyer	S	
Rodney M. Gamble	H 1961	
Charles Gardiner	V 1981	
Felix Gardner	R	
William Gibbs	H	
Annabel Gibson	S 2010	
Alan G. Gill	W 1954	
Humphrey W. Gill	S 1957	
John Gill	W 1962	
Rupert Gill	W 1990	
Richard Gilliat	G 1963	
George Gilligan-Court	R	
Georgia Gilmore	G 2009	
Peter Gimson	G	
Anthony Gladstone-Thompson	R 1962	
Richard Goddard	R 1959	
D.R. Goldschmidt	W 1960	
James Goldsmith	D 1989	
Jemima Goodwin	g 2007	
Theodora Goodwin	g 2010	
John S. Gordon	R 1953	
J.M.C. Gordon	V 1960	
Howard Gordon-Martin	V 1962	
R.A. Gordon-Smith	Brooke Hall 1982–97	
Jonathan Gough	V 1986	
Sam Gough	V 1993	
Toby Gough	V 1988	
Matthew Gowar	H 1989	
Hugh Gracey	D 1985	
Simon Gracey	D 1990	
Hugh Grainger	g 1954	
Mark C. Gray	W 1988	
Andrew Green	R 1954	
Chris Goetz	P	
Hunter Goetz	R	
Jack Goetz	R 2009	
T. Elmer Grantham	V 1929	
Andrew Green	L 1992	
Andrew Curtis Green	R 1954	
Malcolm Green	L 1960	
Marcus Green	L 1997	
John Greenwood	G 1966	
C.L. Greig	G 1947	
Ian Groom	R 1975	
Guy Gross	L 1957	
Major A.R. Gurney	g 1939	
Robert Gygax	V 1986	
Lord David Hacking	G 1956	
Nicholas Guy Melville Hacking	P 1974	
Christopher Hadfield	g 1974	
Hisham Halawi	V 1987	
M.F. Hall	D 1945	
Mike Hall-Taylor	H 1986	
J.P. Hamilton	H 1967	
J.H.M. Handley	V 2007	
P.M.C. Handley	W 2003	
W. Handley		
George James Barnard Hankey	L 1999	
Oliver Hare	S 1982	
Kachaphol Harinsuit	G 1996	
M.G. Harrap	R 1970	
Alan J.F. Harris	D 1960	

Adeline Sophie Hartmann	B 1997	
Julia Hartmann (Mrs Pollert)	H 1990	
B.F. Hartshorne	G 1863	
B.K.J.B. Hartshorne	R 1898	
B.K.S.B. Hartshorne	G 1942	
D.J.M. Hartshorne	G 1972	
Holly Hartshorne	P 2000	
T.G.M. Hartshorne	G 2002	
Ian Harvey-Samuel	H 1983	
Captain J. Harvey-Samuel, Royal Navy	H 1953	
Christopher B. Harvie	W 1982	
Jeremy J.O. Harwood	G 1976	
Stewart Hawkins	R 1956	
Rosemary H. Hawley		
Hilary R. Haydon		
Felix George Hamer	R	
William (Bill) Haynes	D 1952	
Guy Hayward-Cole	G 1980	
A.G. Hazan	L 1966	
Stephen Hearn	Brooke Hall 1985–	
Jeffrey Hedges	R 1972	
Anil Ram Hemnani	S 1989	
Ravi Ram Hemnani	S 1990	
W. Henderson	S 1980	
Andrew Hendry	G 1971	
Raymond Henley	B 1963	
Paul Herbert	V 1957	
John Maclaren Herington	g 1961	
Christopher Hewett	S 1956	
James Hickman	V 2009	
Jack Hillcox	P	
Benjamin Himpe-Depuydt	B	
William Himpe-Depuydt	B	
Anthony Hines	V 1953	
A.R. Hippisley	S 1956	
Adrian Ho	V	
David Hodges	P 1985	
Peter J.D. Hodgson CBE DL	H 1965	
Julian Crandall Hollick	D 1965	
Christopher J. Hollis	G 1978	
Christopher Hollis	G 2010	
Tom Hollis	G 2008	
Tony Holt	W 1947	
Jonathan G. Hooper	G 1971	
Jonathan Horne	G 1969	
J.A.D. Howard	R 1981	
Peter J. Howard	G 1964	
C.J. Hudson	g 1949	
Ed Hughes	B 2007	
Richard J.M. Hughes	H 1976	
William Hughes	H 2010	
Michael C. Hughesdon	R 1956	
Brandon C.H. Hui	P	
M.G. Humphery	G 1947	
Dr J.P. Hunt	S 1965	
R.B. Hunt	S 1946	
Ailsa P. Hurst (Mrs Guidi)	S 1993	
J.K. Hutchinson	P 1967	
Tim Hutton	V 1972	
Rob Ingram	Brooke Hall 1971–2006	
Donald Innes	S 1959	
Alan C. Jackson	D 1964	
James N.B. Jackson	G 2000	

Nicholas S.B. Jackson	G 2001	
John E. James	W 1997	
Dr Peter J. James	R 1967	
Dariush Naghavi	H 1975	
Philip J.C. Jefferies	B 1992	
Charles Jenkins	D 1987	
Henry Jenkins	S 2010	
Samuel Jenkins	S	
M. David C. Jenks	B 1950	
Dennis Jenks	H 1946	
Christopher Jenner	R 1999	
David Jimenez-Blanco	g	
Ben Jobson	S	
John A. Johnson	W 1939	
Thomas K. Johnson	P 1950	
Frederick Johnson	R	
Sir Geoffrey Johnson Smith DL	g 1942	
Michael Johnston	V 1991	
Peter Johnstone	L 1966	
Richard Johnstone	G 1962	
Christopher Jonas CBE	G 1959	
Donald Louis Jones	P 1943	
G.E. Jones	Brooke Hall 1967–87	
George T. Jones	V 2010	
Daryl Jones	B 1978	
Sophie Jordan (Mrs Arnold)	S 1991	
Ramzi Joukhadar	H 1991	
Rachel Jubb (Mrs Whiting)	S 2002	
The Very Revd Peter Judd	L 1967	
Harvey Jullien	D	
Martin Kadhim	W 1997	
Elizabeth Kahn	P 2010	
Jonathan Kahn	P	
Stephen Kahn	D	
Anthony Kane	g	
Jehangir Dara Karanjavala	L 1973	
Sam Kazemi	B 2005	
Graham Kelly	g 1951	
Michael Kelly	P	
Nick Kelly	g 1981	
Simon Kelly	g 1979	
Anthony Kemball Price	L 1952	
Michael Kempner	D 1970	
Nigel Justin Kempner	G 1974	
A.M. Keat	S 1960	
C.N. Kenyon	B 1959	
P.C. Kenyon	P 1984	
David Kerr	W 1957	
K.M. Kershaw	V 1958	
Dr Robert Kershaw	D 1930	
Peter Keymer	G 1960	
Yuki Kidani (Mrs Beardmore-Gray)	D 1982	
Charlotte King	P 1989	
Christopher King	P 1961	
Timothy King	P 1990	
Tom Kinsey	H 2001	
David Kirke-Smith	D 1966	
A.C.H. Kirkman	B 2008	
R.J.H. Kirkman	B 2010	
Charles Kitching	D	
Simon Kitching	D 1980	
Bryan Knight	L 1953	
Belinda Knox	B 1978	

H.M.O. Knox .... B 1927
R.O. Knox .... B 1953
T.O. Knox .... B 1955
Aswin Kongsiri .... G 1963
Dr Michael Koehler
Visnu Kongsiri .... G 1961
Lana Kovacevic .... H
Dr Stephan Kusick .... H 1998
Kelvin Kwok Ho-Man (Hoi) ...... H 2007
Olivia Lace-Evans .... P 2010
Richard W. Lack .... D 1949
J.J. Lack .... L 1952
Lt Col Robin Laird .... L 1950
Dr D. Lancefield .... Brooke Hall 2006–
Edward Langley .... H
Sven-Erik Larsen .... B 1961
Sir Anthony Laughton .. Governing Body 1981–2000
William Lawrie .... P 2004
George Frederick Louis Lawson ...... g
Jerry Lawson .... R 1990
Maximilian Gordon Henry Lawson . S 2008
Neil Lawson-Smith .... R 1976
James Le Couilliard .... H 1983
Alain Le Jeune .... V 1977
Richard Le Jeune .... V 1981
Johnathan Leathers .... W 1992
Delman Lee .... S 1985
Weng Hon Lee .... B 1985
Sir David Lees .... L 1955
Martin Lesourd .... P 2010
Toby Leston .... R 2009
Anthony Leung CH .... G
Constance Leung .... B
Peter L. Levy OBE .... R 1958
Charles Lewis .... W 1956
Miranda Lewis .... R 2004
P.G.T. Lewis .... Brooke Hall 1963–94
Stephen C. Lewis .... W 1958
Branton Li .... S
David Lidderdale .... G 1963
William Lidstone .... W 1996
John M. Lightbody .... G 1958
Ka-Ming Lim .... H 1983
Chi-Fu Lin .... S 1985
Stephen Llewellyn .... L 1980
David W. Lloyd .... D 1943
Ben Lockwood .... H 1960
John Loftus .... D 1966
Mark Lovill .... G 1978
Stephen K.K. Loo .... g 1995
Brian S. Lowe .... H 1931
Fotis Lykiardopulo .... S
Michael F. Lykiardopulo .... S 1978
Nicholas F. Lykiardopulo ...... S 1976
Nicholas M. Lykiardopulo .... S
Alex Macdonald .... g 2009
Ian Macdonald .... W 1946
C.W.D. Macey .... P 1972
Frederick Mack .... B
Roderick Mackay .... W 1959
J.C.S. Mackie .... R 1944
Lachlan Mackinnon .... G 1974
Will MacLaren .... W 1995

P.J.L. MacLure .... D 1961
G.I. MacMillan .... V 1988
C.W.S. Macrae .... P 1967
Charles Mahalski .... S
Antony Maitland .... P 1964
Mahyar Makhzani .... P 1976
Henry Mallin .... W
William Mallin .... W
Richard Mallinson .... D 1956
N.J.K. Mark .... D 1960
Andrew Marks .... H
N.A. Marks .... W 1960
Stephen P. Marks .... W 1957
Tom Markwell .... S
David Marriott .... W 1953
Hugh Marsden .... R 1960
Alan Marsh .... S 1954
Alison Marsh (Mrs Power) ...... P 1979
Charles Marsh .... H
Jamie Marsh .... H
Julian Marsh .... V 1989
Nico Marsh .... H
Roger P.T. Marshall .... V 1970
Richard Martin .... G 1978
Francis Marx .... W 1940
Michelle Mather (Mrs Bradburn) Brooke Hall 1978–83
Janet Mathews .... Brooke Hall 1985– 2006
S. Jeffrey Matthews .... g 1962
Oliver J.H. Maunder .... R 1989
Charlie Mawer .... L 1987
Brigadier John Maxwell .... D 1950
D.P. Simon (Paddy) McCormick .. D 1964
Dr Peter D. McCall .... P 1961
Michael McClure .... R 1971
Dr Anton S. McCourtie .... B 1993
Euan McDougall .... W
Rory McDougall .... W
Katherine (Katie) McFadden .... L 2010
C.A. McGleughlin .... S
Fergal McGuire .... B
Tom McIlwaine .... R 1996
Angus J.F. McIsaac .... G 1994
Ian McIsaac .... G 1962
Robert G.H. McIsaac .... G 2007
Tom McKay .... P 2009
Thomas McMahon .... B 2009
Stanley Meares .... g 1947
R.D.M. Metcalf .... V 1973
J.R.H. Middleton .... B 1970
Oli Millard .... V 1999
David Miller .... D 1953
Noel Miller .... S 1983
H.T. Miller .... L 1960
James Miller .... P 1985
Hugo Millington-Drake .... S 2008
Luke Millington-Drake V
Alexander James Eaton Mills ... D 2002
Frederick Mills .... g 2010
George Mills .... S 2009
Neville Mills .... P 1944
Nigel Mills .... S 1975
A.M. Mitchell .... V 1966
Peter Mitchell .... D 1955

Richard Mitton .... P 1971
Christopher Mole .... D 1979
Richard Mole .... D 1982
A.F.T. Monck-Mason .... H 1952
Andrew Charles Malcolm Moncrieff .. D 1980
Tom Monfries .... g 1984
His Honour Judge E.F. Monier-Williams .. g 1937
C.G. Monteath .... S 1939
Paul S. Montgomery .... P 1984
Caroline Moore (Mrs Donald) ... S 1991
John R.M. Moore .... G 1960
R.M. More .... S 1952
Peter Morel .... V 1987
D.Ll. Morgan .... S 1951
Juliet Tomoko Morrice .... B 2000
Nicholas Morris .... G 1958
Henry F.R. Morton L
Jock Moss .... W 1933
Richard Munro .... B 1996
Warren Mutch .... W 2002
Takanori Nakazawa .... F
Olga Naprasnikova .... D
P.G. Nathan OBE DL .... H 1947
Tom Nauta .... H 2006
Dr Rupert P.M. Negus .... P 1979
Mark Nesbitt .... W 1979
Palmer Newbould .... L 1947
John Newell .... W 1947
Roger E.P. Newhall .... H 1967
Hedley Newton .... V 1954
Edward (Ted) Noble .... L 1965
Charlie Noel-Johnson .... W 1994
P.M.R. Norris .... B 1972
Richard Norris .... L 1979
Canon Dr P.E.P. Norton .... V 1957
Dr J.R. Noyce .... R 1971
Fergus O'Brien .... V 2005
Mark O'Brien .... L 1978
Michael O'Brien .... V 1953
S. O'Brien .... V 1982
Charlotte Oliver .... G
James Oliver .... S
N.J. Orgill .... G 1993
Nicholas Orr .... W
Sean Ostro .... H 2009
Tom Otley .... V 1956
Nigel Ottley .... L 1974
H.C.N.M. Oulton .... W 1937
Nicholas Oulton .... W 1979
Tim Palmer .... H 1984
Prinn Panitchpakdi .... R 1996
Andrew N. Parker .... S 1981
Ian Parker .... S 1944
Dr W.N.B. Parker .... P 1945
John Parsons .... Brooke Hall 1992–
Alec Paterson .... S 1997
David Paton .... W 1979
Ian Paton .... W 1949
Guy Alexander Partridge .... g 2009
The Revd Charles Patterson .... G 1958
Lucy Pattinson .... S 1981
R.S.R. Pattison .... V 1969
Elizabeth J. Paul

203

John Pearmund	B 1971
Thomas J. Pearson Chisman	W 1989
Christopher Pease	g 1990
Henry Pease	G 1995
Geoffrey Peck	W 1951
Geoffrey Peek	G 1963
Ben C.E. Peers	D
Captain Hugh R.L. Peers	D 1954
John Peers	D 1950
Ronald Peet	G 1976
Andrew Peile	S 1954
Charles Peirson	H
George Peirson	L
Darryl Penrose	G 1990
L.D. Penrose	G 1988
Rory Peplow	W
Brigadier M.J. Perkins CBE	R 1949
John W. Perrin	V 1947
Ron Perrin .... Head Groundsman 1972–2003
J.N. Perryer	V 1943
Richard Peskin	R 1962
Charles Peters	H 1987
Alan Petrides	G 1962
Benjamin Phillips	g
Robin Phillips	g 1976
Roger Phillips	g 1966
Robert D.A. Pick	L 1961
Rupert J.W. Pick	L 1993
Matija D.K. Pisk	R
Michael Pickavance	H 1969
J.N.M. Pickersgill	g 1949
R.C.E. Pigott	S 1966
Christopher J. Pittam	G 1955
Ben Plant	W 2005
Oliver Plant	D 2006
A.M. Pleass	g 1953
Joshua Plummer	L 2008
Oliver Plummer	L
Julia Podedworny	V 2007
A.J.G. Polhill	S 1974
The Rev. Dr John Pollock	S 1941
Tony Pool	V 1957
Anthony Potter	D 1961
Sebastian Potter	D 1994
Chris Potts	P
Brigadier George Powell	H 1944
H.G.L. Powell	B 1963
Michael Power	g 1978
Michael R. Power	V 1970
Paul Poynter-Smith	g 1990
Hugh Cowper Pratt	H 1950
Lord James Prior	S 1945
Angus Procter	L 2006
James Procter	L 2008
Robert Procter	L 2008
Phillip Pulfrey	V 1972
William Pye	L 1956
David Raeburn	P 1943
Alexis Ralli	V
Christopher Ralling	R 1947
Edward R.J. Ramsay	P 2005
Rupert G.A. Ramsay	B 2005
Devesh D. Rasgotra	R 2009

C.T.A. Ray .... D 1942, Brooke Hall 1965–85
Daniel J. Ray	H 1998
Martin Read	H 1981
Brian Rees	Headmaster 1973–81
Harry Briggs Reeve	D 2008
Peter Reeves	Brooke Hall 1984–2006
James Register	G
James Reid	B 1983
Dr P.G.E. Reid	G 1962
H.B. Reynolds	B 1976
Tim Reynolds	D 1967
Archie Rhind-Tutt	g 2010
Owen E. Riddett	L 1931
D.C. Ridley	G 1956
John Rigg	g 1960
Ben Rinck	D 2009
Andrew Rintoul	g 1968
John Callender Ritchie	W 1915
A.C. Robertson	S 1944
E.M.W. Robinson	H 1953
Jeremy Robinson	W 1959
John Robinson	H 1971
Jonathon Myles Robinson	H 2005
Michael J.C. Robinson	H 1968
Andrew P.M. Robson	G 1979
Charlie Rogers	V 1976
Dr Alan Rogerson .... Brooke Hall 1966–1969
Elizabeth Rose-Innes	P
Timothy Rose-Innes	S 2010
Dr Kirsty Ross (Mrs Hutchison)	G 2000
Peter Roth	D 1974
William Rothery	V 1974
Russell M Routh	P 1938
Christopher Jack Bristowe Rowe	P 1957
Gerry Rowe-Ham	G 1993
M.W.M. Rowlandson	B 1960
Dr W.M.J. Rowlandson	B 1994
Andrew Rowntree	V 1948
Ashley Rudd	D 2003
Miss Nicky Rudd	R 2003
Richard Rudden	g 2007
Annabel Rudebeck	V 1995
Brian Russell OBE	g 1945
Charles Russell-Jones	V 2010
Emma Russell-Jones	B 2008
Dr D.J. Russell-Weisz	H 1982
Julian Ryder Richardson	H 1953
His Excellency M.A.F. Al-Saad	P 1974
A.F. Sabin	R 1941
W.F.J. Samengo-Turner	S 2001
C.K. Samuleson	L 1977
K.V. Samuelson	B 1936
Francis Sandison	S 1967
Nicholas Sando	B 2010
John Sargeant	P 1968
Nicholas Saynor	S 1954
James Scholefield	V 1989
Lisa Scholefield	V 1991
Michael M. Scott	W 1956
Jack Sears	g 1948
D.N. Seaton	V 1940
Patrick Seaver	P 1968
Michael Sechiari	W 1951

John J.B. Segar	B 2008
Michael C. Seligman	H 1956
D.J. Sendall	W 1964
Major John Sergison-Main .... Brooke Hall 1994–
Helen Shakespeare (née Wreford-Brown)
Justin Sham	S 1998
Geoffrey G.G. Sharp	D 1986
John Martin Thorndike Shaw	D 1976
Adam D. Shepard	R 1985
Sir John Shepherd	W 1961
Robert Shepherd	P 1971
Robert Shepherd	P 2001
Timothy Shepherd	P 2000
W. Adrian Shepherd	B 1978
Alam Sher	W 1947
Azam Sher	W 1974
Sanjana Shetty	S
Dr Fiona Morven Shields	G 1990
Catriona Mary Shields	G 1997
E.J. Shipton	G 1981
John Shipton	G 1951
M.R. Shipton	G 1984
W.K. Shipton	G 1980
Patrick Shovelton CB CMG	L 1938
Pawat Silawattakun	G
A.J. Silver	B 1978
Paul Silver	B 1979
V.K.C. Simmonds
(Mrs Lyon Taylor)	H 1995
Keith Simmons	D 1958
D.J. Simms	G 1948
Scott Simpkin	S
Keith E. Simpson	S 1961
Hugh Sinclair	V 1991
A. Sington	G 1972
Alexander Skinner	L 2006
Douglas Skinner	L 2009
Charles Skinner	W 1977
Nathan A. Smith	R 1982
Nicholas Smith	G 1989
Rachel Smith	H 1994
Robert Smith	B 1944
Theo Smith	V 1968
Toby Smith	L 1995
Edward Smith-Suarez	L 2010
O.R.H. Smyth	H 1980
Simon Snook	W 1982
Olukorede Solomon	H
Michael Sommer	S 1959
Hari Sood	S
Jaya Sood	R
J.A.V. Sopher	G 1983
Brian R. Souter .... Brooke Hall 1970–2004
Air Marshal Sir Freddie Sowrey	V 1940
Hammy Sparks .... Brooke Hall 1968–2005
Charles Spencer	L 1972
Simon Spooner	R 2001
Sir Greville Spratt	g 1945
Peter M. Stafford	P 1960
Andrew Stainer	V 1970
D.L. Stallabrass	P 1942
R. Standring	G 1956
Dr Guy Steed	P 1957

M.L.H. Stent	V 1946
Chris Sterling-Manson	P 1972
Andrew Stevens	P 1958
S. Stevenson	H 1951
A.K.J. Stewart	R 1980
Charles Stewart	g 1959
J.R.S. Stilwell	B 1957
Robert Stokes	W 2007
David G. Stone	L 1955
John J. Stork	S 1953
Duncan Street	P 2008
Andrew G. Summers	g 2008
Peter H. Summers	g 2005
Rodney Sutton	S 1957
Jeremy Sutton-Pratt	V 1967
Keith Swabey	L 1979
D.J. Sword	S 1946
Jonathan Tam	S 2003
Tien-Chung Tang	Brooke Hall 1976–1982
Alison F.B. Taylor	D 2005
J.P. Lyon Taylor	L 1954
Justin E. Lyon Taylor	W 2001
Laurent Taylor	D 2005
Oliver W. Taylor	P 2003
R.P. Lyon Taylor	W 1995
A.A. Teape	V 1954
Adrian Tellwright	S 1974
William StJ. Temple	L 1996
J. Michael Tennent	S 1947
Chris Terry	W 2010
Nigel Macpherson	W 1974
Christopher J. Thomas	g 1985
Karen E. Thomas	g 1983
Martin C.N. Thompson	g 1958
James Thomson	Master, Sutton's Hospital 2001–
Alan A. Thorman	S 1945
Louise Thornton (Mrs Tinker)	G 1977
Axel Threlfall	L 1986
Jorn Threlfall	L 1986
Victoria Threlfall (Mrs Bathurst)	P 1976
Richard Timmis	S 1961
Peter Tinniswood	G 1969
R.W. Tookey	V 1952
Simon Toombs	H 1981
Lady Elizabeth Toulson	Governing Body 1998–
Henry Toulson	g 1998
Thomas Toulson	g 2002
Christopher Townsend	V 1980
Paul Townsend	V 1983
John Townsend-Rose	W 1967
Simon Tranter	D 1988
Gavin Trechman	D 1960
R.A. Chenevix Trench	D 1939
Peter Tritton	V 1969
Tommy T.K. Tse	S 2002
Christopher Tucker	G 2007
E. Chris Tuckwell	S 1954
Gladwyn Turbutt	S 1946
David Turnbull	W 1972
Peter R. Turner	V 1950
Robin D. Turner	W 1947

Giles Tyler	P
J.J. Ullman	W 1959
Andrew J. Ure	R 1996
Iain S. Ure	R 1999
Roberto Van Meurs	L
D.A.N. Vansittart	R 1950
Guy Varney	S 1980
Michael Vicars-Harris	G 1946
James Vintcent	S 1978
Eric P. Visser	P 1959
Charles Wace	R 1979
Ian Wace	R 1981
J.P. Wainwright	D 1957
Sir Christopher Walford	G 1954
Nicolas Walker	H
Paul Walker	R 1969
Thomas Hay Walker	W 1949
John Walker-Haworth	S 1962
John F. Wallington	V 1990
Andrew Wallis	g 1997
Edward Wallis	G 2002
James Wallis	G 1999
Martin E.B. Walters	V 1960
Nick Walton	R 1959, Brooke Hall 1964–65
Tira Wannamethee	g 1977
Gary Waple	W 1974
A.D. Ward	G 1949
Charles John Nicholas Ward	g 1959
John N. Ward	g 1934
Rodney Ward	g 1962
Simon Warren	R 1980
Euan Watson	H 1949
Michael J.B. Watson	L 1950
Paddy Watson	B 1980
Piers S. Watson	G 1976
Simon Watson	H 1952
F. Weare	W 1881
Susan C. Weaver (Mrs Chapman)	D 1981
Dr E.J. Webb	S 1968
Katy A. Webb	g 2006
Mark J. Webb	g 2008
Alexander Webb-Bowen	B
J.R. Webster	D 1990
R.J. Webster †	D 1992
Patricia Welby-Everard (Mrs Arrowsmith)	L 1993
Richard G.M. Welford	g 1964
Dr Ian Wells	W 1965
Neville M. Wells	S 1943
Robin Wells	Brooke Hall 1965–2003
S.G. West	V 1994
D.J.C. Weston	G 1941
Graham J.P. Weston	L
Tim Weston	G 1958
Lieutenant Colonel Michael Westropp	S 1947
Alexander Wheatley	V
Nick Wheeler	G 1976
Peter Wheeler	D 1975
Charlie Whinney	G 1987
Christopher Whinney	G 1952
Harry Whinney	G 1989
Michael Whinney	G 1948

A.A.H. White	S 1958
Gerald W. White	g 1947
R.H. Whitefield	W 1955
Dr Jervis Whiteley	R 1948
Martin Whitten	D 1987
Anthony Wigram	H 1954
Peter Charles Victor Hubert Wild	g 1960
Roland Wild	R 1968
Nicholas Wilkes	P 1974
Brett D.A. Wilkie	B 1998
Jonathan Neaves Wilkie	W 1959
Ale Wilkinson	L 2005
Cristina Wilkinson	W 2000
David Wilkinson	g 1971
Garth Wilkinson	W 1996
Hugh Wilkinson	P 1944
Mence Wilkinson	P 1943
Michael Wilkinson	G 1952
Robert Wilkinson	L 2003
Samuel J.G. Wilkinson	B 1988
Katie Wilks	S 2005
A.G. Williams	W 1946
Alex Williams	W 1991
Alison L. Williams	S 1999
David Williams	Bursar 2006–
B.H. Williamson	B 1947
Richard F. de L. Willis	B 1954
Cdr David Wilmot Smith MBE	H 1962
Andrew Wilson	Brooke Hall 1975–2002
B.D. Wilson	D 1942
Angus Wilton	G 1995
J.L.C. Winterton	V 1984
John Winther	H 1955
Nigel P. Wisden	G 1956
Sir Peter Womersley Bt	H 1960
James K.S. Wong	P 2007
Alan Woo	P 1996
Sebastian Wood	V 1984
Sophie Wood	R 1999
Benjamin Woods	D
Alice Woodwark (Mrs McIlwaine)	G 1996
Benjamin Woolf	H
D. Worth	g 1953
Anthony Wright	G 1973
Timothy Wright	G 1982
James Wyatt	g 1983
Peter Wynne-James	g 1951
Josh Wynter	L 2005
Mackenzie Xu	P
Nelson Xu	P
M.H. Yeats	W 1974
Tim Yeo	S 1963
C.M.K. Yonge	V 1996
David T. Young	S 1955
Richard Zerny	P 1962
Alexander Zervos	L 1987
Matthew Zervos	L 1981
Nicholas Zervos	L 1977
Sharif Ali Zu'Bi	H 1981

Index of Names and Places

advantage whatsoever of him the said Si
late in the tenure or occupaton of the
ularly and at large appeareth; And
re Indenture under theire handes and See
led in his said high Courte of Chancery at
nire and unto the said John wotton their
res and appurtenances in the County of D
one of them or of theire or some of theire
whatsoever yearely and from tyme to ty
m Abbott Esquire Justinian Abbott and to
Hartland aforesaid late were parcell of
and Trees whatsoever in and vpon the
Soyle thereof, And all and singuler Sta
owne vnderwood tythes of Corne and th
ment for tythes or oblatons right mise
it appurtenances whatsoever to the said
ed or emoved, And the reversion and re
demise or grantes of the said Rectory an
sons donations free dispositons and ri
ever of the said last mentoed premisses b
ng by the said last mentoed Indenture o

is mentioned in and by the said
Aldworth and John wotton for the consi
to the said Samuell marton, John Clark
ory Tythes mesuages mansion Houses bu
said eleaventh day of June in the said
t before mentoed or recited Indenture be
singuler the premisses and of every parte
Richard Aldworth and John wotton or o
them in the foresaid County of Yorke, a
marsh Cappett and Vetney or in any
mesuages land tent and hereditame
Sutton Richard Aldworth and John wott
ent yssues and proffitt reserved vpon a
Clayme and demannd whatsoever whice
hane of mor to all and singuler the pu
interpart of leases writings, munument
mannors Sites ffarmes Grantes Jo
er parte and parcell thereof with the a
ever to the only proper vse and behoofe
ate the said eleaventh day of June in th
made and provided, inrolled in our high
h day of November in the said fifth year
ught of theone parte, and the foresaid S
Richard Sutton for the consideratons the
eires and Assignes. All that the Site
tuff in and vpon the said Site and all

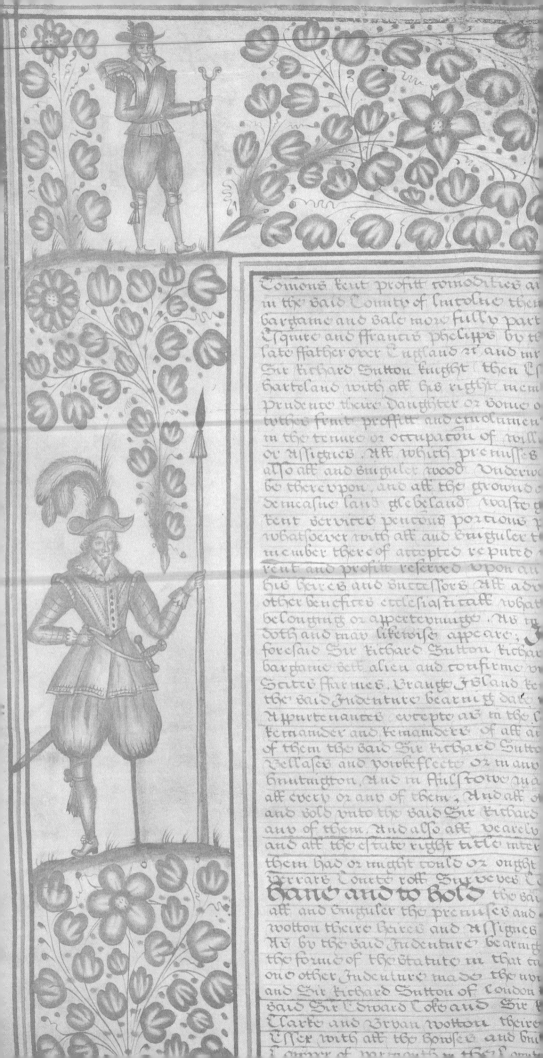

Comons rent profitt comodities a[...]
in the said County of Lincolne then[...]
bargaine and sale more fully part[...]
Esquire and ffrancis phelipps by t[...]
late ffather over Rutland 21 and m[...]
Sir Richard Sutton knight then Es[...]
hartland with all his right mem[...]
Prudence theire daughter or sonne o[...]
tuthes frute proffitt and emolument[...]
in the tenure or occupacon of will[...]
or Assignes. All which premisses[...]
also all and singuler wood vnderwo[...]
be thereupon, and all the ground [...]
demeasne land glebeland waste g[...]
rent services pencons porcions p[...]
whatsoever with all and singuler t[...]
member thereof accepted reputed[...]
rent and profitt reserved vpon a[...]
his heires and successors All ad[...]
other benefitts ecclesiasticall what[...]
belonging or apperteyninge. As [...]
doth and may likewise appeare; [...]
foresaid Sir Richard Sutton Richard[...]
bargaine sell alien and confirme[...]
Statts ffurnes. Brauge Island [...]
the said Indenture bearing date[...]
Appurtenances excepte as in the [...]
Remainder and Remainders of all a[...]
of them the said Sir Richard Sutto[...]
Bellasse and Yorkefleete or in any[...]
huntington. And in ffulstowe and[...]
all every or any of them, And all[...]
and sold vnto the said Sir Richard[...]
any of them. And also all yearely[...]
and all the estate right title inter[...]
them had or might could or ought[...]
ferrars Courte roll Sir ves [...]

hand and to hold the sai[...]
all and singuler the premisses and[...]
wotton theire heires and Assignes[...]
As by the said Indenture bearing[...]
the forme of the Statute in that [...]
one other Indenture made the [...]
and Sir Richard Sutton of London[...]
said Sir Edward Coke and Sir[...]
Clarke and Bryan wotton theire[...]
Essex with all the howses and bu[...]
County of yarmouth 1651 an[...]